D0855230

INTRODUCTION TO ANALYSIS

W. Vance Underhill
East Texas State University

University Press of America

University Press
of America™

To Charlotte

P R E F A C E

For some time now there has been a trend toward "intuitive" calculus courses, that is, courses
which stress techniques, applications, and problem
solving. Students going on to study more advanced
mathematics are required at many universities to
take an intermediate course which emphasizes a rigorous and logical development of those concepts
common to elementary analysis. This book is designed for that transition course.

All the standard topics of one-dimensional
calculus are covered as well as some advanced material not usually taken up at that level. The
presentation is rigorous, yet leisurely. After an
introductory chapter devoted to exploring certain
properties of real numbers which often cause difficulty, the principal ideas of calculus are developed systematically and rigorously in the remaining
seven chapters.

All mathematics books must be read with pen-
cil and paper at hand. It should be the goal of
anyone using this book to work out the examples
and prove the theorems on his own, looking at the
printed solutions and proofs only when necessary.
Mathematics is not a spectator sport! There is
nothing wrong with skipping over a proof and continuing to work on it from time to time while
going on to new material.

Although the book is designed especially for
those who have already been exposed to calculus,
it is virtually self-contained and can be read by
anyone with a knowledge of elementary algebra and
trigonometry. There are 212 completely worked
examples to illustrate the material plus more than
500 exercises. Most of these deal with theoretical questions though a few are computational.
There are answers or hints to more than one-third
of the exercises.

v

Definitions are stated in the form, "A is true provided B is true," which is equivalent to the more usual, "A is true if and only if B is true." Theorems and definitions are numbered together consecutively within each chapter; for example, there is either a Definition 3.8 or a Theorem 3.8 but not both. Examples are not given chapter numbers. An exercise which begins, "prove or disprove" requires a proof if the given statement is true and a counterexample if it is false. All exercises marked with an asterisk should be done, for they contain facts essential to the development of later material.

I would like to express in print my deepest gratitude to Marcia Lair for her superb job of typing the manuscript.

TABLE OF CONTENTS

CHAPTER 1

Every mathematical work must begin by regarding certain things as being known. This book deals exclusively with the real number system, and the elementary properties of real numbers will be taken for granted. Certain properties of real numbers which are not so elementary will be considered in detail.

A thorough understanding of inequalities is essential to any serious study of analysis. The very word "inequality" implies, of course, the symbols $<$, $\leq$, $>$, and $\geq$, whose definitions will be taken for granted.

The following elementary properties of inequalities will be assumed here, though in a formal development of the real number system each is a theorem whose proof depends on the axioms being used.

(1) If a, b, c are numbers such that $a \leq b$ and $b \leq c$, then $a \leq c$.

(2) If a and b are numbers such that $a \leq b$, then $a + c \leq b + c$ for any number c.

(3) If a and b are numbers such that $a \leq b$ and c is a positive number, then $ac \leq bc$.

(4) If a and b are numbers such that $a \leq b$ and c is a negative number, then $ac \geq bc$.

Theorem 1.1:

(a) If a, b, c, d are numbers such that $a \leq b$ and $c \leq d$, then $a + c \leq b + d$.

(b) If a, b, c, d are numbers such that $a \leq b$, $c \leq d$, $b \geq 0$, and $c \geq 0$, then $ac \leq bd$.

1

(c)   If a and b are numbers such that $a \leq b$, then $-b \leq -a$.

(d)   If a and b are positive numbers such that $a \leq b$, then $\frac{1}{b} \leq \frac{1}{a}$.

(e)   If a and b are non-negative numbers such that $a \leq b$, then $a^2 \leq b^2$.

(f)   If a and b are non-negative numbers such that $a \leq b$, then $\sqrt{a} \leq \sqrt{b}$.

(g)   If a and b are any non-negative numbers, then $\sqrt{ab} \leq \frac{a + b}{2}$.

Proof of (a):   By (2) we can add c to both sides of $a \leq b$, so

$$a + c \leq b + c.$$

Using (2) again and adding b to both sides of $c \leq d$, we get

$$b + c \leq b + d.$$

Since $a + c \leq b + c$ and $b + c \leq b + d$ we conclude from (1) that

$$a + c \leq b + d. \qquad \square$$

Proof of (b):   Left as an exercise.

Proof of (c):   Left as an exercise.

Proof of (d):   Since a and b are positive, both $\frac{1}{a}$ and $\frac{1}{b}$ are positive. Using (3) we can multiply both sides of $a \leq b$ by $\frac{1}{b}$, getting

$$\frac{a}{b} \leq 1.$$

Multiplying both sides of this last inequality by $\frac{1}{a}$ and using (3) again,

$$\frac{1}{b} \leq \frac{1}{a} . \qquad \square$$

Proof of (e): Left as an exercise.

Proof of (f): Left as an exercise.

Proof of (g): Since the square of every real number is non-negative,

$$0 \leq (\sqrt{a} - \sqrt{b})^2.$$

Therefore

$$0 \leq a - 2\sqrt{ab} + b$$

$$2\sqrt{ab} \leq a + b$$

$$\sqrt{ab} \leq \frac{a + b}{2} . \qquad \square$$

Example 1: Determine all values of x for which

$$\frac{2}{x + 1} < x.$$

We cannot simply multiply both sides of the inequality by x + 1, for we don't know whether x + 1 is positive or negative and therefore don't know whether (3) or (4) should be used. (One method would be to consider two separate cases, but the problem will be done another way.) Since $x \neq -1$, $(x + 1)^2 > 0$. Using (3) with $(x + 1)^2$ as the multiplier produces

$$2(x + 1) < x(x + 1)^2.$$

It follows that $0 < x(x + 1)^2 - 2(x + 1)$

3

and $\qquad$ $0 < (x - 1)(x + 1)(x + 2).$

The indicated product is positive if all three factors are positive or if exactly one of the three is positive. Thus there are four cases:

Case 1: $x - 1 > 0$ and $x + 1 > 0$ and $x + 2 > 0$
Case 2: $x - 1 > 0$ and $x + 1 < 0$ and $x + 2 < 0$
Case 3: $x - 1 < 0$ and $x + 1 > 0$ and $x + 2 < 0$
Case 4: $x - 1 < 0$ and $x + 1 < 0$ and $x + 2 > 0.$

Within each case all three inequalities must be true simultaneously. It's a routine matter to show that Cases 2 and 3 are impossible, while Case 1 requires $x > 1$ and Case 4 requires $-2 < x < -1$. Thus the original inequality is satisfied if either $x > 1$ or if $-2 < x < -1$.

Definition 1.2: The absolute value of a number a, denoted $|a|$, is defined by

$$|a| = \begin{cases} a \text{ if } a \geq 0 \\ -a \text{ if } a < 0. \end{cases}$$

We see that the absolute value of zero is zero while the absolute value of every other number is positive. Note that an equivalent definition would be $|a| = \sqrt{a^2}$ since the symbol $\sqrt{}$ always denotes the non-negative root. Note also that $-|a| \leq a \leq |a|$ for every number a.

Theorem 1.3:

(a) If a is any number, then $|a| = |-a|$.

(b) If a and b are any numbers, then $|ab| = |a||b|$. In particular, $|a^2| = |a|^2 = a^2$.

4

(c)   If a is any number and b is any non-zero num-
      ber, then $\left|\dfrac{a}{b}\right| = \dfrac{|a|}{|b|}$.

(d)   If a is a non-negative number, then $|x| \leq a$ if
      and only if $-a \leq x \leq a$.

(e)   If a and b are any numbers, then $|a + b| \leq |a| + |b|$.

(f)   If a and b are any numbers, then $\big||a| - |b|\big| \leq |a + b|$.

Proof of (a):   Left as an exercise.

Proof of (b): $|ab| = \sqrt{(ab)^2} = \sqrt{a^2b^2} = \sqrt{a^2}\,\sqrt{b^2} = |a||b|.$ □

Proof of (c):   Left as an exercise.

Proof of (d):   Left as an exercise.

Proof of (e):

$$|a + b|^2 = (a + b)^2 \qquad\qquad \text{by (b)}$$
$$= a^2 + 2ab + b^2$$
$$\leq a^2 + 2|a||b| + b^2 \qquad \text{since } x \leq |x|$$
$$= |a|^2 + 2|a||b| + |b|^2 \quad \text{by (b)}$$
$$= (|a| + |b|)^2$$
$$|a + b| \leq |a| + |b| \qquad\qquad \text{by Theorem 1.1 (f)}\;□$$

5

<u>Proof of (f)</u>: Since a = a - b + b, $|a| \leq |a - b|$ + $|b|$. Since b represents any number, we can re-place b by -b. Hence

$$|a| \leq |a + b| + |b|$$

and therefore

$$|a| - |b| \leq |a + b|.$$

Interchanging a and b,

$$|b| - |a| \leq |a + b|.$$

From the last inequality

$$-|a + b| \leq |a| - |b|.$$

Therefore

$$-|a + b| \leq |a| - |b| \leq |a + b|.$$

By Theorem 1.3 (d)

$$\Big||a| - |b|\Big| \leq |a + b|. \qquad\qquad \square$$

<u>Example 2</u>: Determine all values of x for which

$$\left|\frac{x + 1}{2x - 3}\right| < 2.$$

This   is   equivalent to

$$-2 < \frac{x + 1}{2x - 3} < 2.$$

That is,   we must satisfy both

$$(1) \qquad -2 < \frac{x + 1}{2x - 3}$$

and $(2) \qquad \dfrac{x + 1}{2x - 3} < 2$

6

simultaneously. Multiplying both sides of (1) by $(2x - 3)^2$ we get

$$-2(2x - 3)^2 < (x + 1)(2x - 3)$$

which reduces to

$$(3) \qquad 0 < (2x - 3)(x - 1).$$

There are two cases to consider: (a) both factors are positive, (b) both factors are negative. It is easily seen that the solution of the former is $x > \frac{3}{2}$, and the solution of the latter is $x < 1$. Putting this aside for the moment, we turn to (2). Multiplying both sides by $(2x - 3)^2$ produces

$$(x + 1)(2x - 3) < 2(2x - 3)^2$$

which reduces to

$$(4) \qquad 0 < (2x - 3)(3x - 7).$$

Again there are two cases: (a) both factors are positive, (b) both factors are negative. The solution of the former is $x > \frac{7}{3}$, and the solution of the latter is $x < \frac{3}{2}$. The problem of solving the original inequality has been reduced to satisfying (1) and (2) simultaneously. Thus we must have either $x > \frac{3}{2}$ or $x < 1$ and at the same time either $x > \frac{7}{3}$ or $x < \frac{3}{2}$. Certainly $x > \frac{3}{2}$ and $x > \frac{7}{3}$ can occur together as can $x < 1$ and $x < \frac{3}{2}$, while the other two cases are impossible. Therefore the original inequality is satisfied for

$$x > \frac{7}{3}$$

and also for $\qquad x < 1$

but for no other values of x.

Theorem 1.4 (Cauchy-Schwarz Inequality): If n is a positive integer and a_1, a_2, . . . , a_n and b_1, b_2, . . . , b_n are any numbers, then

$$\left(\sum_{k=1}^{n} a_k b_k \right)^2 \leq \left(\sum_{k=1}^{n} a_k^2 \right) \left(\sum_{k=1}^{n} b_k^2 \right).$$

Proof: We begin by observing that, since the square of a real number cannot be negative,

$$\sum_{k=1}^{n} (a_k x + b_k)^2 \geq 0$$

for every number x. Consequently

$$\sum_{k=1}^{n} a_k^2 x^2 + \sum_{k=1}^{n} 2a_k b_k x + \sum_{k=1}^{n} b_k^2 \geq 0$$

and with the notations

$$A = \sum_{k=1}^{n} a_k^2 \, , \quad B = \sum_{k=1}^{n} a_k b_k \, , \quad C = \sum_{k=1}^{n} b_k^2$$

we have $\quad Ax^2 + 2Bx + C \geq 0$.

Since this inequality is true for all x, it is true for $x = -\frac{B}{A}$. Hence

$$A\left(-\frac{B}{A}\right)^2 + 2B\left(-\frac{B}{A}\right) + C \geq 0$$

$$-\frac{B^2}{A} + C \geq 0$$

$$B^2 \leq AC$$

that is,

$$\left(\sum_{k=1}^{n} a_k b_k \right)^2 \leq \left(\sum_{k=1}^{n} a_k^2 \right) \left(\sum_{k=1}^{n} b_k^2 \right). \qquad \square$$

Example 3: If n is a positive integer, let

$$a_k = \sqrt{k} \quad \text{and} \quad b_k = \frac{1}{\sqrt{k}}$$

for each integer k, $1 \le k \le n$. Using the Cauchy-Schwarz Inequality

$$\left(\sum_{k=1}^{n} \sqrt{k} \cdot \frac{1}{\sqrt{k}} \right)^2 \le \left(\sum_{k=1}^{n} k \right) \left(\sum_{k=1}^{n} \frac{1}{k} \right).$$

That is,

$$n^2 \le (1 + 2 + \cdots + n)(1 + \frac{1}{2} + \cdots + \frac{1}{n})$$

for each positive integer n.

In a rigorous development of the real number system one begins with a set of axioms for the natural numbers (positive integers). In one form or another the following statement is one of those axioms.

Axiom of Mathematical Induction: Suppose S is a set of positive integers with the following two properties:

(i) 1 is in S;

(ii) whenever S contains a positive integer k, S also contains k + 1.

Then S is the set of all positive integers.

It is often desirable to show that a certain proposition P(n) is true for every positive integer n. A typical "proof by mathematical induction" takes the following form: first show P(1) is true; then show that if P(k) is true* P(k + 1) must also be true. If both of these steps can be accomplished,

*The assumption that P(k) is true is often called the "induction hypothesis."

9

then P(n) is true for every positive integer n, for we need only let S denote the set of positive integers for which the proposition is true and apply the axiom.

Example 4: Show that $1^2 + 2^2 + 3^2 + \cdots + n^2 = \dfrac{n(n + 1)(2n + 1)}{6}$ for every positive integer n. The proposition P(n), of course, is the equation above. For n = 1 the left side is $1^2 = 1$, and the right side is $\dfrac{1 \cdot 2 \cdot 3}{6} = 1$, so P(1) is true. Assuming P(k) is true, that is,

$$1^2 + 2^2 + 3^2 + \cdots + k^2 = \frac{k(k + 1)(2k + 1)}{6}$$

we must show that P(k + 1) is true, that is,

$$1^2 + 2^2 + 3^2 + \cdots + k^2 + (k + 1)^2$$

$$= \frac{(k + 1)[(k + 1) + 1][2(k + 1) + 1]}{6}$$

$$= \frac{(k + 1)(k + 2)(2k + 3)}{6} \; .$$

Adding $(k + 1)^2$ to both sides of the equation for P(k) we get

$$1^2 + 2^2 + 3^2 + \cdots + k^2 + (k + 1)^2$$

$$= \frac{k(k + 1)(2k + 1)}{6} + (k + 1)^2$$

$$= \frac{k + 1}{6} [k(2k + 1) + 6(k + 1)]$$

$$= \frac{k + 1}{6} (2k^2 + 7k + 6)$$

$$= \frac{(k + 1)(k + 2)(2k + 3)}{6}$$

which establishes the fact that P(k + 1) is true.

Example 5: Show that if n is a positive integer, then $\frac{1}{3}(n^3 + 2n)$ is a positive integer. Certainly P(1) is true since $\frac{1}{3}(1^3 + 2 \cdot 1)$ is the integer 1. If P(k) is true, then

$$\frac{1}{3}(k^3 + 2k) = s$$

where s is a positive integer. We must show that P(k + 1) is true, i.e., $\frac{1}{3}[(k + 1)^3 + 2(k + 1)]$ is a positive integer.

$$\frac{1}{3}[(k + 1)^3 + 2(k + 1)] = \frac{1}{3}(k^3 + 3k^2 + 5k + 3)$$

$$= \frac{1}{3}(k^3 + 2k)$$

$$+ \frac{1}{3}(3k^2 + 3k + 3)$$

$$= s + (k^2 + k + 1)$$

Since both s and $k^2 + k + 1$ are positive integers, the right side is a positive integer.

It may very well happen that a proposition P(n) is false for a finite number of positive integers but is true for all others. A proof by mathematical induction is still possible, as in the following example.

Example 6: Show that $2^n \leq n!$ for every integer $n \geq 4$.* This is equivalent to the inequality

*The symbol n!, called "n factorial," is defined to be the product $1 \cdot 2 \cdot 3 \cdots (n - 1) \cdot n$ for each positive integer n. Also 0! = 1 by a separate definition.

11

$2^{n+3} \leq (n + 3)!$ for $n > 1$. Strictly speaking, the axiom of mathematical induction applies to the latter but not to the former. Clearly, however, this is merely a change of notation and not a substantive change, so it suffices to work the problem in its original form. For the first positive integer under consideration,

$$16 = 2^4 \leq 4! = 24.$$

We assume   (1) $2^k \leq k!$

and try to show $2^{k+1} \leq (k + 1)!$.

If $k \geq 4$, then certainly

$$(2) \qquad 2 < k + 1$$

and multiplication of (1) and (2) as allowed by Theorem 1.1 (b) produces

$$2^{k+1} \leq (k + 1)!$$

which was to be shown.

As another example of mathematical induction, we will establish the following very useful inequality.

Theorem 1.5 (Bernoulli's Inequality): If n is any positive integer and $x > -1$, then $(1 + x)^n \geq 1 + nx$.

Proof: If $n = 1$, the left side is $(1 + x)^1 = 1 + x$, and the right side is $1 + (1)x = 1 + x$. We assume that

$$(1 + x)^k \geq 1 + kx$$

and must show

$$(1 + x)^{k+1} \geq 1 + (k + 1)x.$$

Since $x > -1$, $1 + x > 0$. Multiplying both sides of the induction hypothesis by $1 + x$, we get

$$(1 + x)^{k+1} \geq (1 + kx)(1 + x)$$

$$= 1 + (k + 1)x + kx^2$$

$$\geq 1 + (k + 1)x \quad \text{since } kx^2 \geq 0$$

and the proof is complete. $\square$

Corollary: If n is any positive integer and $x > -1$, then $(1 + x)^n > nx$.

Our final proof by mathematical induction will be the famous binomial theorem. The following notation is customarily used in connection with that theorem.

Definition 1.6: If n and k are non-negative integers and $k \leq n$, the symbol $\binom{n}{k}$, called a binomial coefficient, is defined by

$$\binom{n}{k} = \frac{n!}{k!(n - k)!} .$$

Example 7:

(a) $\binom{11}{3} = \frac{11!}{3!8!} = \frac{11 \cdot 10 \cdot 9}{3 \cdot 2 \cdot 1} = 165$

(b) $\binom{n}{0} = \frac{n!}{0!n!} = 1$ for each non-negative integer n

(c) $\binom{n}{n-1} = \frac{n!}{(n - 1)!1!} = n$ for each non-negative integer n.

13

Lemma: If n and k are non-negative integers and k ≤ n, then

$$\binom{n}{k} + \binom{n}{k+1} = \binom{n+1}{k+1} .$$

Proof:

$$\binom{n}{k} + \binom{n}{k+1} = \frac{n!}{k!(n-k)!} + \frac{n!}{(k+1)!(n-k-1)!}$$

$$= \frac{n!(k+1)}{(k+1)!(n-k)!} + \frac{n!(n-k)}{(k+1)!(n-k)!}$$

$$= \frac{(k+1+n-k)n!}{(k+1)!(n-k)!}$$

$$= \frac{(n+1)!}{(k+1)!(n-k)!}$$

$$= \binom{n+1}{k+1} \qquad \qquad \square$$

Theorem 1.7 (Binomial Theorem): If a and b are any numbers and n is a positive integer, then

$$(a+b)^n = \sum_{i=0}^{n} \binom{n}{i} a^{n-i} b^i .$$

Proof: If n = 1 the left side is $(a+b)^1 = a + b$ and the right side is $\binom{1}{0} a^1 b^0 + \binom{1}{1} a^0 b^1 = a + b$. The induction hypothesis is

$$(a+b)^k = \sum_{i=0}^{k} \binom{k}{i} a^{k-i} b^i$$

and we must show

14

$$(a + b)^{k+1} = \sum_{i=0}^{k+1} \binom{k+1}{i} a^{k+1-i} b^i.$$

Multiplying both sides of the induction hypothesis by $(a + b)$ we get

$$(a + b)^{k+1} = \sum_{i=0}^{k} \binom{k}{i} a^{k-i} b^i (a + b)$$

$$= \sum_{i=0}^{k} \binom{k}{i} a^{k+1-i} b^i + \sum_{i=0}^{k} \binom{k}{i} a^{k-i} b^{i+1}$$

$$= \binom{k}{0} a^{k+1} + \sum_{i=1}^{k} \binom{k}{i} a^{k+1-i} b^i$$

$$+ \sum_{i=0}^{k-1} \binom{k}{i} a^{k-i} b^{i+1} + \binom{k}{k} b^{k+1}$$

$$= a^{k+1} + \sum_{i=1}^{k} \binom{k}{i} a^{k+1-i} b^i$$

$$+ \sum_{i=1}^{k} \binom{k}{i-1} a^{k+1-i} b^i + b^{k+1}$$

$$= a^{k+1} + \sum_{i=1}^{k} \left[\binom{k}{i-1} + \binom{k}{i} \right] a^{k+1-i} b^i$$

$$+ b^{k+1}$$

$$= a^{k+1} + \sum_{i=1}^{k} \binom{k+1}{i} a^{k+1-i} b^i + b^{k+1}$$

$$= \sum_{i=0}^{k+1} \binom{k+1}{i} a^{k+1-i} b^i \qquad \square$$

The following inequality is often useful (see problem 13 of the exercises for a stronger result).

Example 8: If n is any positive integer and $x \geq 0$, show that

$$(1 + x)^n > \frac{1}{2} n(n - 1)x^2 .$$

The inequality clearly holds for n = 1 and n = 2. For n > 2

$$(1 + x)^n = 1 + nx + \frac{1}{2} n(n - 1)x^2 + \ldots + x^n$$

$$> \frac{1}{2} n(n - 1)x^2$$

since each individual term of the binomial expansion is non-negative.

Before continuing our study of certain aspects of the real number system, we pause for some notation. In mathematics one often speaks of a "set" as a collection of things having a common property. On an elementary level the idea of a set is intuitive and remains undefined. The things that make up the set are called its "elements." The notation $x \; \varepsilon \; A$ is used to indicate that the element x belongs to the set A. In this book set notation is minimal and is used only to simplify statements that would otherwise be awkward. The notation {x:P}, where P is a statement about x, is used to denote the set of all x for which statement P is true.

As an example of this notation consider the following, where a is a number less than b.

$$[a,b] = \{x: \quad a \leq x \leq b\}$$
$$(a,b] = \{x: \quad a < x \leq b\}$$
$$[a,b) = \{x: \quad a \leq x < b\}$$
$$(a,b) = \{x: \quad a < x < b\}$$

16

We call [a,b] a "closed interval" and (a,b) an "open interval." The "length" of each of the four intervals in the example is b - a.

Definition 1.8: Suppose A and B are sets.

    (1)   The statement that B is a subset of A, denoted B $\subseteq$ A, means that every element of B is an element of A.

    (2)   The union of A and B, denoted A $\cup$ B, is the set defined by

$$A \cup B = \{x: \ x \ \varepsilon \ A \ \text{or} \ x \ \varepsilon \ B\}.*$$

    (3)   The intersection of A and B, denoted A $\cap$ B, is the set defined by

$$A \cap B = \{x: \ x \ \varepsilon \ A \ \text{and} \ x \ \varepsilon \ B\}.$$

    (4)   The complement of A, denoted C(A), is the set of all elements which do not belong to A.

For the remainder of the book it will be understood, unless something is said to the contrary, that every set is a non-empty set of real numbers.

Definition 1.9: The set A is said to be bounded above provided there exits a number K such that x < K for every x in A (and K is called an upper bound for A). The set A is said to be bounded below provided there exists a number L such that L < x for every x in A (and L is called a lower bound for A). Finally, the set A is called bounded provided it is both bounded above and bounded below, that is, provided there exists a number M such that $|x| \leq M$ for every x in A.

*To say that x ε A or x ε B is not to exclude the possibility that x ε A and x ε B.

Definition 1.10: Suppose A is a set which is bounded above. The number b is called a least upper bound (or supremum) for A provided the following two conditions are satisfied:

>   (i) b is an upper bound for A;
>
>   (ii) no number smaller than b is an upper bound for A.

Definition 1.11: Suppose A is a set which is bounded below. The number b is called a greatest lower bound (or infimum) for A provided the following two conditions are satisfied:

>   (i) b is a lower bound for A;
>
>   (ii) no number larger than b is a lower bound for A.

The final property of the real number system to be considered here can be stated in several ways. For our purposes it takes the following form.

Axiom of Completeness: Every set which is bounded above has a least upper bound.

Intuitively this axiom says that the real number system has no "holes" in it--wherever there should be a number there is one. This is in sharp contrast to the set of rational numbers, say, which has lots of holes. It would seem that we need a similar axiom for greatest lower bounds. Actually this is not so, for the following theorem is easily proved.

Theorem 1.12: Every set which is bounded below has a greatest lower bound.

Proof: Left as an exercise.

18

It should be clear from the definitions that a set cannot have more than one least upper bound (abbreviated "sup") nor more than one greatest lower bound (abbreviated "inf"). Also, neither the least upper bound nor the greatest lower bound of a set is necessarily an element of that set.

Theorem 1.13:   Suppose A and B are bounded sets and c is a number.

If $A + B = \{a + b: \ a \in A \text{ and } b \in B\}$

and $cA = \{ca: \ a \in A\}$,

then   (a) $\sup (A + B) = \sup A + \sup B$

(b) $\inf (A + B) = \inf A + \inf B$

(c) $\sup (cA) = \begin{cases} c \sup A & \text{if } c \geq 0 \\ c \inf A & \text{if } c < 0 \end{cases}$

(d) $\inf (cA) = \begin{cases} c \inf A & \text{if } c \geq 0 \\ c \sup A & \text{if } c < 0. \end{cases}$

Proof of (a):   Let $u = \sup A$, $v = \sup B$, and $w = u + v$. We must show: (i) $x \leq w$ for every x in $A + B$; and (ii) if $w' < w$, there exists a number x in $A + B$ such that $x > w'$. If x is any element of $A + B$, then $x = a + b$ for some a in A and some b in B. Since $a \leq u$ and $b \leq v$, $x = a + b \leq u + v = w$. For the second part, suppose $w' < w$ and let $w - w' = \varepsilon$, where, of course, $\varepsilon > 0$. Now u is the least upper bound for A, so $u - \frac{\varepsilon}{2}$ is not an upper bound. Hence there exists some a in A such that $a > u - \frac{\varepsilon}{2}$. By the same reasoning there exists some b in B such that $b > v - \frac{\varepsilon}{2}$. Adding the inequalities and letting $x = a + b$,

$$x = a + b > (u + v) - \varepsilon = w - \varepsilon = w'. \qquad \square$$

Proof of (c): If c = 0, the conclusion is obvious. If c > 0, let u = sup A and w = cu. We must show: (i) x $\leq$ w for every x in cA; and (ii) if w' < w, there exists a number x in cA such that x > w'. Since a $\leq$ u for every a in A and since c > 0, x = ca $\leq$ cu = w for every x in cA. Letting w - w' = ε we can assert the existence of some a in A such that a > u - $\frac{ε}{c}$. Therefore

$$x = ca > cu - ε = w - ε = w'.$$

If c < 0, let v = inf A and w = cv. Again (i) and (ii) above must be shown. Since v is the greatest lower bound for A, for every a in A, v $\leq$ a and consequently -a $\leq$ - v. Since c < 0, -ca $>$ - cv and therefore x = ca $\leq$ cv = w for every x in cA. With ε = w - w' we observe that v - $\frac{ε}{c}$ > v since c < 0. Since no number greater than v is a lower bound for A, there exists some a in A such that a < v - $\frac{ε}{c}$. It follows that

$$x = ca > cv - ε = w - ε = w'. \qquad \square$$

Proof of (b) and (d): Left as an exercise.

Definition 1.14: A function f from a set A to a set B is a correspondence whereby with each element x of A is associated a unique element y of B. The element y is called the value of f at x and is denoted by f(x). The domain of f is the set A, and the range of f is the set {y: y = f(x) for some x in A}.

Certainly the concept of function underlies all of mathematics. Some comments are in order concerning this most important idea. A function f is a rule or correspondence between two sets A and B. This correspondence is often specified by an equation, but it could be given in other ways, say by a verbal description or simply a table of x's and

y's. Although with each element of A there is associated a unique element of B, there may be one
or more elements of B associated with many elements
of A. Also, there could be elements of B which are
not associated with any elements of A. Thus, though
the range of f is a subset of B, it need not be all
of B (in the case of a "constant" function it is a
set containing only one element). Note that there
is nothing in the definition concerning the nature
of the elements of A and B--they could be anything
(even functions!). Unless something is said to the
contrary, however, both A and B will be understood
to be sets of real numbers. Finally, a word about
notation. If f is a function, then $f(x)$ denotes
the value of f at x. In other words, the symbol f
represents a function, and the symbol $f(x)$ represents a number. Once it was common for $f(x)$ to
stand for both number and function, but now it is
customary to distinguish between the symbols.
Still, there are certain functions whose notation
is so well established that this convention is vio-
lated. One speaks, for example, of "the function
sin x" and not "the function sin."

Definition 1.15: Suppose f is a function from A
to B.

    (1)   f is said to be onto provided the range
           of f is B.

    (2)   f is said to be one-to-one provided $f(x_1)$
           and $f(x_2)$ are different elements of B
           whenever x_1 and x_2 are different elements
           of A.

    There are several ways of combining functions
to produce other functions. For the moment we will
consider only one; the others are defined in later
sections.

Definition 1.16: Suppose f is a function from A
to B and g is a function from B to C. The composition of g with f, denoted $g(f)$, is the function

from A to C defined by

$[g(f)](x) = g(f(x))$ for every x in A.*

Example 9:   Suppose $f(x) = x^3 + 8$ for $x \geq -2$ and $g(x) = \sqrt{x}$.   Then

$$[f(g)](x) = x^{3/2} + 8, \ x \geq 0$$

and $[g(f)](x) = \sqrt{x^3 + 8}, \ x \geq -2.$

Note that if no restriction is placed on the domain of f, then f(g) is defined but g(f) is not.

We close this chapter with a brief introduction to a concept that is relatively new in the long history of mathematics.

Definition 1.17:   Two sets A and B are said to be equivalent, denoted A ∼ B, provided there is a function from one to the other which is both onto and one-to-one.

Example 10:   The sets A = {t,z,u,c} and B = {*,$,%,#} are equivalent, for the function f from A to B defined by f(t) = %, f(z) = *, f(u) = #, f(c) = $ is both one-to-one and onto.

Definition 1.18:   The set A is said to be infinite provided, for every positive integer n, A contains a subset with n elements.   A set which is not infinite is called finite.

As can be seen from the simple example above, equivalent sets need not have the same elements or even the same kind of elements.   Rather, the concept of equivalence is used to compare the "number"

*An alternate notation for g(f) is g∘f.

of elements in two sets. It is only in the case
of infinite sets that this idea is really interesting.

The revolutionary work of Georg Cantor in the
late nineteenth century showed that there are different "levels" of infinite sets, that infinite
sets, in fact, can be arranged in a sort of hierar-
chy. The following definition is fundamental in
this regard.

Definition 1.19: Any set which is equivalent to
the set of positive integers is called countable.*
An infinite set which is not countable is called
uncountable.

Example 11: If A denotes the set of positive integers and B denotes the set of all integers, consider the function f from A to B defined by

$$
f(n) = \begin{cases} \dfrac{n-1}{2} & n = 1,3,5, \ldots \\[2ex] -\dfrac{n}{2} & n = 2,4,6, \ldots \end{cases}
$$

It's a routine matter to show that f is one-to-one
and onto. From this we conclude that A $\sim$ B and B
is countable.

Cantor was able to show, among many other
things, that the set of rational numbers is countable. Loosely speaking, this means that there are
no more rational numbers than there are positive
integers, appearances notwithstanding. He was
also able to show that the set of real numbers is
uncountable. Thus, despite the fact both sets are
infinite, the set of real numbers is "more numer-
ous" than the set of positive integers. His

*A countable set is simply one whose elements can
be arranged in a sequence (see Definition 2.1).

demonstrations of these facts are ingenious and
yet simple to understand. In order to allow you
the pleasure of discovery, the proofs are not shown
here. Hints are given in case you get stuck.

Theorem 1.20: The set of positive rational numbers
is countable.

Proof: Left as an exercise.

Corollary: The set of all rational numbers is
countable.

Proof: Left as an exercise.

Theorem 1.21: The set $\{x: 0 \leq x \leq 1\}$ is uncountable.

Proof: Left as an exercise.

Corollary: The set of all real numbers is uncountable.

Proof: Left as an exercise.

24

Exercise 1.1

1. Solve the equation $|2x^2 - x - 1| = 2$.

2. Prove (b), (c), (e), and (f) of Theorem 1.1.

3. Determine all values of x for which $\dfrac{x + 1}{x} \geq 2x - 1$.

4. Prove (a), (c), and (d) of Theorem 1.3.

5. If $|2x - 9| \leq 3$, find the smallest and largest values of $|x - 2|$.

6. Determine all values of x for which $|x + 4| > |1 - 3x|$.

7. If $a_1, a_2, \ldots, a_n$ are any numbers, prove that $\left| \sum_{k=1}^{n} a_k \right| \leq \sum_{k=1}^{n} |a_k|$.

8. Conjecture a formula for $1 + 2 + \ldots + n$ and prove it by mathematical induction.

9. Show that $1^3 + 2^3 + \ldots + n^3 = (1 + 2 + \ldots + n)^2$ for every positive integer n.

10. Prove that if n is a positive integer, then $\frac{1}{7}n^7 + \frac{1}{3}n^3 + \frac{11}{21}n$ is a positive integer.

11. By examining special cases "guess" a formula for the product $(1 - \frac{1}{2})(1 - \frac{1}{3})(1 - \frac{1}{4}) \ldots (1 - \frac{1}{n})$ and prove it by mathematical induction.

12. Prove that the number of points of intersection of n lines in a plane cannot exceed $\frac{1}{2}n(n - 1)$.

13. If n is a positive integer, prove that

  (a) $(1 + x)^n \leq 1 + nx + \frac{1}{2}n(n - 1)x^2$ if $-1 < x \leq 0$;

  (b) $(1 + x)^n \geq 1 + nx + \frac{1}{2}n(n - 1)x^2$ if $x > 0$.

14. Find the smallest positive integer for which $n^2 + n + 41$ is not a prime.

15. Prove that $1 + \frac{1}{4} + \frac{1}{9} + \ldots + \frac{1}{n^2} < 2 - \frac{1}{n}$ for every integer $n \geq 2$.

16. Show that if $x \neq y$, then $x - y$ is a factor of $x^n - y^n$ for every positive integer n.

17. With the same hypothesis as in the Cauchy-Schwarz Inequality, prove <u>Minkowski's Inequality</u>:

$$\sqrt{\sum_{k=1}^{n} (a_k + b_k)^2} \leq \sqrt{\sum_{k=1}^{n} a_k^2} + \sqrt{\sum_{k=1}^{n} b_k^2}.$$

18. Let $P(n)$ denote the proposition $1 + 3 + 5 + \ldots + (2n - 1) = n^2 + 4$. Show that $P(k)$ implies $P(k + 1)$, but the proposition is not true for any integer n.

19. Show that $(1 + \frac{1}{n - 1})^n > (1 + \frac{1}{n})^{n+1}$ for every integer $n \geq 2$.

*20. Prove that $a + ar + ar^2 + \ldots + ar^{n-1} = \frac{a(1 - r^n)}{1 - r}$ for any number a, any number $r \neq 1$, and any positive integer n.

21. Prove the <u>Well-Ordering Principle</u>. Every (non-empty) set <u>S of positive integers</u> contains a smallest element.

22. "Guess" a formula for $1 \cdot 1! + 2 \cdot 2! + 3 \cdot 3! + \ldots + n \cdot n!$ and prove it by mathematical induction.

23. Prove that the sum of the interior angles of a polygon of n sides is $180(n - 2)$ degrees.

24. Prove the <u>Second Principle of Mathematical In-</u><u>duction</u>. Suppose $P(n)$ is a proposition such that: (i) $P(1)$ is true, and (ii) for each integer $m > 1$, if $P(1)$, $P(2)$, ... , $P(m - 1)$ are all true, then $P(m)$ is true. Then $P(n)$ is true for every positive integer n.

25. Prove that every integer greater than one is either a prime or a product of primes.

*26. Show that $\binom{n}{0} + \binom{n}{1} + \binom{n}{2} + \ldots + \binom{n}{n} = 2^n$ for every non-negative integer n.

27. Prove Theorem 1.12.

28. Prove that b is the least upper bound for A if and only if, for each positive number ε, (i) $x < b + \varepsilon$ for every x in A and (ii) there is at least one x in A for which $x > b - \varepsilon$.

29. If A and B are sets such that no element of A exceeds any element of B, prove that sup A $\leq$ inf B.

30. Prove or disprove: if $b = \sup A$ and ε is any positive number, there is an element x of A such that $b - \varepsilon < x < b$.

31. Prove <u>Dedekind's Theorem</u>. Suppose A and B are (non-empty) sets whose union contains every number. Suppose also that every element of A is less than every element of B. Then there exists a number z such that if $x > z$ then $x \in B$ and if $x < z$ then $x \in A$.

32. Prove (b) and (d) of Theorem 1.13.

33. Prove or disprove: the least upper bound of a (non-empty) set A is the greatest lower bound of the set of all upper bounds for A.

*34. Prove <u>Abel's Summation by Parts Formula</u>. Suppose $a_1, a_2, \ldots, a_n$ are any numbers and $b_1, b_2, \ldots, b_n$ are any numbers, where n is some positive integer. If $s_k = a_1 + a_2 + \ldots + a_k$, $1 \leq k \leq n$, then

$$\sum_{k=1}^{n} a_k b_k = s_n b_{n+1} + \sum_{k=1}^{n} s_k (b_k - b_{k+1}).$$

35. If $f(x) = \sqrt{x}$ and $g(x) = x^2$, (a) find a formula for $f(g)$, giving the domain and range; (b) find a formula for $g(f)$, giving the domain and range.

36. If $f(x) = \dfrac{2x - 1}{3}$ and $h(x) = \dfrac{1 - x}{1 + x}$, find g such that $f(g) = h$.

37. For each of the following find a function f from R to R, where R is the set of all numbers, such that

    (a) f is one-to-one and onto;

    (b) f is one-to-one but not onto;

    (c) f is onto but not one-to-one;

    (d) f is neither one-to-one nor onto.

38. Prove or disprove: if f is a one-to-one function from A to B and g is a one-to-one function from B to C, then g(f) is a one-to-one function from A to C.

39. Show that every infinite subset of a countable set is countable.

40. Prove Theorem 1.20.

41. Prove the corollary to Theorem 1.20.

42. Prove Theorem 1.21.

43. Prove the corollary to Theorem 1.21.

CHAPTER 2

1. Convergence

One of the best ways of reaching the heart of real analysis is by means of sequences. The present chapter is devoted to a detailed study of this important topic.

Definition 2.1: A sequence is a function whose domain is the set of positive integers.

It should be noted that the range of a sequence can be any set whatsoever. As far as our study is concerned, however, it will be understood that the range of a sequence is a set of real numbers.

Notation: Using the ordinary functional notation, a sequence f might be defined as follows:

$$f(n) = 3n + 2$$

for each positive integer n. Thus, $f(1) = 5$, $f(2) = 8$, $f(3) = 11$, $f(4) = 14$, and so on. Since the function is undefined for all numbers except positive integers, we can describe the sequence above just as accurately by writing

$$\{5, 8, 11, 14, \ldots\}$$

provided we understand that the first number represents $f(1)$, the second number $f(2)$, and in general the nth number $f(n)$. Each of the numbers in the range is called a term of the sequence and is labeled according to the position it occupies. Hence 5 is the first term, 8 the second term, 11 the third term, and so on. A notation like

$$\{5, 8, 11, 14, \ldots\}$$

with no other information given is open to some criticism, however, for it requires that a person discern the "pattern" in order to know the terms

that are not explicitly given. Since more than
one "pattern" is possible, an incorrect conclusion
could result. It would be much better to write

$$\{5, 8, 11, 14, \ldots, 3n + 2, \ldots\}$$

where the expression $3n + 2$ is understood to represent the nth term. If a formula is given for
the nth term, though, it's quite unnecessary to
identify any terms of the sequence explicitly.
Since n stands for any positive integer, a symbol
like

$$\{3n + 2\}$$

describes the entire sequence if we understand
that the terms of the sequence are "generated"
by substituting successively for n the positive
integers 1, 2, 3, ... In practice both notations

$$\{3n + 2\}$$

and

$$\{5, 8, 11, 14, \ldots\}$$

are common, the latter being used only when there
is no danger of misunderstanding. (In this notation the number of terms explicitly given is a
matter of personal preference.)

   Further examples are as follows:

$$\{n^2\} = \{1, 4, 9, 16, 25, \ldots\}$$
$$\{\frac{1}{n + 3}\} = \{1/4, 1/5, 1/6, 1/7, \ldots\}$$
$$\{(-1)^n\} = \{-1, 1, -1, 1, \ldots\}$$
$$\{2 \sin \frac{(2n - 1)\pi}{4}\} = \{\sqrt{2}, \sqrt{2}, -\sqrt{2}, -\sqrt{2}, \ldots\}$$

When referring to an arbitrary sequence, we will
use a notation such as $\{a_n\}$, that is, $\{a_1, a_2,$
$a_3, \ldots\}$.

There are several important properties that a particular sequence may or may not possess. We will be considering these properties throughout the remainder of the chapter and especially the relationships between them. Probably the simplest is given in the following definition.

Definition 2.2: A sequence $\{a_n\}$ is said to be bounded above provided there exists a number K such that

$$a_n \leq K$$

for every positive integer n. A sequence $\{a_n\}$ is said to be bounded below provided there exists a number L such that

$$L \leq a_n$$

for every positive integer n. Finally, we say that a sequence is bounded if it is both bounded above and bounded below. That is, $\{a_n\}$ is bounded provided there is a number M such that

$$|a_n| \leq M$$

for every positive integer n.

Without a doubt the most important property a sequence may possess is that of "convergence." We will first give the formal definition and then analyze its meaning.

Definition 2.3: The sequence $\{a_n\}$ is said to converge to the number A provided the following condition is satisfied:

if ε is any positive number, there exists a positive integer N such that for every integer $n \geq N$

$$|a_n - A| < \varepsilon.$$

In trying to get at the real meaning of this definition, let us look at an example.

Example 1: Let $\{a_n\} = \{\frac{n+3}{2n}\}$. By calculating the first five terms we find that

$$\{\frac{n+3}{2n}\} = \{2, 5/4, 1, 7/8, 4/5, \ldots\}.$$

Examining the first few terms is not particularly helpful in identifying the number that plays the role of A in the definition. However, if we observe that the 10th term is 13/20, the 100th term is 103/200, and the 1000th term is 1003/2000, it appears that A = 1/2. At the present this is only a conjecture. To prove that this particular sequence does indeed converge to 1/2, we must show, according to the definition, the following:

> if ε is any positive number, there exists a positive integer N such that for every integer $n \geq N$
> $$\left|\frac{n+3}{2n} - 1/2\right| < \varepsilon.$$

Note carefully that the number ε is "given to us," as it were; we have absolutely no control over its value. Once knowing ε, however, we are free to choose N in any manner we like. The criterion for choosing N is governed by the inequality above. For all $n \geq N$ (N not yet determined) we require

$$(1) \qquad \left|\frac{n+3}{2n} - 1/2\right| < \varepsilon.$$

If (1) is true, then we have the following:

$$\left|\frac{n+3-n}{2n}\right| < \varepsilon$$

$$\left|\frac{3}{2n}\right| < \varepsilon$$

$$\frac{3}{2n} < \varepsilon \qquad \text{since n is positive}$$

$$(2) \qquad \frac{3}{2\varepsilon} < n.$$

34

This last inequality appears to tell us how N
should be chosen--let N be any integer greater
than $\frac{3}{2\varepsilon}$. There is one logical difficulty, though.
We obtained (2) by assuming that (1) was true,
whereas in reality we want just the reverse--we
need to be able to say that (1) is a necessary
consequence of (2). This is not automatic from
what we have done. The logically correct argument
follows. Let N be any (fixed) integer such that

$$\frac{3}{2\varepsilon} < N,$$

and let n be any integer satisfying $n \geq N$. Then
we have

$$\frac{3}{2\varepsilon} < N \leq n$$

$$3 < 2n\varepsilon$$

$$\frac{3}{2n} < \varepsilon$$

$$\left|\frac{3}{2n}\right| < \varepsilon$$

$$\left|\frac{n + 3 - n}{2n}\right| < \varepsilon$$

$$\left|\frac{n + 3}{2n} - 1/2\right| < \varepsilon.$$

You should convince yourself, from your knowledge
of inequalities, that each step above is indeed a
valid one. The steps used in going from (1) to (2)
are important from a practical point of view, for
they tell us now to choose N. Logically, however,
they can be considered as "scratch work." The
only important thing is to show that the chosen N,
however it was obtained, has the desired property.

There are several important things to be noted
about the definition of convergence of a sequence.
The number A is an intrinsic property of the sequence itself. This is in contrast to the positive
integer N which is a function of ε (except for very

special cases). Notice too, that having found one integer with the property required of N, we can see that any larger integer also has this property.

Following are more examples of convergent sequences. You should be able to show in each case, directly from the definition, that the sequence converges to the number given.

Example 2:

    (a) $\{\frac{1}{n}\}$ converges to 0.

    (b) $\{\frac{n + 4}{n - 1/2}\}$ converges to 1.

    (c) $\{\frac{(-1)^n}{n} - 2\}$ converges to -2.

    (d) $\{\tan \frac{(3n - 2)\pi}{3}\}$ converges to $\sqrt{3}$.

    (e) $\{\frac{n + 2}{n^2}\}$ converges to 0.

Example 3: Let $\{a_n\} = \{c^n\}$ where c is a number such that $0 < c < 1$. We will show that this sequence converges to 0. Suppose that ε is any positive number. There is a positive number h such that

$$c = \frac{1}{1 + h} \cdot$$

By Bernoulli's Inequality $(1 + h)^n > nh$ for every positive integer n. Let N be an integer such that $N > \frac{1}{\varepsilon h}$. Then for every integer $n \geq N$ we have

$$|c^n - 0| = |c^n| = c^n = \frac{1}{(1 + h)^n} < \frac{1}{nh} \leq \frac{1}{Nh} < \varepsilon \cdot$$

The last step is obtained by rewriting $N > \frac{1}{\varepsilon h}$.

Example 4: Let $\{a_n\} = \{\sqrt{1 + \frac{c}{n}}\}$ where c is any positive number. We will show that this sequence converges to 1. Suppose ε is any positive number. Let N be a positive integer such that $N > \frac{c}{\varepsilon}$. For all $n \geq N$ we have

$$\left|\sqrt{1 + \frac{c}{n}} - 1\right| = \left|\left(\sqrt{1 + \frac{c}{n}} - 1\right) \frac{\sqrt{1 + \frac{c}{n}} + 1}{\sqrt{1 + \frac{c}{n}} + 1}\right|$$

$$= \left|\frac{\frac{c}{n}}{\sqrt{1 + \frac{c}{n}} + 1}\right|$$

$$= \frac{\frac{c}{n}}{\sqrt{1 + \frac{c}{n}} + 1} \qquad \text{since } c > 0$$

$$< \frac{\frac{c}{n}}{1} \qquad \text{since } \sqrt{1 + \frac{c}{n}} > 0$$

$$\leq \frac{c}{N}$$

$$< \varepsilon.$$

One way of looking at the definition of convergence is to regard each term of the sequence as an approximation to the number A. For any desired accuracy (the positive number ε) it's possible to go far enough out in the sequence (the positive integer N) so that all terms from there on approximate A with the desired accuracy

($|a_n - A| < \varepsilon$ for $n \geq N$). We note again that how far out we have to go in the sequence to achieve a particular accuracy depends on how severe that accuracy is--the smaller the ε, the larger the N (in general). In describing convergence one might be tempted to say something like, "the terms of the sequence get closer and closer to A." What objection would you have to this kind of language?

Another method of considering the idea of convergence uses the neighborhood concept. Accordingly, we have the following definition.

Definition 2.4: Suppose x is a number. A neighborhood of x is any open interval whose midpoint is x.

Notice that the definition does not refer to a neighborhood by itself but rather to a neighborhood of some number (point). Obviously every number has infinitely many neighborhoods, and every open interval is a neighborhood of one particular number (its midpoint). It follows from the definition that if D is a neighborhood of x, then $D = (x - t, x + t)$ for some positive number t.

Theorem 2.5: The sequence $\{a_n\}$ converges to the number A if and only if every neighborhood of A contains all terms of $\{a_n\}$ with the possible exception of a finite number.

Proof: Suppose $\{a_n\}$ converges to A. Let D be any neighborhood of A. Then $D = (A - t, A + t)$ for some positive number t. Because of convergence, for the positive number $\varepsilon = t$ there is a positive integer N such that

38

$$|a_n - A| < t \text{ for all } n \geq N.$$

This is equivalent to

$$A - t < a_n < A + t \text{ for all } n \geq N.$$

That is, a_n is in D for all $n \geq N$. Hence D contains all terms of $\{a_n\}$ with the possible exception of the finite set $\{a_1, a_2, a_3, \ldots, a_{N-1}\}$. (Actually some or even all of these terms may be in D; it doesn't matter.) Suppose, on the other hand, that every neighborhood of A contains all terms of $\{a_n\}$ with the possible exception of a finite number. We want to show that $\{a_n\}$ converges to A. Let ε be any positive number. By hypothesis only finitely many terms of $\{a_n\}$, at most, are outside the neighborhood D = (A - ε, A + ε). If none are outside, there is nothing to prove, so let a_{N-1} denote the term outside D having largest subscript. (Since the set of terms outside D is finite, this is possible.) Then a_N, a_{N+1}, a_{N+2}, $\ldots$ are in D, that is,

$$|a_n - A| < \varepsilon \text{ for all } n \geq N$$

and therefore $\{a_n\}$ converges to A. $\qquad\qquad\Box$

For ease in referring to the matters at hand we make the following definition.

Definition 2.6: A sequence $\{a_n\}$ is said to <u>converge</u> (or be <u>convergent</u>) provided there is a number A such that $\{a_n\}$ converges to A. Otherwise $\{a_n\}$ is said to <u>diverge</u> (or be <u>divergent</u>).

A further understanding of convergent sequences may perhaps be provided by examining some sequences which are not convergent.

Example 5:

    (a) $\{2n + 3\} = \{5, 7, 9, 11, \ldots\}$.

Clearly this sequence diverges.

    (b) $\{a_n\}$ where $a_n = \begin{cases} 0 & \text{if } n \text{ is odd} \\ n & \text{if } n \text{ is even} \end{cases}$.

That is, $\{a_n\} = \{0, 2, 0, 4, 0, 6, 0, 8, \ldots\}$.   Even
though all of the odd-numbered terms have the same
value, this sequence also diverges.

    (c) $\{\cos n\pi\} = \{-1, 1, -1, 1, \ldots\}$.

This sequence seems to be better behaved than the
previous two, yet it also diverges. You should
convince yourself that neither +1 nor -1 can
play the part of the number A in the definition
of convergence.

Theorem 2.7: A sequence cannot converge to more
than one number.

Proof: An indirect proof is indicated. Assume
that A and B are different numbers and that $\{a_n\}$
converges to both A and B. We want to show that
this assumption leads to a contradiction. Let
$\varepsilon = |A - B|$. (Note that $\varepsilon > 0$ since $A \neq B$.)
Since $\{a_n\}$ converges to A, there is a positive
integer N_1 such that $|a_n - A| < \varepsilon/2$ for all $n \geq N_1$.
Since $\{a_n\}$ converges to B, there is a positive
integer N_2 such that $|a_n - B| < \varepsilon/2$ for all $n \geq N_2$.
Let N be the larger of N_1 and N_2. Then we have
both

$$|a_N - A| < \varepsilon/2 \text{ and } |a_N - B| < \varepsilon/2.$$

From $\qquad$ $B - A = (B - a_N) + (a_N - A)$

we get

$|B - A| \leq |B - a_N| + |a_N - A| < \varepsilon/2 + \varepsilon/2 = \varepsilon.$

Our conclusion here is $|B - A| < \varepsilon$, whereas we know that $|B - A| = \varepsilon$. This contradiction establishes the theorem. $\qquad$ □

The result above prompts the following definition.

Definition 2.8: If $\{a_n\}$ is a convergent sequence, the (unique) number A to which it converges is called the limit of $\{a_n\}$.

Having a better understanding now of what convergence of a sequence is all about, we might look for conditions which are either necessary or sufficient for convergence. In the light of our previous examples the following statement should come as no surprise.

Theorem 2.9: Every convergent sequence is bounded.

Proof: Left as an exercise.

Example 6: Let $\{a_n\} = \{c^n\}$ where c is a number such that $c > 1$. We will show that this sequence diverges. The contrapositive of the previous theorem says that no unbounded sequence converges. Therefore, if we can show $\{c^n\}$ is unbounded, its divergence will follow. Assume that $\{c^n\}$ is bounded. Then, for some positive number M,

$$|c^n| \leq M \text{ for all n.}$$

41

Denote by h the positive number such that $c = 1 + h$. Let N be any integer satisfying $N > \frac{M}{h}$. Then we have

$$|c^N| = c^N = (1 + h)^N > Nh > M$$

where the step $(1 + h)^N > Nh$ is a consequence of Bernoulli's Inequality. This contradicts our boundedness assumption above. Hence $\{c^n\}$ is un-bounded and therefore divergent.

Exercise 2.1

1. Write the first four terms of each of the following sequences:

   (a) $\{\frac{2n - 1}{n + 3}\}$ (b) $\{\sum_{i=1}^{n} \frac{1}{i}\}$ (c) $\{(1 + \frac{1}{n})^n\}$

2. Find a formula for the nth term of each of the following sequences.

   (a) $\{2, -5, 8, -11, 14, \ldots\}$
   (b) $\{2, 7/4, 5/4, 13/16, 1/2, 19/64, \ldots\}$
   (c) $\{2, 7, 14, 23, 34, \ldots\}$

3. (a) Determine the smallest positive integer N such that

      $\left|\frac{n + 4}{n - 1/2} - 1\right| < 1/2$ for all $n \geq N$.

   (b) Determine the smallest positive integer N such that

      $\left|\frac{n + 4}{n - 1/2} - 1\right| < 1/50$ for all $n \geq N$.

In problems 4-8 show directly from the definition of convergence that the sequence converges to the given number.

4. Example 2(a).

5. Example 2(b).

6. Example 2(c).

7. Example 2(d).

8. Example 2(e).

9. Prove that the sequence $\{a_n\} = \{\frac{1 - 2n}{n + (-1)^{n+1}}\}$

43

has the property that $|a_n| \leq 3$ for every positive integer n.

10. A sequence $\{a_n\}$ is defined as follows:

    $a_1 = \sqrt{2}$ and $a_{n+1} = \sqrt{2 + a_n}$ for $n \geq 1$.

    Use mathematical induction to show that $a_n < 2$ for every positive integer n.

11. Prove Theorem 2.9.

12. Give an example to show that the converse of Theorem 2.9 is false.

*13. Prove that $\{a_n\}$ converges to 0 if and only if $\{|a_n|\}$ converges to 0.

14. Prove that if $\{a_n\}$ converges to A, then $\{|a_n|\}$ converges to $|A|$.

15. Prove or disprove: if $\{a_n\}$ is a sequence such that $\{|a_n|\}$ converges, then $\{a_n\}$ converges.

*16. If c is a number such that $-1 < c < 0$, show that $\{c^n\}$ converges to 0.

17. Show that if $\left\{\dfrac{a_n}{n}\right\}$ converges to a non-zero number, then $\{a_n\}$ is unbounded.

2. Algebra of Sequences

If two convergent sequences are combined by means of one of the four arithmetic operations, we would hope that the resulting sequence "inherits" the property of convergence. The next group of theorems shows that this does happen in each case.

<u>Theorem 2.10</u>: If $\{a_n\}$ converges to A and $\{b_n\}$ converges to B, then $\{a_n + b_n\}$ converges to A + B.

<u>Proof</u>: Suppose ε is any positive number. We must show the existence of a positive integer N such that

$$|(a_n + b_n) - (A + B)| < \varepsilon \text{ for all } n \geq N.$$

Since $\{a_n\}$ converges to A, there exists a positive integer N_1 such that

$$|a_n - A| < \varepsilon/2 \text{ for all } n \geq N_1.$$

Since $\{b_n\}$ converges to B, there exists a positive integer N_2 such that

$$|b_n - B| < \varepsilon/2 \text{ for all } n \geq N_2.$$

Let N be the larger of N_1 and N_2. Then for any integer $n \geq N$ we have both

$$|a_n - A| < \varepsilon/2 \text{ and } |b_n - B| < \varepsilon/2.$$

Therefore, for all $n \geq N$,

$$|(a_n + b_n) - (A + B)| = |(a_n - A) + (b_n - B)|$$

$$\leq |a_n - A| + |b_n - B|$$

45

$$< \varepsilon/2 + \varepsilon/2$$

$$= \varepsilon. \qquad \qquad \square$$

Theorem 2.11: If $\{a_n\}$ converges to A and $\{b_n\}$ converges to B, then $\{a_n b_n\}$ converges to AB.

Proof: Suppose ε is any positive number. We must show the existence of a positive integer N such that

$$|a_n b_n - AB| < \varepsilon \text{ for all } n \geq N.$$

(Before reading any further, you should try to complete the proof yourself. The simple technique of the preceding proof does not quite work here. If you get stuck, make use of the following hint: $a_n b_n - AB = (a_n b_n - Ab_n) + (Ab_n - AB).$) The sequence $\{b_n\}$ is convergent and therefore bounded by Theorem 2.9. Let M denote a positive number such that

$$|b_n| \leq M \text{ for all } n.$$

Since $\{a_n\}$ converges to A, there exists a positive integer N_1 such that

$$|a_n - A| < \frac{\varepsilon}{2M} \text{ for all } n \geq N_1.$$

Since $\{b_n\}$ converges to B, there exists a positive integer N_2 such that

$$|b_n - B| < \frac{\varepsilon}{2|A| + 1} \text{ for all } n \geq N_2.$$

Define N to be the larger of N_1 and N_2, and let n be any integer satisfying $n \geq N$. For such an integer n we have

46

$$|a_n b_n - AB| = |(a_n b_n - Ab_n) + (Ab_n - AB)|$$

$$\leq |a_n b_n - Ab_n| + |Ab_n - AB|$$

$$= |a_n - A||b_n| + |A||b_n - B|$$

$$< \frac{\varepsilon}{2M}\,(M) + |A|\,(\frac{\varepsilon}{2|A| + 1})$$

$$< \frac{\varepsilon}{2} + \frac{\varepsilon}{2}$$

$$= \varepsilon. \qquad\qquad \square$$

It's important to remember that the above sequence of steps is not valid for an arbitrary integer n, but only for $n > N$. (The reason for using $2|A| + 1$ instead of $2|\overline{A}|$ is to avoid 0 in the denominator in case $A = 0$. The problem didn't arise with the other expression since M was positive.)

This proof is quite typical in several respects, and a few more comments are perhaps in order. First of all, the proof would almost certainly not be discovered in the form shown above, but rather by "working backwards." That is, we want $|a_n b_n - AB| < \varepsilon$ for n large enough, and we see what conditions result from this inequality. After some manipulation, it is found that we get the desired result if we can make $|a_n - A||b_n|$ and $|A||b_n - B|$ "arbitrarily small" individually. Each of $|a_n - A|$ and $|b_n - B|$ can be made as small as desired, for n large enough, and therefore both products will be small provided the multiplying factor ($|b_n|$ in one case and $|A|$ in the other) does not get too large as n increases. There is no problem with $|A|$, since it is independent of n. We might worry about $|b_n|$, though, until we remember the necessary boundedness of a convergent sequence. At this point, the rest is easy. Note also that the trick of writing $a_n b_n - AB$

as $(a_n b_n - Ab_n) + (Ab_n - AB)$ was crucial in our proof. This device of adding a term in one place and subtracting it in another will be found useful on many occasions.

Review the proof again under the assumption that $\{a_n\}$ converges to zero. Can you see how to get the conclusion of the theorem with a condition on $\{b_n\}$ much weaker than convergence?

The following result follows easily from Theorem 2.11.

Corollary: If $\{a_n\}$ converges to A and c is any number, then $\{ca_n\}$ converges to cA.

Proof: Left as an exercise.

The following theorem can be proved in a manner analogous to that of Theorem 2.10, but there is an easier way.

Theorem 2.12: If $\{a_n\}$ converges to A and $\{b_n\}$ converges to B, then $\{a_n - b_n\}$ converges to A - B.

Proof: By the corollary above the sequence $\{(-1)b_n\}$ converges to -B. By Theorem 2.10 the sequence $\{a_n + (-1)b_n\}$, that is, $\{a_n - b_n\}$, converges to A - B. □

Let us now consider the problem of division. If $\{a_n\}$ converges to A and $\{b_n\}$ converges to B, can we say that $\{\frac{a_n}{b_n}\}$ converges to $\frac{A}{B}$? Since $\frac{a_n}{b_n}$

48

can be regarded as a product $a_n(\frac{1}{b_n})$, it suffices to show that $\{\frac{1}{b_n}\}$ converges to $\frac{1}{B}$ and then use Theorem 2.11. Clearly we must require $B \neq 0$ and $b_n \neq 0$ for all n. Even then the result is not obvious, for consider the following scratch work. To make

$$\frac{1}{b_n} - \frac{1}{B} = \frac{B - b_n}{Bb_n}$$

small for large enough n, we can certainly make the numerator small, but if the denominator becomes small too, we have no assurance that the quotient of two small numbers is small. It is essential to know that the denominator does not get "arbitrarily close" to zero. A precise statement of what we require is the following.

Lemma: Suppose that $\{b_n\}$ converges to B and $B \neq 0$. There exists a positive number c and a positive integer N such that

$$|b_n| > c \text{ for all } n \geq N.$$

Proof: Let $c = \frac{1}{2}|B|$. By Theorem 2.5 there exists a positive integer N such that the neighborhood $(B - c, B + c)$ contains all b_n for $n \geq N$. For $n \geq N$, then, we have the following:

if $B > 0$, $c = \frac{1}{2}B$, $B = 2c$, $B - c = c$, so
$c = B - c < b_n < B + c$

if $B < 0$, $c = -\frac{1}{2}B$, $B = -2c$, $B + c = -c$, so
$B - c < b_n < B + c = -c$

and the conclusion follows in either case. □

49

Because of the previous result, a sequence which converges to a non-zero number is said to be "bounded away from zero." (You might try to construct a proof which does not require consideration of the two separate cases $B > 0$ and $B < 0$.) Armed with the lemma above, we can now prove the following theorem.

Theorem 2.13: If $\{b_n\}$ converges to B, $B \neq 0$, and $b_n \neq 0$ for every positive integer n, then $\{\frac{1}{b_n}\}$ converges to $\frac{1}{B}$.

Proof: Suppose ε is any positive number. There exists a positive number c and a positive integer N_1 such that

$$|b_n| > c \text{ for all } n \geq N_1.$$

Since $\{b_n\}$ converges to B, there exists a positive integer N_2 such that

$$|b_n - B| < |B| c \varepsilon \text{ for all } n \geq N_2.$$

Suppose N is the larger of N_1 and N_2. If n is any integer satisfying $n \geq N$, then

$$\left| \frac{1}{b_n} - \frac{1}{B} \right| = \left| \frac{B - b_n}{Bb_n} \right|$$

$$= \frac{|b_n - B|}{|B||b_n|}$$

$$< \frac{|b_n - B|}{|B|c}$$

$$< \frac{|B| c\ \varepsilon}{|B| c}$$

$$= \varepsilon. \qquad \qquad \square$$

<u>Corollary</u>: If $\{a_n\}$ converges to A, $\{b_n\}$ converges to B, $B \neq 0$, and $b_n \neq 0$ for each n, then $\{\frac{a_n}{b_n}\}$ converges to $\frac{A}{B}$.

<u>Proof</u>: By Theorem 2.13 $\{\frac{1}{b_n}\}$ converges to $\frac{1}{B}$. By Theorem 2.11 the sequence $\{a_n(\frac{1}{b_n})\} = \{\frac{a_n}{b_n}\}$ converges to $A(\frac{1}{B}) = \frac{A}{B}$. $\qquad \square$

By using one or more of the last four theorems, we can often show convergence of a sequence without the tedious inequalities required in a direct application of the definition.

<u>Example 7</u>: Consider the sequence $\{\frac{2n^2 - n + 5}{1 - n^2}\}$. It is helpful to rewrite this as

$$\left\{ \frac{2 - \frac{1}{n} + \frac{5}{n^2}}{\frac{1}{n^2} - 1} \right\} .$$

We have already noted that $\{\frac{1}{n}\}$ converges to 0. By Theorem 2.11 $\{\frac{1}{n^2}\}$ converges to 0 also, and the limit of $\{\frac{5}{n^2}\}$ is therefore 0 by the corollary to that theorem. The sequence $\{2\}$ (a sequence every term of which is 2) obviously converges to 2.

51

Hence the limit of

$$(\{2\} - \{\tfrac{1}{n}\}) + \{\tfrac{5}{n^2}\} = \{2 - \tfrac{1}{n}\} + \{\tfrac{5}{n^2}\} = \{2 - \tfrac{1}{n} + \tfrac{5}{n^2}\}$$

is $2 - 0 + 0 = 2$ by Theorems 2.12 and 2.10. By a similar argument the limit of $\{\tfrac{1}{n^2} - 1\}$ is -1. Finally, from the corollary to Theorem 2.13, we conclude that the original sequence, considered as $\{2 - \tfrac{1}{n} + \tfrac{5}{n^2}\}$ divided by $\{\tfrac{1}{n^2} - 1\}$, has limit $\tfrac{2}{-1}$, that is, -2. Notice that we could not use the same reasoning on $\{2n^2 - n + 5\}$ divided by $\{1 - n^2\}$, for both of these sequences are divergent. It should be clear to you from this example how to find the limit of any sequence whose general term is a polynomial in n divided by a polynomial in n. Even if polynomials are not involved, the previous theorems are still often useful.

Example 8: Consider the sequence $\{\sqrt{n^2 + 3n} - n\}$.
We rewrite the general term as follows:

$$\sqrt{n^2 + 3n} - n = (\sqrt{n^2 + 3n} - n)\,\frac{\sqrt{n^2 + 3n} + n}{\sqrt{n^2 + 3n} + n}$$

$$= \frac{3n}{\sqrt{n^2 + 3n} + n}$$

$$= \frac{3n}{n\sqrt{1 + \tfrac{3}{n}} + n}$$

$$= \frac{3}{\sqrt{1 + \tfrac{3}{n}} + 1}\quad.$$

52

Therefore $\{\sqrt{n^2 + 3n} - n\} = \dfrac{\{3\}}{\{\sqrt{1 + \frac{3}{n}}\} + \{1\}}$. With

the help of Example 4 we find the limit to be

$\dfrac{3}{1 + 1} = \dfrac{3}{2}$.

Several other results which aid in showing convergence can be considered at this time.

Theorem 2.14: Suppose $\{a_n\}$ converges to A and $\{b_n\}$ converges to B. Suppose also that there is a positive integer N such that $a_n \leq b_n$ for all $n \geq N$. Then A $\leq$ B.

Proof: Left as an exercise.

A similar and perhaps more useful result is the following theorem, sometimes known as the "squeeze theorem."

Theorem 2.15: Suppose $\{b_n\}$ and $\{c_n\}$ are convergent sequences having the same limit L. Suppose $\{a_n\}$ is a sequence with the property that for some positive integer N we have $b_n \leq a_n \leq c_n$ for all $n \geq N$. Then $\{a_n\}$ converges to L.

Proof: Let D be any neighborhood of L. Then $D = (L - \varepsilon, L + \varepsilon)$ for some positive number ε. Since $\{b_n\}$ converges to L, there is a positive integer N_1 such that D contains every b_n for $n \geq N_1$. Since $\{c_n\}$ converges to L, there is a positive integer N_2 such that D contains every

c_n for $n \geq N_2$. Let M be the largest of N_1, N_2, and N. For all $n \geq M$ we have

$$L - \varepsilon < b_n \leq a_n \leq c_n < L + \varepsilon$$

and $\{a_n\}$ converges to L by Theorem 2.5. $\qquad\qquad$ □

<u>Example 9</u>:   Consider the sequence $\{a_n\}$, where
$$a_n = \frac{1}{\sqrt{n^2 + 1}} + \frac{1}{\sqrt{n^2 + 2}} + \ldots + \frac{1}{\sqrt{n^2 + n}} .$$
Make sure you understand the nature of the general term.   The first three terms are

$$a_1 = \frac{1}{\sqrt{2}} , \quad a_2 = \frac{1}{\sqrt{2}} + \frac{1}{\sqrt{6}} , \quad a_3 = \frac{1}{\sqrt{2}} + \frac{1}{\sqrt{6}} + \frac{1}{\sqrt{12}} .$$

On the   one   hand we know that

$$a_n < \frac{1}{\sqrt{n^2}} + \frac{1}{\sqrt{n^2}} + \ldots + \frac{1}{\sqrt{n^2}} \quad (n \text{ terms in all})$$

or
$$a_n < \frac{n}{\sqrt{n^2}} = 1,$$

and on the other hand

$$a_n \geq \frac{1}{\sqrt{n^2 + n}} + \frac{1}{\sqrt{n^2 + n}} + \ldots + \frac{1}{\sqrt{n^2 + n}}$$

(n terms in all) or

$$a_n \geq \frac{n}{\sqrt{n^2 + n}} .$$

Thus we have $\dfrac{n}{\sqrt{n^2 + n}} \leq a_n \leq 1$, $n \geq 1$.

The sequence {1} obviously converges to 1, and the sequence $\dfrac{n}{\sqrt{n^2 + n}} = \dfrac{1}{\sqrt{1 + \dfrac{1}{n}}}$ also converges to 1. By Theorem 2.15 $\{a_n\}$ converges to 1.

Sequences having the limit zero occur often enough to warrant a special name.

Definition 2.16: Any sequence which converges to zero is called a null sequence.

There are several useful theorems dealing with null sequences. One of the simplest is the following.

Theorem 2.17: If $\{a_n\}$ is a null sequence and $\{b_n\}$ is bounded, then $\{a_n b_n\}$ is a null sequence.

Proof: Suppose ε is any positive number. Let M be a positive number such that $|b_n| \leq M$ for all n. Since $\{a_n\}$ converges to 0, there is a positive integer N such that $|a_n| < \dfrac{\varepsilon}{M}$ for all $n \geq N$. If $n \geq N$,

$$|a_n b_n - 0| = |a_n b_n| = |a_n||b_n|$$

$$\leq M|a_n|$$

$$< M(\dfrac{\varepsilon}{M})$$

$$= \varepsilon$$

and convergence to 0 is established directly from Definition 2.3. $\square$

55

The following theorem is helpful in showing that certain sequences converge to zero. The proof gives us another opportunity to employ the squeeze principle used in the previous example.

Theorem 2.18: Suppose $\{a_n\}$ is a sequence each term of which is positive. If there exists a (fixed) number r satisfying $0 < r < 1$ and a positive integer N such that

$$\frac{a_{n+1}}{a_n} \leq r \text{ for all } n \geq N,$$

then $\{a_n\}$ is a null sequence.

Proof: From the hypothesis we have

$$a_{N+1} \leq r a_N$$

$$a_{N+2} \leq r a_{N+1} \leq r(r a_N) = r^2 a_N$$

$$a_{N+3} \leq r a_{N+2} \leq r(r^2 a_N) = r^3 a_N$$

.

.

.

and in general $\quad a_{N+k} \leq r^k a_N$.

Define a sequence $\{c_n\}$ by

$$c_n = \begin{cases} 0 & \text{if } n \leq N \\ r^{n-N} a_N & \text{if } n > N \end{cases}$$

and let $\{b_n\}$ be the sequence consisting entirely

56

of zeros. Then

$$b_n \leq a_n \leq c_n \text{ for } n \geq N + 1.$$

From Example 3 and the corollary to Theorem 2.11 we know that $\{c_n\}$ converges to 0 (the fact that $r < 1$ is crucial). Since $\{b_n\}$ clearly converges to 0, we conclude from Theorem 2.15 that $\{a_n\}$ is also a null sequence. $\quad\square$

Example 10: Let $\{a_n\} = \{\frac{c^n}{n!}\}$ where c is any posi-tive number. Suppose N is a positive integer such that $N > 2c - 1$. For all $n \geq N$ we have

$$\frac{a_{n+1}}{a_n} = \frac{\dfrac{c^{n+1}}{(n + 1)!}}{\dfrac{c^n}{n!}} = \frac{c}{n + 1}$$

$$\leq \frac{c}{N + 1}$$

$$< \frac{c}{2c} \text{ since } N + 1 > 2c$$

$$= \frac{1}{2}$$

and $\{a_n\}$ is a null sequence by the previous theo-rem.

   As a special case of Example 10, consider $\{\frac{1000^n}{n!}\}$. Even though many terms at the beginning are enormous, the sequence nevertheless converges to zero. This is a striking illustration of the fact that, as far as convergence is concerned, the

57

behavior of any finite number of terms is unimportant.

Exercise 2.2

1. Prove the corollary to Theorem 2.11.

In each of Problems 2-9 determine convergence or divergence, and in the case of convergence evaluate the limit.

2. (a) $\{\frac{1 - 2n}{5n + 3}\}$ (b) $\{\frac{4n + 3}{n^2 + 2}\}$ (c) $\{\frac{(n - 1)^3}{3n - 1}\}$

3. $\{\frac{\cos n}{n}\}$ 4. $\{\frac{1}{\sqrt{n}}\}$ 5. $\{\sqrt{n^2 + n} - n\}$

6. $\{\frac{n!}{1 \cdot 3 \cdot 5 \cdots (2n - 1)}\}$ 7. $\{n - \sqrt{n}\}$

8. $\{\frac{n^2}{2^n}\}$ 9. $\{\frac{1}{n^2 + 1} + \frac{1}{n^2 + 2} + \ldots + \frac{1}{n^2 + n}\}$

10. Give an example of divergent sequences $\{a_n\}$ and $\{b_n\}$ such that $\{a_n + b_n\}$ is convergent.

11. Prove Theorem 2.14.

*12. Prove that if $\{a_n\}$ and $\{b_n\}$ both converge and $\{a_n - b_n\}$ is a null sequence, then $\{a_n\}$ and $\{b_n\}$ have the same limit.

13. Prove or disprove: if $\{a_n b_n\}$ is a null sequence and $\{b_n\}$ is bounded, then $\{a_n\}$ is a null sequence.

*14. If $\{a_n\}$ converges to A and all terms of $\{a_n\}$ are non-negative, show that $\{\sqrt{a_n}\}$ converges to $\sqrt{A}$.

15. Give an example of convergent sequences $\{a_n\}$ and $\{b_n\}$, having limits A and B, respectively,

such that $a_n < b_n$ for all n and $A = B$.

16. Prove or disprove: if $\{a_n\}$ is bounded and $\{a_{n+1} - a_n\}$ is a null sequence, then $\{a_n\}$ converges.

17. Suppose $\{a_n\}$ is a sequence each term of which is positive. If there exists a number $r > 1$ and a positive integer N such that $\frac{a_{n+1}}{a_n} \geq r$ for all $n \geq N$, prove that $\{a_n\}$ diverges.

18. Find three pairs of null sequences $\{a_n\}$ and $\{b_n\}$, each satisfying one of the following:
    (a) $\{\frac{a_n}{b_n}\}$ diverges   (b) $\{\frac{a_n}{b_n}\}$ converges to zero

    (c) $\{\frac{a_n}{b_n}\}$ converges to a non-zero number

19. Suppose $\{a_n + b_n\}$ converges to C and $\{a_n - b_n\}$ converges to D. Show that $\{a_n b_n\}$ must converge, and find the limit.

20. Prove or disprove: if $\{na_n\}$ is bounded, then $\{a_n\}$ is a null sequence.

21. (a) Give an example of a null sequence $\{a_n\}$, all terms positive, such that $\{\frac{a_{n+1}}{a_n}\}$ converges to 1.

    (b) Give an example of a divergent sequence $\{a_n\}$, all terms positive, such that $\{\frac{a_{n+1}}{a_n}\}$ converges to 1.

22. If $\{a_n\}$ is any sequence, define a sequence $\{\rho_n\}$ by

$$\rho_n = \frac{a_1 + a_2 + \ldots + a_n}{n}$$

for each positive integer n. Prove that if $\{a_n\}$ converges to A, then $\{\rho_n\}$ also converges to A.

3. Monotonic Sequences

Definition 2.19: The sequence $\{a_n\}$ is said to be increasing provided there exists a positive integer N such that $a_{n+1} \geq a_n$ for all $n \geq N$. The sequence $\{a_n\}$ is said to be decreasing provided there exists a positive integer N such that $a_{n+1} \leq a_n$ for all $n > N$. A sequence which is either increasing or decreasing is said to be monotonic.

Example 11: Consider $\{\frac{2^n}{n!}\}$. Then $a_n = \frac{2^n}{n!}$ and $a_{n+1} = \frac{2^{n+1}}{(n+1)!}$. This sequence can be shown to be decreasing by the following reasoning.

If
$$1 < n$$

then
$$2 < n+1$$

$$2n! < (n+1)!$$

$$2^n(2n!) < 2^n(n+1)!$$

$$2^{n+1}n! < 2^n(n+1)!$$

$$\frac{2^{n+1}n!}{(n+1)!} < 2^n$$

$$\frac{2^{n+1}}{(n+1)!} < \frac{2^n}{n!} \quad .$$

Consequently $a_{n+1} < a_n$ for $n \geq 2$. Just as in Example 1 the steps involved in establishing the desired inequality would actually be discovered by working backwards.

<u>Example 12</u>: Let $\{a_n\} = \{(1 + \frac{1}{n})^n\}$. We will show
that this important sequence is increasing. Using
the Binomial Theorem,

$$a_n = 1 + n(\frac{1}{n}) + \frac{n(n-1)}{2!}(\frac{1}{n})^2$$

$$+ \frac{n(n-1)(n-2)}{3!}(\frac{1}{n})^3 + \ldots + \frac{n!}{n!}(\frac{1}{n})^n$$

or

$$a_n = 1 + 1 + \sum_{k=2}^{n} \frac{n(n-1)(n-2)\ldots(n-k+1)}{k!}(\frac{1}{n})^k$$

for $n \geq 2$. We can also say

$$a_n = 2 + \sum_{k=2}^{n} \frac{\frac{n}{n} \cdot \frac{n-1}{n} \cdot \frac{n-2}{n} \ldots \frac{n-k+1}{n}}{k!} \quad (n \geq 2)$$

and therefore

$$a_n = 2 + \sum_{k=2}^{n} \frac{(1-\frac{1}{n})(1-\frac{2}{n})\cdots(1 - \frac{k-1}{n})}{k!} \quad (n \geq 2).$$

Since this expression represents any term of the
sequence (except the first one), we can get a re-
presentation for a_{n+1} by simply replacing n by
n + 1:

$$a_{n+1} = 2 + \sum_{k=2}^{n+1} \frac{(1-\frac{1}{n+1})(1-\frac{2}{n+1})\cdots(1 - \frac{k-1}{n+1})}{k!} \quad (n \geq 1).$$

Notice that each factor in the numerator of the summation for a_{n+1} is greater than the corresponding
factor in the numerator of the summation for a_n.

That is,

$$1 - \frac{1}{n+1} > 1 - \frac{1}{n}$$

$$1 - \frac{2}{n+1} > 1 - \frac{2}{n}$$

.
.
.

$$1 - \frac{k-1}{n+1} > 1 - \frac{k-1}{n} .$$

(The easiest way to see this is to observe that in each term on the left a smaller number is being subtracted from 1 than in the corresponding term on the right.) In addition, the summation for a_{n+1} has one more (positive) term than the summation for a_n, the one for which $k = n + 1$. Certainly, then, we can say that $a_{n+1} > a_n$ for $n \geq 1$. This example will be found useful in several future problems.

The principal importance of monotonic sequences is given by the following two theorems.

Theorem 2.20: If a sequence is both increasing and bounded above, it is convergent.

Proof: Suppose $\{a_n\}$ is an increasing sequence which is bounded above. Since every set which is bounded above has a least upper bound, let A denote the least upper bound of the set

$$S = \{a_n: \quad n = 1, 2, 3, \ldots \}.$$

64

Let D be any neighborhood of A. Then $D = (A - \varepsilon, A + \varepsilon)$ for some positive number ε. Since A is an upper bound for S, $a_n \leq A$ for every positive integer n. Since A is also the least upper bound for S, no number smaller than A is an upper bound. In particular, $A - \varepsilon$ is not an upper bound for S. Therefore, for some positive integer N, $A - \varepsilon < a_N$. But $\{a_n\}$ is an increasing sequence, so $a_N \leq a_n$ for all $n \geq N$. Hence, we have the following:

$$A - \varepsilon < a_N \leq a_n \leq A < A + \varepsilon \text{ for all } n \geq N.$$

We conclude from Theorem 2.5 that $\{a_n\}$ converges to A.   □

Even though the proof tells us what the limit is, namely the least upper bound of the range of the sequence, finding this least upper bound is usually no easier than finding the limit directly. Ordinarily we will use the theorem by showing that a sequence is both increasing and bounded above and conclude convergence without ever knowing the actual limit. Similar comments apply to the next theorem.

Theorem 2.21: If a sequence is both decreasing and bounded below, it is convergent.

Proof: Left as an exercise.

Example 13: The sequence $\{\frac{2^n}{n!}\}$ was shown to be decreasing in Example 11. Since each term is obviously positive, the sequence is bounded below by 0 and therefore convergent by Theorem 2.21.

Example 14: The sequence $\{a_n\} = \{(1 + \frac{1}{n})^n\}$ was shown to be increasing in Example 12. We obtained there the expression

65

$$a_n = 2 + \sum_{k=2}^{n} \frac{(1-\frac{1}{n})(1-\frac{2}{n})\ldots(1-\frac{k-1}{n})}{k!} \quad (n \geq 2).$$

Since $1 - \frac{i}{n} < 1$, $i = 1, 2, \ldots, k - 1$

we see that

$$a_n < 2 + \sum_{k=2}^{n} \frac{(1)(1) \ldots (1)}{k!} \ ;$$

that is,

$$a_n < 2 + \frac{1}{2!} + \frac{1}{3!} + \ldots + \frac{1}{n!} \ .$$

To obtain an upper bound we reason as follows. For $n \geq 2$,

$$a_n < 2 + \frac{1}{1\cdot 2} + \frac{1}{1\cdot 2\cdot 3} + \frac{1}{1\cdot 2\cdot 3\cdot 4} + \ldots + \frac{1}{1\cdot 2\cdot 3\cdots n}$$

$$< 2 + \frac{1}{1\cdot 2} + \frac{1}{1\cdot 2\cdot 2} + \frac{1}{1\cdot 2\cdot 2\cdot 2} + \ldots + \frac{1}{1\cdot 2\cdot 2\cdots 2\cdot 2}$$

$$= 2 + \frac{1}{2} + \frac{1}{4} + \frac{1}{8} + \ldots + \frac{1}{2^{n-1}}$$

$$= 2 + (1 - \frac{1}{2^{n-1}})$$

$$< 2 + 1$$

$$= 3$$

where we use the algebraic identity

$$a + ar + ar^2 + \ldots + ar^{k-1} = \frac{a(1 - r^k)}{1 - r}$$

66

with $a = \frac{1}{2}$, $r = \frac{1}{2}$, $k = n - 1$. The argument above applied only to a_n for which $n \geq 2$. However, $a_1 = (1 + \frac{1}{1})^1 = 2$, so $a_1 < 3$ also. Therefore $\{(1 + \frac{1}{n})^n\}$ is increasing and bounded above and consequently convergent by Theorem 2.20. The limit of this sequence is actually e, the base of natural logarithms.

The fact that a particular sequence is monotonic can sometimes be established by mathematical induction. This is often the case with sequences which are defined recursively. A typical example follows.

Example 15: Define $a_1 = 1$ and $a_{n+1} = \sqrt{1 + a_n}$ for $n \geq 1$. We find that

$$\{a_n\} = \{1, \sqrt{2}, \sqrt{1 + \sqrt{2}}, \sqrt{1 + \sqrt{1 + \sqrt{2}}}, \ldots\}$$

and "guess" that the sequence is increasing. To prove that this conjecture is correct we need to show that: (1) $a_1 < a_2$ and (2) if $a_{k-1} < a_k$, then $a_k < a_{k+1}$. Certainly $a_1 < a_2$ since $1 < \sqrt{2}$. For part (2) we have

$$a_{k-1} < a_k$$

$$1 + a_{k-1} < 1 + a_k$$

$$\sqrt{1 + a_{k-1}} < \sqrt{1 + a_k}$$

$$a_k < a_{k+1} \ .$$

We next need to show that $\{a_n\}$ is bounded above. By examining the first few terms of the sequence, one might try 2 as an upper bound. To establish this we must show: (1) $a_1 < 2$ and (2) if $a_k < 2$, then $a_{k+1} < 2$. Obviously (1) is true. Assuming $a_k < 2$ we get

$$
\begin{aligned}
a_{k+1} &= \sqrt{1 + a_k} \\
&< \sqrt{1 + 2} \\
&= \sqrt{3} \\
&< \sqrt{4} \\
&= 2.
\end{aligned}
$$

Hence $\{a_n\}$ converges since it is both increasing and bounded above. Theorem 2.20 gives us no help in finding the limit, but the limit can nevertheless be determined (in this case, anyway) by the following useful device. Let A denote the limit. From $a_{n+1} = \sqrt{1 + a_n}$ we get

$$a_{n+1}^2 = 1 + a_n$$

so that

$$\{a_{n+1}\}^2 = \{1\} + \{a_n\}.$$

Clearly $\{a_{n+1}\}$ has the same limit as $\{a_n\}$. Therefore

$$A^2 = 1 + A$$

and consequently $A = \dfrac{1 + \sqrt{5}}{2}$. Since the limit can't be negative ($a_n \geq 1$ for all n), we conclude that

$$A = \frac{1 + \sqrt{5}}{2} \ .$$

Note carefully that the last part of the discussion does not in any way prove convergence. It does enable us to find the limit provided the limit is already known to exist.

Example 16: Suppose c is any positive number. Define $\{a_n\}$ as follows: a_1 is any positive number and

$$a_{n+1} = \frac{1}{2} (a_n + \frac{c}{a_n}) \text{ for } n \geq 1.$$

It is not hard to see that each term of the sequence is positive. (This can quickly be proved by mathematical induction, if need be.) For every integer $n \geq 2$ we have

$$a_n^2 - c = \left[\frac{1}{2} (a_{n-1} + \frac{c}{a_{n-1}}) \right]^2 - c$$

$$= \frac{1}{4} (a_{n-1}^2 + 2c + \frac{c^2}{a_{n-1}^2}) - c$$

$$= \frac{1}{4} (a_{n-1}^2 - 2c + \frac{c^2}{a_{n-1}^2})$$

$$= \frac{1}{4} (a_{n-1} - \frac{c}{a_{n-1}})^2$$

$$\geq 0.$$

Furthermore, for $n \geq 2$,

$$a_n - a_{n+1} = a_n - \frac{1}{2} (a_n + \frac{c}{a_n})$$

$$= \frac{1}{2} (a_n - \frac{c}{a_n})$$

$$= \frac{1}{2} (\frac{a_n^2 - c}{a_n})$$

$$\geq 0 \text{ since } a_n > 0 \text{ and } a_n^2 - c \geq 0.$$

In other words $a_n \geq a_{n+1}$ for $n \geq 2$, so the sequence is decreasing. It is bounded below by zero and therefore convergent by Theorem 2.21. If A denotes the limit, then

$$A = \frac{1}{2} (A + \frac{c}{A}).$$

Elementary algebra shows that $A^2 = c$, and consequently $\{a_n\}$ converges to $\sqrt{c}$. This example is of more than passing interest, for the sequence given above is actually a very efficient algorithm for computing square roots. The closer a_1 is to $\sqrt{c}$, the more rapid is the convergence. But $\{a_n\}$ converges to $\sqrt{c}$ for any positive number a_1!

Before leaving monotonic sequences, a few comments are in order. Every increasing sequence is automatically bounded below (by its first term), and every decreasing sequence is automatically bounded above (by its first term). Therefore the conditions "bounded above" in Theorem 2.20 and "bounded below" in Theorem 2.21 can both be replaced by "bounded" without any change in meaning. The two theorems can then be combined into the following simpler statement: "Every bounded monotonic sequence converges." The importance of this result is that we are able to show many sequences

70

convergent (those which are monotonic and bounded) without ever knowing the limit. Since finding the limit is often difficult if not impossible, this is a great advantage. The requirement that a sequence be monotonic, of course, is rather strict. Later we will examine a different sufficient condition for convergence which applies to a larger class of sequences.

We next consider a topic which is important in its own right and which also has important consequences for the study of sequences.

Definition 2.22: The number x is said to be a limit point of the set S provided every neighborhood of x contains infinitely many points of S.

The terms "cluster point" and "point of accumulation" are often used instead of "limit point". This language is perhaps more descriptive, for it expresses the fact that such a point is a point around which elements of the set congregate. Note carefully that x does not have to be an element of S just because x is a limit point of S.

Example 17:

    (a)   Let $S = \{x: \ 1 < x < 2\}$. The set of limit points of S is $\{x: \ 1 \leq x \leq 2\}$.

    (b)   Let $S = \{x: \ x = \frac{1}{n}$, n a positive integer$\}$. The only limit point of S is 0.

    (c)   Let $S = \{x: \ 1 < x < 2$ and x is rational$\}$. The set of limit points of S is $\{x: \ 1 \leq x \leq 2\}$.

    (d)   Let S denote the set of positive integers. Then S has no limit points.

Theorem 2.23: The number x is a limit point of the set S if and only if the following condition is satisfied:

there exists a sequence $\{a_n\}$ of mutually distinct elements of S, each different from x, such that $\{a_n\}$ converges to x.

Proof: Suppose that $\{a_n\}$ converges to x, $a_n \neq x$ for all n, and $a_m = a_n$ only if m = n. We want to show that x is a limit point of S. Let D be any neighborhood of x. We know by Theorem 2.5 that there exists a positive integer N such that D contains every a_n for $n \geq N$. Since no two terms of $\{a_n\}$ are equal, but each is an element of S, D contains infinitely many elements of S. Thus x is a limit point of S, and half of the theorem is proved.

Suppose next that x is a limit point of S. For each positive integer n let D_n denote the neighborhood $(x - \frac{1}{n}, x + \frac{1}{n})$. Remember that, since x is a limit point of S, every neighborhood of x contains infinitely many points of S. Certainly D_1 contains a point a_1 of S distinct from x (we don't know whether x belongs to S or not). Similarly D_2 contains a point a_2 of S distinct from x and such that $a_2 \neq a_1$. Furthermore D_3 contains a point a_3 of S such that $a_3 \neq x$, $a_3 \neq a_2$, and $a_3 \neq a_1$. In general D_n contains a point a_n of S which is distinct from x and distinct from $a_1, a_2, \ldots a_{n-1}$. Since each neighborhood of x contains infinitely many points of S, there must be one point (infinitely many, actually) with this property. The sequence $\{a_n\}$ thus defined clearly

72

has mutually distinct elements of S, each different from x. Note that for each positive integer
n, D_n contains a_n, a_{n+1}, a_{n+2}, $\cdots$. Let D be
any neighborhood of x. Then D = $(x - \varepsilon, x + \varepsilon)$
for some positive number ε. If N is any integer
satisfying N > $\frac{1}{\varepsilon}$, then $\frac{1}{N} < \varepsilon$ and D_N is a subset of
D. Since D_N contains a_N, a_{N+1}, a_{N+2}, $\cdots$, it
follows that D contains every a_n for n $\geq$ N. Hence
$\{a_n\}$ converges to x by Theorem 2.5, and the proof
is complete. $\square$

We now come to a theorem which is one of the
cornerstones of analysis. This theorem was first
proved by the Czechoslovakian priest Bolzano about
1817. It was not until many years later, however,
that the importance of this result was recognized
and publicized by the German mathematician Weierstrass. Despite the imposing name and big build-
up, the proof of the theorem is within the reach
of anyone who has followed the development so far.
If you've never seen it proved, by all means try
to provide a proof yourself before reading the one
in the book. Give yourself plenty of time, and
keep in mind the various results already established.
Even if you fail, you will gain a greater apprecia-
tion of this wonderful theorem.

Theorem 2.24 (Bolzano-Weierstrass Theorem): Every
bounded infinite set has at least one limit point.

Proof: Let S be any bounded infinite set. Since
S is bounded, there exists a closed interval I_0 =
$[a_0, b_0]$ which contains S. Thus we have the infinitely many points of S somehow distributed
along the interval I_0 of finite length. It seems
reasonable that some "arbitrarily small" part of

the interval must have a heavy concentration of
points of S--in other words, a limit point. But
knowing nothing else about S, how can we possibly
determine the location of such a point? This is
the heart of the problem.

Let m_0 denote the midpoint of I_0. At least
one of the two intervals $[a_0,m_0]$ and $[m_0,b_0]$ must
contain infinitely many elements of S, for if this
were not so S would be a finite set. Let I_1 =
$[a_1,b_1]$ be whichever of the two intervals has this
property; if they both do, let I_1 be either one.
(The change in subscripts is for notational convenience. If $I_1 = [a_0,m_0]$, then $a_1 = a_0$ and if
$I_1 = [m_0,b_0]$, then $b_1 = b_0$.) Let m_1 denote the
midpoint of I_1. Let $I_2 = [a_2,b_2]$ be whichever of
the two intervals $[a_1,m_1]$ and $[m_1,b_1]$ contains
infinitely many elements of S. One of the two
certainly has this property by the same reasoning
as before. Continuing this argument, we obtain
for each positive integer n an interval $I_n = [a_n,b_n]$
such that I_n contains infinitely many elements of
S and I_n is a subset of I_{n-1}. The situation might
look something like this:

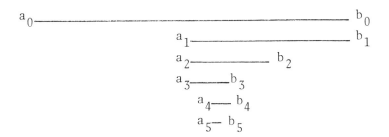

From the manner in which the intervals are determined we know that

$$a_0 \leq a_1 \leq a_2 \leq a_3 \leq$$
$$\cdots \leq a_n \leq \cdots \leq b_n \leq$$
$$\cdots \leq b_2 \leq b_1 \leq b_0.$$

Furthermore, since the length of each interval is
half the length of the preceding one, it is not
hard to show that

$$(1) \quad b_n - a_n = \frac{b_0 - a_0}{2^n}.$$

The sequence $\{a_n\}$ is increasing and bounded above
(by b_0) and consequently convergent by Theorem 2.20.
The sequence $\{b_n\}$ is decreasing and bounded below
(by a_0) and therefore convergent by Theorem 2.21.
Let A denote the limit of $\{a_n\}$ and B the limit of
$\{b_n\}$. The sequence $\{\frac{1}{2^n}\}$ is easily seen to be a
null sequence, so $\{(b_0 - a_0) \frac{1}{2^n}\}$ is a null sequence
also. Therefore, from (1) above, $\{b_n - a_n\}$ is a
null sequence. Furthermore, Problem 12 of Exercise 2.2 tells us that A = B. It follows that
$a_n \leq A \leq b_n$ for every n since A is the limit of
both monotonic sequences.

We have only to show that A is a limit point
of S. Let D be any neighborhood of A. Then D =
$(A - \varepsilon, A + \varepsilon)$ for some positive number ε. Let N
be an integer such that $b_N - a_N < \varepsilon$. Then the
interval I_N is a subset of D. Since I_N contains
infinitely many elements of S, so does D. Hence
A is a limit point of S.   □

75

There are several worthwhile observations to be made about the argument just given. This is a "constructive" as opposed to an "existence" proof. That is, we are not only assured that every bounded infinite set has a limit point, but we are given a method for finding such a point (theoretically, that is, since infinitely many steps could not actually be carried out). Notice that the method of the proof might produce many limit points. If both halves of some subinterval I_n contain infinitely many elements of S, we are allowed to choose either half in our argument. It seems likely that the two choices would lead to different limit points. Finally, notice how heavily the proof depends on the fact that every bounded monotonic sequence converges. Since the latter result was obtained by using the least upper bound axiom, perhaps that principle could be used if a different proof of the Bolzano-Weiertrass Theorem were desired.

Exercise 2.3

1. Give an example of a convergent sequence which is not monotonic.

2. Prove Theorem 2.21.

3. If $\{a_n\} = \{\dfrac{n - 6}{n^2 + 1}\}$, determine the smallest positive integer N such that $a_{n+1} < a_n$ for all $n \geq N$.

4. Show that if S is any set, the set of limit points of S cannot be the rational numbers.

5. Suppose S is a set and S' is the set of limit points of S. Prove that if x is a limit point of S', then x is a limit point of S.

6. Give an example of an unbounded countable set which has a limit point.

7. Define a sequence $\{a_n\}$ as follows: $a_1 = 1$ and $a_{n+1} = \dfrac{1}{4}(2a_n + 1)$ for $n \geq 1$. Use Theorem 2.21 to show that $\{a_n\}$ converges. Then find the limit.

8. Using the fact that $\{(1 + \dfrac{1}{n})^n\}$ converges to e, determine the limit of each of the following sequences.

(a) $\{(1 + \dfrac{1}{n + 1})^n\}$ (b) $\{(1 + \dfrac{1}{n})^{n+5}\}$

(c) $\{(1 + \dfrac{2}{n})^n\}$ (d) $\{(1 + \dfrac{1}{n})^{\frac{n}{2}}\}$

In Problems 9-14 determine convergence or divergence of each sequence. In the case of convergence, find the limit if possible.

9. $\{\frac{1 \cdot 3 \cdot 5 \cdots (2n - 1)}{2 \cdot 4 \cdot 6 \cdots (2n)}\}$ 10. $\{\frac{1 + 2 + \ldots + n}{n^2}\}$

11. $\{\frac{n!}{n^n}\}$ 12. $\{\frac{1}{n + 1} + \frac{1}{n + 2} + \ldots + \frac{1}{2n}\}$

13. $\{a_n\}$ where $a_1 = 0$, $a_{n+1} = \sqrt{2a_n + 3}$ for $n \geq 1$

14. $\{a_n\}$ where $a_1 = 1$, $a_{n+1} = \frac{3a_n - 1}{a_n + 2}$ for $n \geq 1$

*15. Suppose S is a set which is bounded above [bounded below]. Show that the least upper bound [greatest lower bound] of S is either an element of S or a limit point of S.

16. Suppose $\{a_n\}$ and $\{b_n\}$ are any increasing sequences. Determine whether or not each of the following sequences is necessarily increasing.

(a) $\{a_n + b_n\}$ (b) $\{a_n - b_n\}$

(c) $\{a_n b_n\}$ (d) $\{\frac{a_n}{b_n}\}$

17. Same as the preceding problem with "increasing" replaced by "monotonic."

18. Determine whether or not there exists a bounded set whose set of limit points is countable.

19. Letting $c = 2$ and $a_1 = 1$, calculate the next four terms of the sequence in Example 16. Using a table of square roots, determine to how many decimal places of accuracy each of these

78

numbers approximates $\sqrt{2}$.

20. Prove the Bolzano-Weierstrass Theorem without using Theorems 2.20 and 2.21.

*21. Prove that the sequence $\{\sqrt[n]{n}\}$ converges to one.

4. Cauchy Sequences

Definition 2.25: Suppose $\{a_n\}$ is a sequence and $\{i_n\} = \{i_1, i_2, i_3, \ldots\}$ is an increasing sequence of mutually distinct positive integers. For each positive integer n define b_n by $b_n = a_{i_n}$. Then the sequence $\{b_n\}$ is called a <u>subsequence</u> of $\{a_n\}$.

The idea of a subsequence is very simple, though notationally a bit of a problem. If from a sequence we select any infinite collection of terms, the result is a subsequence provided the order of the chosen terms is the same as it was in the original sequence. (Do you think the set of all subsequences of a sequence is countable or uncountable?) Note also that every sequence is a subsequence of itself.

Example 18: Some subsequences of $\{n^2\} = \{1, 4, 9, 16, 25, 36, \ldots\}$ are given below.

    (a) $\{(2n - 1)^2\} = \{1, 9, 25, 49, \ldots\}$

    (b) $\{(2n)^2\} = \{4, 16, 36, 64, \ldots\}$

    (c) $\{(3n + 1)^2\} = \{16, 49, 100, 169, \ldots\}$

    (d) $\{1, 9, 36, 100, 225, 441, \ldots\}$ where the pattern is: pick one, omit one; pick one, omit two; pick one, omit three; etc.

Theorem 2.26: If $\{a_n\}$ converges to A, every subsequence $\{a_{i_n}\}$ of $\{a_n\}$ also converges to A.

80

Proof: Suppose ε is any positive number. There exists a positive integer N such that $|a_n - A| < \varepsilon$ for all $n > N$. It follows immediately that $|a_{i_n} - A| < \varepsilon$ for all $i_n \geq N$ since every element of $\{a_{i_n}\}$ is an element of $\{a_n\}$. Thus, $\{a_{i_n}\}$ converges to A. $\qquad\qquad\qquad\qquad\qquad\qquad\square$

Certainly a divergent sequence can have a convergent subsequence. For example, $\{(-1)^{n+1}\} = \{1, -1, 1, -1, \ldots\}$ has both $\{1, 1, 1, \ldots\}$ and $\{-1, -1, -1, \ldots\}$ as convergent subsequences. However, if all subsequences of a sequence converge, then the sequence itself converges for it is in fact one of the subsequences. The discussion of convergent subsequences is facilitated by the following terminology.

Definition 2.27: The number x is said to be a limiting point of the sequence $\{a_n\}$ provided some subsequence of $\{a_n\}$ converges to x.

Notice that we speak of a "limiting point" of a sequence and a "limit point" of a set. The two concepts are similar but different.

Example 19:

(a) The sequence $\{(-1)^{n+1}\}$ has only +1 and -1 as limiting points.

(b) The sequence $\{\frac{n + 1}{1 - 2n}\}$ has only $-\frac{1}{2}$ as a limiting point.

(c) The sequence $\{\sqrt{n}\}$ has no limiting points.

81

(d) The sequence $\{\cos \frac{n\pi}{2}\}$ has only 0, +1, and -1 as limiting points.

(e) Every positive integer (and no other number) is a limiting point of the sequence
$$\{1+1, \ 1+\frac{1}{2}, \ 2+\frac{1}{2}, \ 1+\frac{1}{3}, \ 2+\frac{1}{3}, \ 3+\frac{1}{3}, \ 1+\frac{1}{4},$$
$$2+\frac{1}{4}, \ 3+\frac{1}{4}, \ 4+\frac{1}{4}, \ . \ . \ . \ , \ 1+\frac{1}{n}, \ 2+\frac{1}{n},$$
$$3+\frac{1}{n}, \ . \ . \ . \ , \ n+\frac{1}{n}, \ . \ . \ .\}.$$

A natural question to consider is "how many" limiting points a sequence can have. If no restriction is placed on the sequence, the examples above show that the answer is anywhere from none to infinitely many. It is an immediate consequence of Theorem 2.26 that every convergent sequence has exactly one limiting point. From the Bolzano-Weierstrass Theorem we might conjecture that a bounded sequence has at least one limiting point. This is, in fact, true, and you should be able to give a proof at this time, probably using Theorem 2.24. The proof is almost trivial, however, after the following interesting result has been established.

Theorem 2.28: Every sequence has a monotonic subsequence.

Proof: Suppose $\{a_n\}$ is any sequence. For each positive integer n define a subsequence S_n of $\{a_n\}$ as follows: $S_n = \{a_n, \ a_{n+1}, \ a_{n+2}, \ . \ . \ . \}$. We consider two cases.

Case 1: Every one of the subsequences S_n has a largest element, that is, a term whose value is

82

exceeded by no other term of S_n (the same maximum value could occur as more than one term of S_n.) In this case a decreasing subsequence of $\{a_n\}$ can be constructed in the following way. Let a_{i_1} be the largest term of S_1 (if several terms have the same largest value, pick any one of them). Let a_{i_2} be the largest term of S_{i_1+1}. Note that $i_1 < i_1 + 1 \leq i_2$. Notice also that $a_{i_2} \leq a_{i_1}$, for if we had $a_{i_2} > a_{i_1}$, then a_{i_2} would have been chosen as the largest element of S_1. Let a_{i_3} be the largest term of S_{i_2+1}. Then $i_2 < i_2 + 1 \leq i_3$ and $a_{i_3} \leq a_{i_2}$. Continuation of the same argument yields a decreasing subsequence $\{a_{i_n}\}$ of $\{a_n\}$.

Case 2: Not every one of the subsequences S_n has a largest element. Then for some particular positive integer N, S_N does not have a largest element. The implication of this fact is as follows: for any element x of S_N there are infinitely many elements of S_N larger than x (if there were only finitely many larger than x, the largest of this finite number would be the largest element of S_N). Let a_{n_1} be any element of S_N (hence $n_1 \geq N$). By our reasoning above there is an element a_{n_2} of S_N such that $a_{n_2} > a_{n_1}$ and $n_2 > n_1$. Likewise there exists an element a_{n_3} of S_N such that $a_{n_3} > a_{n_2}$ and $n_3 > n_2$. Continuation of this argument yields an increasing subsequence $\{a_{i_n}\}$ of $\{a_n\}$ $\qquad\square$

Theorem 2.29: Every bounded sequence has a convergent subsequence.

Proof: Suppose $\{a_n\}$ is any bounded sequence. By
Theorem 2.28 $\{a_n\}$ has a monotonic subsequence $\{a_{i_n}\}$
(note that the boundedness of $\{a_n\}$ is not needed
here). The sequence $\{a_{i_n}\}$ is bounded (see Problem
1 of Exercise 2.4). But every bounded monotonic
sequence converges.   □

An equivalent formulation of the preceding
theorem would be, "Every bounded sequence has at
least one limiting point." A sequence can sometimes be shown convergent by consideration of certain of its subsequences. The following theorem
gives one way of doing this.

Theorem 2.30: Suppose $\{a_n\}$ is a sequence satisfying the following three conditions:

   (a) $\{a_{2n-1}\}$ is increasing [decreasing];

   (b) $\{a_{2n}\}$ is decreasing [increasing];

   (c) $\{a_{n+1} - a_n\}$ is a null sequence.

Then $\{a_n\}$ converges.

Proof: We assume that the range of $\{a_n\}$ is infinite, since otherwise there is nothing to prove.
From the hypothesis we know that there is a positive integer N such that

   $a_{2n-1} \leq a_{2n+1}$ and $a_{2n+2} \leq a_{2n}$ for $n \geq N$.

Suppose that for some $M \geq N$ we had $a_{2M} < a_{2M-1}$.

Then, since $\{a_{2n}\}$ is decreasing and $\{a_{2n-1}\}$ is increasing, we would have

$$\cdots \leq a_{2M+4} \leq a_{2M+2} \leq a_{2M}$$
$$< a_{2M-1} \leq a_{2M+1} \leq a_{2M+3} \leq \cdots \cdots$$

Therefore

$$|a_{n+1} - a_n| \geq a_{2M-1} - a_{2M} \text{ for all } n \geq 2M - 1.$$

Since $a_{2M-1} - a_{2M}$ is a fixed positive number, $\{a_{n+1} - a_n\}$ would not be a null sequence. This contradiction tells us that the relationship of the terms must be as follows:

$$a_{2N-1} \leq a_{2N+1} \leq a_{2N+3} \leq \cdots \leq \cdots \leq a_{2N+4} \leq a_{2N+2} \leq a_{2N}.$$

Hence both sequences $\{a_{2n-1}\}$ and $\{a_{2n}\}$ are bounded and consequently convergent. Let A_1 denote the limit of $\{a_{2n-1}\}$ and A_2 the limit of $\{a_{2n}\}$. Assume $A_1 \neq A_2$. Let $|A_1 - A_2| = \varepsilon$. There exists a positive integer L such that

$$|a_{2n-1} - A_1| < \varepsilon/3 \text{ for } n \geq L$$
$$|a_{2n} - A_2| < \varepsilon/3 \text{ for } n \geq L$$
$$|a_{2n} - a_{2n-1}| < \varepsilon/3 \text{ for } n \geq L.$$

The first two of these inequalities follow from the convergence of $\{a_{2n-1}\}$ and $\{a_{2n}\}$ and the last from the hypothesis. From $A_2 - A_1 = (A_2 - a_{2n}) + (a_{2n} - a_{2n-1}) + (a_{2n-1} - A_1)$ we get, for $n \geq L$,

$$|A_2 - A_1| \leq |A_2 - a_{2n}| + |a_{2n} - a_{2n-1}|$$
$$+ |a_{2n-1} - A_1| < \varepsilon/3 + \varepsilon/3 + \varepsilon/3 = \varepsilon$$

85

which contradicts the fact that $|A_2 - A_1| = \varepsilon$.
Hence $A_1 = A_2$. Since both $\{a_{2n-1}\}$ and $\{a_{2n}\}$ converge to A_1, and since every term of $\{a_n\}$ has either an even or odd subscript, it follows that $\{a_n\}$ converges to A_1 also. (A similar proof can be provided for the case where $\{a_{2n-1}\}$ is decreasing and $\{a_{2n}\}$ is increasing.) $\qquad\square$

Example 20: Let $\{a_n\}$ be defined by $a_1 = 0$, $a_2 = 1$, and $a_{n+2} = \dfrac{a_{n+1} + a_n}{2}$ for $n \geq 1$. The first eight terms of the sequence are easily found to be
0, 1, 1/2, 3/4, 5/8, 11/16, 21/32, 43/64. Hence
$\{a_{2n-1}\} = \{0, 1/2, 5/8, 21/32, \ldots\}$ and $\{a_{2n}\} = \{1, 3/4, 11/16, 43/64, \ldots\}$. It seems likely that $\{a_{2n-1}\}$ is increasing and $\{a_{2n}\}$ is decreasing.
Mathematical induction is needed to prove these conjectures. For $\{a_{2n-1}\}$ the induction is started with $0 < \dfrac{1}{2}$. We assume $a_{2k-1} < a_{2k+1}$ and try to show $a_{2k+1} < a_{2k+3}$.

$$a_{2k-1} < a_{2k+1}$$

$$a_{2k} + a_{2k-1} < a_{2k} + a_{2k+1}$$

$$\frac{a_{2k} + a_{2k-1}}{2} < \frac{a_{2k} + a_{2k+1}}{2}$$

$$a_{2k+1} < a_{2k+2}$$

$$a_{2k+1} + a_{2k+1} < a_{2k+1} + a_{2k+2}$$

86

$$\frac{2a_{2k+1}}{2} < \frac{a_{2k+1} + a_{2k+2}}{2}$$

$$a_{2k+1} < a_{2k+3}$$

The proof that $\{a_{2n}\}$ is decreasing is similar and is left as an exercise. By direct calculation we find the following: $a_2 - a_1 = 1$, $a_3 - a_2 = -1/2$, $a_4 - a_3 = 1/4$, $a_5 - a_4 = -1/8$, $a_6 - a_5 = 1/16$. On the basis of this evidence we conjecture $a_{n+1} - a_n = \frac{(-1)^{n-1}}{2^{n-1}}$. This will now be proved by induction. If $n = 1$, the formula gives $\frac{(-1)^0}{2^0} = 1$, which is $a_2 - a_1$. Assuming that $a_{k+1} - a_k = \frac{(-1)^{k-1}}{2^{k-1}}$, we need to show $a_{k+2} - a_{k+1} = \frac{(-1)^k}{2^k}$.

$$
\begin{aligned}
a_{k+2} - a_{k+1} &= \frac{a_{k+1} + a_k}{2} - a_{k+1} \\
&= \frac{a_k - a_{k+1}}{2} \\
&= -\frac{a_{k+1} - a_k}{2} \\
&= -\frac{1}{2} \cdot \frac{(-1)^{k-1}}{2^{k-1}} \\
&= \frac{(-1)^k}{2^k}
\end{aligned}
$$

From previous results it's clear that $\{a_{n+1} - a_n\} = \left\{ \frac{(-1)^{n-1}}{2^{n-1}} \right\}$ is a null sequence. All conditions of Theorem 2.30 are met, so $\{a_n\}$ converges

We have seen that finding the limit of a sequence is often difficult, if not impossible. Nevertheless, such a sequence can sometimes be shown convergent by such theorems as 2.20, 2.21, or 2.30. The hypothesis of each of these, however, is quite stringent. What we need is a more general sufficient condition for convergence. Loosely speaking, in a convergent sequence the terms get closer and closer to a fixed number, the limit. Therefore the terms get closer and closer to each other. Thinking along these lines the French mathematician Augustin-Louis Cauchy investigated the following condition, which has come to bear his name.

<u>Definition 2.31</u>: The sequence $\{a_n\}$ is said to be a <u>Cauchy Sequence</u> provided the following condition is satisfied:

> if ε is any positive number, there exists a positive integer N such that for any integers $m \geq N$ and $n \geq N$ we have
>
> $$|a_m - a_n| < \varepsilon.$$

<u>Theorem 2.32</u>: Every convergent sequence is a Cauchy Sequence.

<u>Proof</u>: Left as an exercise.

The last statement is not unexpected. What is more interesting is that the converse is true: every Cauchy Sequence is a convergent sequence. This is not obvious, and we need the following result to prove it.

<u>Theorem 2.33</u>: Every Cauchy Sequence is bounded.

Proof: Corresponding to the positive number 1
there exists a positive integer N such that for
any integers m $\geq$ N and n $\geq$ N,

$$|a_m - a_n| < 1.$$

(There is no particular reason for using 1 here;
any other positive number would do just as well.)
Therefore, letting m = N,

$$|a_N - a_n| < 1 \text{ for all } n \geq N.$$

That is, every term of the sequence from a_N on
is inside the neighborhood $(a_N - 1, a_N + 1)$.   Let
M_1 be the largest of the numbers

$$|a_1|, |a_2|, \; . \; . \; . \; , |a_{N-1}|$$

and let M_2 be the larger of the numbers $|a_N - 1|$
and $|a_N + 1|$.   If M is the larger of M_1 and M_2,
then

$$|a_n| \leq M \text{ for all } n \geq 1. \qquad \square$$

Theorem 2.34:   Every Cauchy Sequence converges.

Proof: Suppose $\{a_n\}$ is a Cauchy Sequence.   We
know from Theorem 2.33 that $\{a_n\}$ is bounded.   Furthermore, from Theorem 2.29, $\{a_n\}$ has a convergent
subsequence $\{a_{i_n}\}$.   Let A denote the limit of
$\{a_{i_n}\}$.   We will show that $\{a_n\}$ converges to A.
Suppose ε is any positive number.   Since $\{a_n\}$ is
a Cauchy Sequence, there exists a positive integer
M such that for all integers m $\geq$ M and n $\geq$ M we
have

$$(1) \quad |a_m - a_n| < \varepsilon/2.$$

89

Since $\{a_{i_n}\}$ converges to A, there exists a positive integer $N \geq M$ belonging to the set $\{i_1, i_2, i_3, \ldots\}$ such that

$$|a_N - A| < \varepsilon/2.$$

Since $N \geq M$, (1) tells us that $|a_N - a_n| < \varepsilon/2$ for all $n \geq M$. For $n \geq M$, therefore, we have from $a_n - A = (\bar{a}_n - a_N) + (\bar{a}_N - A)$ that

$$|a_n - A| \leq |a_n - a_N| + |a_N - A|$$

$$< \varepsilon/2 + \varepsilon/2$$

$$= \varepsilon. \qquad \square$$

Our work has shown that there is no difference between a convergent sequence and a Cauchy Sequence--these two ideas are just different expressions of the same concept. The condition of Definition 2.31, incidentally, is often called the Cauchy Criterion. In all honesty it should be stated that the Cauchy Criterion is important mainly for theoretical reasons and not because of its utility in solving problems. The following two examples are illustrations of its use, but ordinarily other methods are easier to apply. In practice the condition is often expressed in the following equivalent form: $\{a_n\}$ is a Cauchy Sequence if and only if for every positive number ε there exists a positive integer N such that for any integer $n \geq N$ and any positive integer k we have $|a_{n+k} - a_n| < \varepsilon$. Convince yourself that this is equivalent to the definition.

Example 21: Consider the sequence $\{\frac{1-n}{n+2}\}$. Then $a_n = \frac{1-n}{n+2}$ and $a_{n+k} = \frac{1-(n+k)}{(n+k)+2}$. Suppose ε is any positive number. Let N be an integer such that $N > \dfrac{3 - 2\varepsilon}{\varepsilon}$. If $n \geq N$ and k is any positive integer,

$$\left| a_{n+k} - a_n \right| = \left| \frac{1 - n - k}{n + k + 2} - \frac{1 - n}{n + 2} \right|$$

$$= \left| \frac{(1 - n - k)(n + 2) - (1 - n)(n + k + 2)}{(n + k + 2)(n + 2)} \right|$$

$$= \left| \frac{-3k}{(n + k + 2)(n + 2)} \right| = \frac{3k}{(n + k + 2)(n + 2)}$$

$$= \frac{3}{\dfrac{n + k + 2}{k}\,(n + 2)} = \frac{3}{(\dfrac{n + 2}{k} + 1)(n + 2)}$$

$$< \frac{3}{n + 2} \quad \text{since } \frac{n + 2}{k} + 1 > 1$$

$$\leq \frac{3}{N + 2}$$

$$< \varepsilon \quad \text{by the way N was chosen.}$$

The difficulty in problems of this kind often lies in showing that $\left| a_{n+k} - a_n \right|$ remains small (for n large enough) even if k increases without bound.

Since the Cauchy Criterion is necessary as well as sufficient for convergence, it's possible to prove a sequence divergent by showing that the condition fails to hold. At this point it might be helpful to state in a positive way the negation of the Cauchy Criterion.

A sequence $\{a_n\}$ is divergent if and only if the following condition is satisfied: there is a positive number ε such that if N is any positive integer, there exists an integer $n \geq N$ and a positive integer k such that $|a_{n+k} - a_n| \geq \varepsilon$.

<u>Example 22</u>: Let $\{a_n\} = \{1 + \frac{1}{2} + \frac{1}{3} + \ldots + \frac{1}{n}\}$. Since

$$a_{n+k} = 1 + \frac{1}{2} + \ldots + \frac{1}{n} + \frac{1}{n+1} + \ldots + \frac{1}{n+k} ,$$

$$|a_{n+k} - a_n| = \frac{1}{n+1} + \frac{1}{n+2} + \ldots + \frac{1}{n+k} .$$

If $k = n$,

$$|a_{2n} - a_n| = \frac{1}{n+1} + \frac{1}{n+2} + \ldots + \frac{1}{2n}$$

$$> \frac{1}{2n} + \frac{1}{2n} + \ldots + \frac{1}{2n} \quad \text{(n terms)}$$

$$= n(\frac{1}{2n})$$

$$= \frac{1}{2} .$$

Thus there is a positive number ε $(= \frac{1}{2})$ such that if N is any positive integer, there exists an integer $n \geq N$ (n can be N or any larger integer) and a positive integer k (=n) such that $|a_{n+k} - a_n| > \varepsilon$. We conclude that $\{a_n\}$ diverges.

Exercise 2.4

*1. Prove that every subsequence of a bounded sequence is bounded.

2. Give an example of an unbounded sequence which has a convergent subsequence.

3. Prove or disprove: if $\{a_n\}$ has exactly one limiting point, then $\{a_n\}$ converges.

4. In Example 20 show that $\{a_{2n}\}$ is decreasing.

5. Determine the limit of $\{a_n\}$ in Example 20.

6. Find all limiting points of each of the following sequences.

(a) $\{n \sin \frac{n\pi}{3}\}$ (b) $\{\frac{4 + (-1)^n n}{3n - 1}\}$

(c) $\left\{ \dfrac{\cos \frac{n\pi}{2}}{(1 + \frac{1}{n})^n} \right\}$

7. Use Theorem 2.30 to show that the sequence $\{\frac{1}{1!} - \frac{1}{2!} + \frac{1}{3!} + \ldots + (-1)^{n+1} \frac{1}{n!}\}$ converges.

8. Prove Theorem 2.29 without using Theorem 2.28.

9. Show that x is a limiting point of $\{a_n\}$ if and only if the following condition is satisfied:

if ε is any positive number and N is any positive integer, there exists an integer $n > N$ such that $|a_n - x| < \varepsilon$.

10. Prove or disprove: every subsequence of a Cauchy Sequence is a Cauchy Sequence.

93

11. Use Theorem 2.34 to show that the sequence $\{\frac{1}{1^2} + \frac{1}{2^2} + \ldots + \frac{1}{n^2}\}$ converges.

12. Prove that if x is a limit point of the range of $\{a_n\}$, then x is a limiting point of $\{a_n\}$. Is the converse true?

13. Prove or disprove: if the monotonic sequence $\{a_n\}$ has a convergent subsequence, then $\{a_n\}$ converges.

In Problems 14-16 determine convergence or divergence of each sequence. In the case of convergence, find the limit if possible.

14. $\{a_n\}$ where $a_1 = 1$, $a_2 = 2$, $a_{n+2} = \frac{2}{3} a_{n+1} + \frac{1}{3} a_n$ for $n \geq 1$.

15. $\{a_n\}$ where $a_1 = 2$, $a_{n+1} = 2 - \frac{1}{a_n}$ for $n \geq 1$.

16. $\{a_n\}$ where $a_1 = 1$, $a_{n+1} = a_n + \frac{1}{a_n}$ for $n \geq 1$.

17. Prove Theorem 2.32.

*18. Prove that if $\{a_n\}$ is a bounded sequence and all of the convergent subsequences of $\{a_n\}$ have the same limit A, then $\{a_n\}$ converges to A.

19. The set of rational numbers on the interval [0,1] is countable and can therefore be arranged in a sequence $\{r_1, r_2, r_3, \ldots\}$. What is the set of limiting points of this sequence?

20. Suppose a sequence $\{a_n\}$ has the following property: if ε is any positive number, there

94

exists a positive integer N such that for all $n \geq N$ we have $|a_{n+1} - a_n| < \varepsilon$. Show that $\{a_n\}$ is not necessarily convergent.

21. Suppose $\{a_n\}$ is a bounded sequence whose set of limiting points is S. Prove that both the least upper bound of S and the greatest lower bound of S are elements of S.

22. Define a sequence $\{a_n\}$ as follows:
$a_1 = 1$, $a_2 = 2$, $a_{n+2} = \sqrt{a_{n+1}a_n}$ for $n \geq 1$.
Taking the convergence of $\{a_n\}$ for granted, determine the limit.

CHAPTER 3

1. Limits of Functions and Limits of Sequences

Broadly speaking, that branch of mathematics
known as "analysis" deals with topics involving
the notion of limit. On this foundation rest the
concepts of continuity, differentiation, integration, and the many ramifications of these important ideas. The definition of limit is given below, perhaps in a more general form than that
usually presented in elementary calculus. It is
understood that the domain of every function occurring in the book is a non-empty set of real numbers.

Definition 3.1: Suppose f is a function having
domain D, and a is a limit point of D. We say
that the limit of f at a is the number L provided
the following condition is satisfied:

> if ε is any positive number, there exists
> a positive number δ such that if x is any
> number in D satisfying $0 < |x - a| < \delta$,
> then
>
> $$|f(x) - L| < \varepsilon.$$

If the above is true, we indicate this fact by the
symbol $\lim_{x \to a} f(x) = L$. (The phrase, "f(x) approaches
L as x approaches a" is used interchangeably with
"the limit of f at a is the number L.")

The next definition simplifies language involving limits.

Definition 3.2: The statement f has a limit at a
(or the limit of f exists at a) means the following:
f is a function, a is a limit point of the domain
of f, and there exists a number L such that the
limit of f at a is L.

Before considering some examples, a few observations are in order. (1) It's quite possible for a function to have a limit at a point not in its domain. (2) No function whose domain is a finite set has a limit at any point. (3) Except for very special cases the number δ depends on ε. (4) The requirement $0 < |x - a|$ is equivalent to $x \neq a$. (5) There may exist numbers x not in the domain of f which nevertheless satisfy $|x - a| < \delta$.

The definition of limit has a natural geometric interpretation. In fact we can state a condition in geometric language which is equivalent to the one in Definition 3.1.

Theorem 3.3: Suppose f is a function having domain D, and a is a limit point of D. The limit of f at a is the number L if and only if the following is true:

> if u and v are any horizontal lines with the point (a,L) between them, there exist vertical lines h and k with (a,L) between them such that every point of the graph of f between h and k, except possibly (a, f(a)), is also between u and v.

Proof: Left as an exercise.

It's worth a few minutes of your time to write out a proof of this theorem. Note that the point (a,L) may or may not be part of the graph of f. Before going too far in our development of limits, we need the following basic result.

Theorem 3.4: A function cannot have more than one limit at a point.

98

Proof: Suppose that f is a function having domain D, and a is a limit point of D. Assume that f has two different limits L_1 and L_2 at a. Let $|L_1 - L_2| = \varepsilon$ and note that $\varepsilon > 0$ since $L_1 \neq L_2$. There exists a positive number δ_1 such that for all x in D satisfying $0 < |x - a| < \delta_1$, we have $|f(x) - L_1| < \varepsilon/2$. There exists a positive number δ_2 such that for all x in D satisfying $0 < |x - a| < \delta_2$, we have $|f(x) - L_2| < \varepsilon/2$. Let δ be the smaller of δ_1 and δ_2. If x_0 is any element of D satisfying $0 < |x_0 - a| < \delta$, then

$$|L_1 - L_2| = |L_1 - f(x_0) + f(x_0) - L_2|$$

$$\leq |L_1 - f(x_0)| + |f(x_0) - L_2|$$

$$< \varepsilon/2 + \varepsilon/2$$

$$= \varepsilon,$$

contradicting the fact that $|L_1 - L_2| = \varepsilon$. $\quad\square$

Example 1: Define a function f by
$$f(x) = \begin{cases} 1 - x & \text{if } 0 \leq x \leq 1 \\ 1 & \text{if } x = 2 \end{cases}.$$
Then f does not have a limit at 2 since 2 is not a limit point of the domain of f. The graph is shown in Figure 3.1.

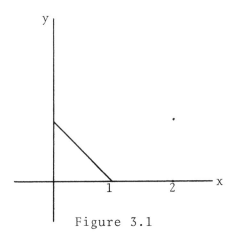

Figure 3.1

Example 2: Define a function f by $f(x) = x + 2$ if $x \neq 1$. Notice that the domain of f is the set of all numbers except 1. Thus the graph consists of the line $y = x + 2$ except for the point $(1,3)$ which is "missing." Even so, f has a limit at 1 and $\lim_{x \to 1} f(x) = 3$. The graph is shown in Figure 3.2.

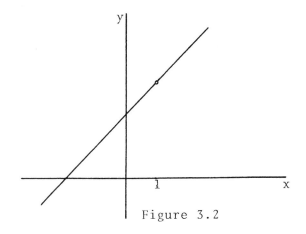

Figure 3.2

Example 3: Define a function f by
$$f(x) = \begin{cases} x + 2 & \text{if } x \neq 1 \\ 2 & \text{if } x = 1 \end{cases}.$$
The only difference between this example and the preceding one is that 1 is in the domain of the function this time. In fact $f(1) = 2$. It is again true that f has a limit at 1 and $\lim_{x \to 1} f(x) = 3$. The graph is shown in Figure 3.3.

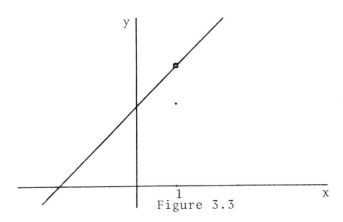

Figure 3.3

Example 4: Define a function f by
$$f(x) = \begin{cases} x + 1 & \text{if } -1 \leq x \leq 0 \\ 2 - x & \text{if } 0 < x \leq 2 \end{cases}.$$
You should be able to show that f fails to have a limit at 0. The graph is shown in Figure 3.4.

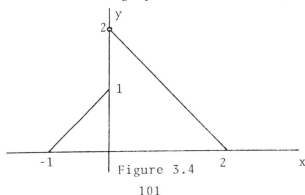

Figure 3.4

101

Example 5: Define a function f by

$$f(x) = x \text{ if } x \text{ is rational}$$

and let f remain undefined for irrational x. The domain D of f is thus the set of rational numbers. The graph of f, which is impossible to draw, consists of all points of the line y = x where x is rational with "holes" at all points of the line where x is irrational. Despite its bizarre appearance, f has a limit at every point. Of course every number a is a limit point of the domain of f. The crucial fact is that, for a particular number δ, we need only consider rational numbers x satisfying $0 < |x - a| < \delta$. You should be able to show that for any number a, rational or irrational,

$$\lim_{x \to a} f(x) = a.$$

We will consider further examples later, including the algebraic manipulation required to show the existence or non-existence of a limit. For the time being this handful of examples should serve to illustrate the major features of the idea of a limit.

There is an intimate relation between the limit of a function at a point and the limit of a sequence. In fact, many of the principal results involving limits of functions can be easily established by using theorems about sequences from the previous chapter. The following two theorems are fundamental in this development.

Theorem 3.5: Suppose f is a function having domain D, a is a limit point of D, and f has the limit L at a. If $\{x_n\}$ is any sequence converging to a with x_n in D and $x_n \neq a$ for all n, then $\{f(x_n)\}$ converges to L.

Proof: Suppose ε is any positive number. By Definition 3.1 there exists a positive number δ such that for all x in D satisfying $0 < |x - a| < \delta$ we have $|f(x) - L| < \varepsilon$. Since $\{x_n\}$ converges to a, there exists a positive integer N such that $|x_n - a| < \delta$ for all $n \geq N$. Since, for each n, x_n is in D and $x_n \neq a$,

$$|f(x_n) - L| < \varepsilon$$

for all $n \geq N$. Therefore $\{f(x_n)\}$ converges to L by Definition 2.3. □

The last result is by no means surprising. If $|f(x) - L| < \varepsilon$ for all x in D satisfying $0 < |x - a| < \delta$, then we can assuredly single out certain of these values of x, namely all the x_n satisfying $|x_n - a| < \delta$, and claim that $|f(x_n) - L| < \varepsilon$. What would be more desirable is to have a converse. In other words, if $\{x_n\}$ converges to a (x_n in D, $x_n \neq a$) and the corresponding sequence $\{f(x_n)\}$ converges, is this enough to assert that f has a limit at a? On the basis of just one such sequence the answer is no. However, we can say the following.

Theorem 3.6: Suppose f is a function having domain D and a is a limit point of D. Suppose that for every sequence $\{x_n\}$ converging to a, x_n in D and $x_n \neq a$ for all n, the corresponding sequence $\{f(x_n)\}$ converges. Then

(a) all of the sequences $\{f(x_n)\}$ have the same limit L

and (b) f has the limit L at a.

103

Proof: Suppose $\{x_n\}$ and $\{y_n\}$ are any two sequences converging to a with each term an element of D and distinct from a. By hypothesis $\{f(x_n)\}$ converges to some number L_1 and $\{f(y_n)\}$ converges to some number L_2. Define a sequence $\{z_n\}$ as follows:

$$z_n = \begin{cases} \dfrac{x_{n+1}}{2} & \text{if n is odd} \\[2em] \dfrac{y_n}{2} & \text{if n is even} \end{cases}.$$

That is, $\{z_n\} = \{x_1, y_1, x_2, y_2, x_3, y_3, \ldots\}$. Certainly each term of $\{z_n\}$ is an element of D and different from a. Moreover, $\{z_n\}$ converges to a. By hypothesis, then, $\{f(z_n)\}$ converges to some number L. Both $\{f(x_n)\}$ and $\{f(y_n)\}$ are sub-sequences of $\{f(z_n)\}$. By Theorem 2.26 they must both have the same limit as $\{f(z_n)\}$. That is, $L_1 = L$ and $L_2 = L$. This proves (a). Assume that (b) is not true. This means the following:

> there exists a positive number ε such that if δ is any positive number, there is a number x in D satisfying $0 < |x - a| < \delta$ such that $|f(x) - L| \geq \varepsilon$.

For each positive integer n let x_n be an element of D satisfying $0 < |x_n - a| < \dfrac{1}{n}$ and such that

$$(1) \quad |f(x_n) - L| \geq \varepsilon.$$

Since $\{x_n\}$ converges to a, $\{f(x_n)\}$ converges. In fact, from part (a), $\{f(x_n)\}$ converges to L. This clearly contradicts (1) above. We conclude that f has the limit L at a. □

Theorem 3.6 can be used to prove the existence of a limit. If it can be shown that for each
sequence $\{x_n\}$ converging to a (x_n in D, $x_n \neq a$) the
sequence $\{f(x_n)\}$ converges, then f has a limit at
a. Of course we're not allowed to choose a particular sequence $\{x_n\}$--it must be arbitrary. On the
other hand, Theorem 3.5 can be used to show that
a limit fails to exist. In reality we use the
contrapositive. If even one sequence $\{x_n\}$ converging to a (x_n in D, $x_n \neq a$) can be found for
which $\{f(x_n)\}$ diverges, then f fails to have a
limit at a. Note that it suffices to find two
sequences $\{x_n\}$ and $\{y_n\}$ converging to a for
which the corresponding function sequences $\{f(x_n)\}$
and $\{f(y_n)\}$ have different limits. For if this
is true, the sequences can be "intertwined" as
in the proof of Theorem 3.6 to produce a divergent sequence.

Our previous examples were fairly simple and
intended mainly to provide an intuitive idea of a
limit. Let's now consider some problems where we
rigorously show in each case that a limit does or
does not exist.

Example 6: Let f(x) = 3 - 5x for every x, and let
a = 1. We will show directly from the definition
that $\lim_{x \to 1} f(x) = -2$. Suppose ε is any positive
number. Let $\delta = \frac{\varepsilon}{5}$, and consider any number x
such that

$$0 < |x - 1| < \delta.$$

Then
$$5|x - 1| < 5\delta$$
$$|5x - 5| < 5(\frac{\varepsilon}{5})$$
$$|5 - 5x| < \varepsilon$$
$$|3 - 5x + 2| < \varepsilon$$
$$|(3 - 5x) - (-2)| < \varepsilon$$
$$|f(x) - (-2)| < \varepsilon.$$

We conclude from Definition 3.1 that f has the limit L = -2 at 1. (Since $|f(1) - (-2)| = 0 < \varepsilon$, we could have considered all x satisfying $|x - 1| < \delta$ instead of $0 < |x - 1| < \delta$.) The procedure used here should be strongly reminiscent of that involved in showing convergence of a sequence from the definition. This time we're hunting a positive number δ instead of a positive integer N. Let it be clearly stated that the steps showing that $\delta = \frac{\varepsilon}{5}$ "works" were actually discovered by working backwards.

Example 7: Let $f(x) = 3x^2 - 2x - 5$ for every number x and a = 2. Suppose ε is any positive number. Let δ be the smaller of the two numbers 1 and $\frac{\varepsilon}{13}$, and consider any number x such that

$$(1) \quad 0 < |x - 2| < \delta.$$

We first observe that, since $\delta \leq 1$,

$$|x - 2| < 1$$
$$1 < x < 3$$
$$3 < 3x < 9$$
$$7 < 3x + 4 < 13$$

and so $(2) \quad |3x + 4| < 13.$

106

Multiplying (1) and (2)

$$|3x + 4||x - 2| < 13\delta$$

$$|3x^2 - 2x - 8| < 13\delta \leq 13(\frac{\varepsilon}{13}) = \varepsilon$$

$$|(3x^2 - 2x - 5) - 3| < \varepsilon$$

$$|f(x) - 3| < \varepsilon.$$

Therefore $\lim_{x \to 2} f(x) = 3.$

You can see that even a fairly simple function like the one in Example 7 calls for considerable manipulation of inequalities if the limit is established by Definition 3.1. We could have come to the same conclusion, however, by appealing to Theorem 3.6. Consider the same problem worked another way.

Example 8: Let $f(x) = 3x^2 - 2x - 5$ for every number x and a = 2. Suppose $\{x_n\}$ is any sequence converging to 2 with $x_n \neq 2$ for each n. (Every number is in the domain of f, so we don't need to require x_n in D.) The sequence $\{x_n \cdot x_n\} = \{x_n^2\}$ converges to 4 by Theorem 2.11. By the corollary to that theorem $\{3x_n^2\}$ converges to 12 and $\{2x_n\}$ converges to 4. The constant term sequence $\{5\}$ certainly converges to 5. Finally, applying Theorem 2.12 twice, the sequence

$$\{3x_n^2\} - \{2x_n\} - \{5\} = \{3x_n^2 - 2x_n - 5\} = \{f(x_n)\}$$

converges to 12 - 4 - 5 = 3. Therefore $\lim_{x \to 2} f(x) = 3$ by Theorem 3.6.

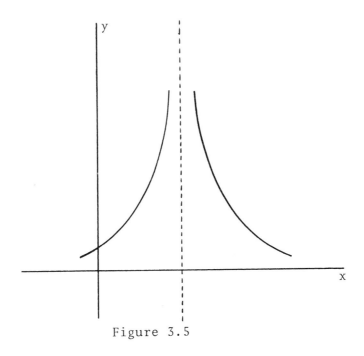

Figure 3.5

<u>Example 9</u>: Let $f(x) = \dfrac{1}{(x-1)^2}$ for each number $x \neq 1$. Let $\{x_n\}$ be the sequence $\{1 + \frac{1}{n}\}$. Certainly each element of $\{x_n\}$ is different from 1 and in the domain of f. Moreover, $\{x_n\}$ converges to 1. Now

$$f(x_n) = \frac{1}{(1 + \frac{1}{n} - 1)^2} = \frac{1}{(\frac{1}{n})^2} = n^2$$

so that $\{f(x_n)\} = \{n^2\}$, a divergent sequence. We conclude from (the contrapositive of) Theorem 3.5 that f fails to have a limit at 1. The graph is shown in Figure 3.5.

108

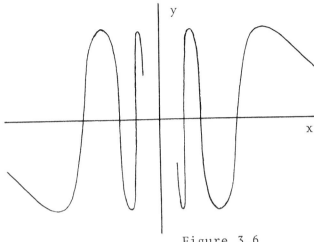

Figure 3.6

Example 10: No discussion of limits would be complete without the classical example $f(x) = \sin \frac{1}{x}$
for each non-zero number x. Examination of the
graph in Figure 3.6 indicates that f does not have
a limit at 0. To verify this conjecture, we pro-
ceed as follows. Let $\{x_n\}$ be the sequence $\{\frac{1}{n\pi}\}$,
and let $\{y_n\}$ be the sequence $\{\frac{2}{(4n - 3)\pi}\}$. Then

$$f(x_n) = \sin \frac{1}{x_n} = \sin n\pi$$

and

$$f(y_n) = \sin \frac{1}{y_n} = \sin \frac{(4n - 3)\pi}{2} .$$

It is easy to see that both $\{x_n\}$ and $\{y_n\}$ converge
to 0, and all terms are non-zero. However $\{f(x_n)\}$
= $\{\sin n\pi\}$ converges to 0 and $\{f(y_n)\}$ =
$\{\sin \frac{(4n - 3)\pi}{2}\}$ converges to 1. Hence f does not
have a limit at 0.

109

Example 11: A function often used to exhibit pathological behavior is "Dirichlet's Function," defined
by

$$f(x) = \begin{cases} 1 \text{ if } x \text{ is rational} \\ 0 \text{ if } x \text{ is irrational} \end{cases}.$$

The graph, of course, consists of all points on
the line y = 1 having rational abscissas and all
points on the line y = 0 having irrational abscis-
as. Because of the many gaps, this has been dubbed
the "salt and pepper graph." Suppose a is any number. One can find a sequence $\{x_n\}$ of rationals
converging to a and a sequence $\{y_n\}$ of irrationals
converging to a. Since $\{f(x_n)\}$ converges to 1 and
$\{f(y_n)\}$ converges to 0, f does not have a limit at
a. (One could also argue directly from the definition of limit.) Despite the fact that its domain
is the set of all numbers, this function does not
have a limit at any point.

Definition 3.7: Suppose S is a set and a is a number. We say that a is a limit point of S from the
left provided every open interval having a as right
end-point contains infinitely many elements of S.
We say that a is a limit point of S from the right
provided every open interval having a as left-end
point contains infinitely many elements of S.

     Recall that a is a limit point of S provided
every open interval containing a contains infinitely many elements of S. The following facts
should be evident: (1) if a is a limit point of
S from either the left or right, then a is a limit point of S; (2) if a is a limit point of S,
then a is a limit point of S from either the left
or right, but not necessarily both.

110

Definition 3.8: Suppose f is a function having domain D, and a is a limit point of D from the left. We say the the left-hand limit of f at a is the number L provided the following condition is satisfied:

if ε is any positive number, there exists a positive number δ such that if x is any number in D satisfying a - δ < x < a, then

$$|f(x) - L| < ε.$$

If the above is true, we indicate this fact by the symbol $\lim_{x \to a^-} f(x) = L$. (The phrase, "f(x) approaches L as x approaches a from the left" is also used.)

Definition 3.9: Suppose f is a function having domain D, and a is a limit point of D from the right. We say that the right-hand limit of f at a is the number L provided the following condition is satisfied:

if ε is any positive number, there exists a positive number δ such that if x is any number in D satisfying a < x < a + δ, then

$$|f(x) - L| < ε.$$

If the above is true, we indicate this fact by the symbol $\lim_{x \to a^+} f(x) = L$. (The phrase, "f(x) approaches L as x approaches a from the right" is also used.)

We will often refer to the limits of Definitions 3.8 and 3.9 as "one-sided limits." The uniqueness of these limits is left to one of the exercises. It should be obvious that either of the one-sided limits can exist without the other. Note also that the limit itself can exist without both of the one-sided limits existing. (This can only happen if a fails to be a limit point of D from both sides.)

111

Theorem 3.10: Suppose f is a function and a is a number.

(1) If $\lim\limits_{x \to a^-} f(x)$ and $\lim\limits_{x \to a^+} f(x)$ both exist and have different values, then f does not have a limit at a.

(2) If $\lim\limits_{x \to a^-} f(x)$ and $\lim\limits_{x \to a^+} f(x)$ both exist and have the same value, then the limit of f at a exists and is that common value.

Proof: Left as an exercise.

The function f of Example 4 illustrates (1) of Theorem 3.10, for $\lim\limits_{x \to 0^-} f(x) = 1$ and $\lim\limits_{x \to 0^+} f(x) = 2$. The following problem shows how (2) might be used.

Example 12: Let $f(x) = \sqrt{|x|}$ for every number x. To investigate the existence of a limit at 0, we might express f by

$$f(x) = \begin{cases} \sqrt{x} & \text{if } x \geq 0 \\ \sqrt{-x} & \text{if } x < 0 \end{cases}.$$

Suppose ε is any positive number. Let $\delta = \varepsilon^2$. If x is any number satisfying $0 < x < \delta$, then

$$|f(x) - 0| = |\sqrt{x}| = \sqrt{x} < \sqrt{\delta} = \varepsilon,$$

so $\lim\limits_{x \to 0^+} f(x) = 0$ by Definition 3.9. For the left-hand limit we again let $\delta = \varepsilon^2$ for any positive number ε. If x is any number satisfying $-\delta < x < 0$, then $\delta > -x > 0$, and

$$|f(x) - 0| = |\sqrt{-x}| = \sqrt{-x} < \sqrt{\delta} = \varepsilon,$$

so lim f(x) = 0 by Definition 3.8. By Theorem
   x→0−
3.10, then, lim f(x) = 0. The graph is shown in
              x→0
Figure 3.7.

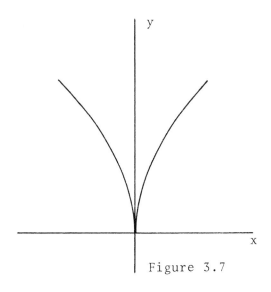

Figure 3.7

Exercise 3.1

1. Let $f(x) = 4x - 1$ for all $x \neq 3$.

   (a) Determine δ so that $|f(x) - 11| < \frac{1}{2}$ for all x satisfying $0 < |x - 3| < \delta$.

   (b) Determine δ so that $|f(x) - 11| < \frac{1}{100}$ for all x satisfying $0 < |x - 3| < \delta$.

   (c) Determine δ so that $|f(x) - 11| < \varepsilon$ for all x satisfying $0 < |x - 3| < \delta$.

2. Prove Theorem 3.3.

3. Show that $\lim_{x \to a} f(x) = L$ if and only if $\lim_{x \to a} [f(x) - L] = 0$.

4. If δ is any number satisfying $0 < \delta < 1$, show that $\left|\frac{x - 5}{2x - 3}\right| < \frac{\delta}{5}$ for all x such that $|x - 5| < \delta$.

5. If $f(x) = \frac{x + 2}{2x - 3}$, show directly from the definition of limit that $\lim_{x \to 5} f(x) = 1$.

6. Explain the similarities and differences between the functions f and g defined by $f(x) = \frac{x^2 - 4}{x - 2}$ and $g(x) = x + 2$.

7. Show that if $0 < |x - 2| < 1$, then $\frac{1}{|x - 4|} < 1$.

8. Give an example of a function f and a number a such that $\lim_{x \to a} f(x)$ exists and either $\lim_{x \to a-} f(x)$ or $\lim_{x \to a+} f(x)$ fails to exist.

114

In Problems 9-13 prove rigorously that the limit of f at a either does or does not exist.

9. $f(x) = 2 - x - x^2$, $a = 1$

10. $f(x) = \dfrac{x + 1}{x^3 + 1}$, $a = -1$

11. $f(x) = px + q$ (p,q constants, $p \neq 0$), a arbitrary

12. $f(x) = \dfrac{x + 3}{2x - 1}$, $a = \dfrac{1}{2}$

13. $f(x) = \dfrac{x}{\sqrt{x + 4} - 2}$, $a = 0$

14. Give an example of a function having all numbers in its domain which has a limit at exactly one point.

15. Prove Theorem 3.10.

16. Prove that if f has a limit at a, then $|f|$ has a limit at a and $\lim_{x \to a} |f(x)| = \left| \lim_{x \to a} f(x) \right|$.

17. Prove or disprove: if f is such that $|f|$ has a limit at a, then f has a limit at a.

18. Explain why each of the following limits fails to exist.

(a) $\lim_{x \to 4^+} \sqrt[10]{64 - x^3}$

(c) $\lim_{x \to 0} x\sqrt{x^2 - 1}$

(b) $\lim_{x \to 1} \text{Arcsin } (3x - 1)$

(d) $\lim_{x \to 0} x^x$

*19. Show that if a is any non-negative number, then $\lim_{x \to a} \sqrt{x} = \sqrt{a}$.

115

20. Define a function f by

$$f(x) = \begin{cases} 2x^2 - x + 2 & \text{if } x > 1 \\ \dfrac{x^2 - 4}{x - 2} & \text{if } x < 1 \end{cases}.$$

Use Theorem 3.10 to show that $\lim\limits_{x \to 1} f(x)$ exists.

21. Define a function f as follows. If x is irrational, let $f(x) = 0$. If x is rational, express x as a quotient of two integers $\dfrac{p}{q}$ (q > 0) in lowest terms, and let $f(x) = \dfrac{1}{q}$. Characterize those points, if any, at which f has a limit.

22. Suppose f is a function and δ is a positive number such that $f(x) > 0$ for all x satisfying $0 < |x - a| < \delta$. Show that if f has a limit L at a, then $L \geq 0$.

23. For the one-sided limits of Definitions 3.8 and 3.9 state and prove theorems analagous to Theorem 3.4.

*24. Suppose f and g are functions having common domain D, and a is a limit point of D from the right. Suppose that for each x in D, $x > a$, there is a number z in D satisfying $a < z < x$ such that $f(z) = g(x)$. Prove that if $\lim\limits_{x \to a+} f(x)$ exists, then $\lim\limits_{x \to a+} g(x)$ also exists and $\lim\limits_{x \to a+} g(x) = \lim\limits_{x \to a+} f(x)$.

2. Algebra of Limits

<u>Definition 3.11</u>: Suppose f is a function with domain D, and S is a set containing at least one point of D. We say that <u>f is bounded above on S</u> provided there exists a number K such that

$$f(x) \leq K$$

for all x in S $\cap$ D. We say that <u>f is bounded below on S</u> provided there exists a number L such that

$$L \leq f(x)$$

for all x in S $\cap$ D. We say that <u>f is bounded on S</u> provided f is both bounded above and bounded below on S, that is, provided there exists a number M such that $|f(x)| < M$ for all x in S $\cap$ D. The statement that <u>f is bounded</u> means that f is bounded on D.

Theorems 3.5 and 3.6 have shown how the limit of a function is related to the limit of a sequence. This relationship will become even more apparent as we consider further theorems concerning limits of functions. Almost every one of these results is the analog of some theorem in Chapter 2 involving sequences.

<u>Theorem 3.12</u>: If f has a limit at a, there exists a neighborhood of a on which f is bounded.

<u>Proof</u>: Let D denote the domain of f and L the limit of f at a. By Definition 3.1 there exists a positive number δ such that for all x in D satisfying $0 < |x - a| < \delta$, we have

$$|f(x) - L| < 1,$$

or $\qquad L - 1 < f(x) < L + 1.$

Hence

$-1 - |L| \leq -1 + L < f(x) < 1 + L \leq 1 + |L|$

that is,

$-(1 + |L|) < f(x) < (1 + |L|)$

so that $|f(x)| < 1 + |L| = M$

for all x in D such that $0 < |x - a| < \delta$.   □

Definition 3.13: Suppose f and g are functions
having in common the domain D. The sum, difference, product, and quotient of f and g, denoted
f + g, f - g, fg, and $\frac{f}{g}$ respectively, are defined
as follows:

    (1) $(f + g)(x) = f(x) + g(x)$ for all x in D

    (2) $(f - g)(x) = f(x) - g(x)$ for all x in D

    (3) $(fg)(x)$ $= f(x) \cdot g(x)$ for all x in D

    (4) $(\frac{f}{g})(x)$ $= \frac{f(x)}{g(x)}$ for all x in D such

        that $g(x) \neq 0$.

    Notice that we do not require f and g to have
the same domain. We do require that the two domains have in common a (non-empty) set D before
the functions can be combined by either of the
four operations above. Suppose now that f and g
both have a limit at some point a. Is it true
that f + g, f - g, fg, and $\frac{f}{g}$ all have a limit at
a? Remembering the corresponding theorems for sequences, it seems reasonable to expect this to be
true (with restrictions likely in the case of division). There is one possible difficulty, though.
In order that f + g, for example, have a limit at
a, it is necessary that a be a limit point of the
domain of f + g. This is not automatic just because a is a limit point of the domains of f and

g individually. (For example, f might be defined for x > 2 and g defined for x < 2 and x > 3, so that f + g is defined for x > 3. Thus 2 is a limit point of the domains of f and g but not a limit point of the domain of f + g.) We must explicitly assume that a is a limit point of the common domain of f and g.

Theorem 3.14: Suppose the functions f and g have common domain D and a is a limit point of D. If $\lim_{x \to a} f(x) = L_1$ and $\lim_{x \to a} g(x) = L_2$, then $\lim_{x \to a} (f + g)(x) = L_1 + L_2$.

Proof: Suppose $\{x_n\}$ is any sequence of elements of D converging to a, $x_n \neq a$ for all n. By Theorem 3.5 $\{f(x_n)\}$ converges to L_1 and $\{g(x_n)\}$ converges to L_2. Theorem 2.10 tells us that the sequence $\{f(x_n) + g(x_n)\} = \{(f + g)(x_n)\}$ converges to $L_1 + L_2$. Using Theorem 3.6 we now conclude that f + g has the limit $L_1 + L_2$ at a. □

Wasn't that painless? Be sure you understand how both Theorems 3.5 and 3.6 are needed--the former because the limits of f and g are known to exist, the latter in order to show that the limit of f + g exists. You shouldn't have any trouble with the next two results.

Theorem 3.15: Suppose the functions f and g have common domain D and a is a limit point of D. If $\lim_{x \to a} f(x) = L_1$ and $\lim_{x \to a} g(x) = L_2$, then $\lim_{x \to a} (f - g)(x) = L_1 - L_2$.

Proof: Left as an exercise.

Theorem 3.16: Suppose the functions f and g have common domain D and a is a limit point of D. If $\lim_{x \to a} f(x) = L_1$ and $\lim_{x \to a} g(x) = L_2$, then $\lim_{x \to a} (fg)(x) = L_1 L_2$.

Proof: Left as an exercise.

Corollary: Suppose the function f has limit L at a. If c is any number, then $\lim_{x \to a} (cf)(x) = cL$.

Proof: Left as an exercise.

Proofs of the last three theorems could be based directly on Definition 3.1, avoiding the use of sequences. If you do this, however, you will find yourself virtually duplicating the proofs of Theorems 2.10, 2.11, and 2.12, a needless waste of energy. Next consider the case of division. The domain D' of $\frac{f}{g}$ may be a proper subset of the common domain D of f and g. Therefore a limit point of D is not necessarily a limit point of D'. The following results show that as long as $\lim_{x \to a} g(x) \neq 0$, a is a limit point of D' whenever it is a limit point of D.

Theorem 3.17: Suppose the function f with domain D has limit L at a. If L > 0, there exist positive numbers c and δ such that if x is any element of D satisfying $0 < |x - a| < \delta$, then $f(x) > c$.

Proof: Since f has the limit L at a, there exists a positive number δ such that if x is any element of D satisfying $0 < |x - a| < \delta$, then

$$|f(x) - L| < \frac{L}{2} .$$

That is, $\qquad L - \frac{L}{2} < f(x) < L + \frac{L}{2} .$

Using only the left half of the inequality, $c = \frac{L}{2} < f(x)$ for all x in D satisfying $0 < |x - a| < \delta$. $\qquad\qquad\qquad\qquad \Box$

Theorem 3.18: Suppose the function f with domain D has limit L at a. If $L < 0$, there exist positive numbers c and δ such that if x is any element of D satisfying $0 < |x - a| < \delta$, then $f(x) < -c$.

Proof: Left as an exercise.

These last two results can be summarized in the following statement.

Corollary: Suppose the function f with domain D has limit L at a. If $L \neq 0$, there exist positive numbers c and δ such that if x is any element of D satisfying $0 < |x - a| < \delta$, then $|f(x)| > c$.

Theorem 3.19: Suppose the functions f and g have common domain D and a is a limit point of D. If $\lim_{x \to a} f(x) = L_1$, $\lim_{x \to a} g(x) = L_2$, and $L_2 \neq 0$, then

$$\lim_{x \to a} \left(\frac{f}{g}\right)(x) = \frac{L_1}{L_2} .$$

121

<u>Proof</u>: The previous result tells us that a is a limit point of the domain of $\frac{f}{g}$. Moreover, there exist positive numbers c and δ such that if x is any element of D satisfying $0 < |x - a| < \delta$, then $|g(x)| > c$. Let $\{x_n\}$ be any sequence of elements of D converging to a, $0 < |x_n - a| < \delta$ for all n. Then $\{f(x_n)\}$ converges to L_1 and $\{g(x_n)\}$ converges to L_2 by Theorem 3.5. Since $g(x_n) \neq 0$ for each n, $\left\{\dfrac{f(x_n)}{g(x_n)}\right\} = \{\frac{f}{g}(x_n)\}$ converges to $\dfrac{L_1}{L_2}$ by the Corollary to Theorem 2.13. We conclude from Theorem 3.6 that $\frac{f}{g}$ has the limit $\dfrac{L_1}{L_2}$ at a. $\qquad\qquad \Box$

<u>Lemma</u>: If $f(x) = x$ for every x and a is any number, $\lim\limits_{x \to a} f(x) = a$.

<u>Proof</u>: Left as an exercise.

<u>Lemma</u>: If a is any number and n is any positive integer, $\lim\limits_{x \to a} x^n = a^n$.

<u>Proof</u>: Mathematical induction is needed. If n = 1 the statement becomes $\lim\limits_{x \to a} x = a$, which is true by the previous lemma. Assume the statement holds for n = k, that is,

$$\lim_{x \to a} x^k = a^k .$$

We must show $\lim\limits_{x \to a} x^{k+1} = a^{k+1}$.

Let $f(x) = x^k$ and $g(x) = x$. Since $\lim\limits_{x \to a} f(x) = a^k$ and $\lim\limits_{x \to a} g(x) = a$, Theorem 3.16 tells us that

$$\lim_{x \to a} (fg)(x) = \lim_{x \to a} x^{k+1} = a^k \cdot a = a^{k+1}. \qquad \square$$

Theorem 3.20: If a is any number and $P(x) = c_n x^n + c_{n-1} x^{n-1} + \ldots + c_1 x + c_0$ is any polynomial, $\lim\limits_{x \to a} P(x) = P(a)$.

Proof: Left as an exercise.

Theorem 3.21: Suppose P and Q are any polynomials. If a is any number such that $Q(a) \neq 0$, then $\lim\limits_{x \to a} \frac{P}{Q}(x) = \frac{P(a)}{Q(a)}$.

Proof: By the previous theorem $\lim\limits_{x \to a} P(x) = P(a)$ and $\lim\limits_{x \to a} Q(x) = Q(a)$. Since $Q(a) \neq 0$, $\lim\limits_{x \to a} \frac{P}{Q}(x) = \frac{P(a)}{Q(a)}$ by Theorem 3.19. $\qquad \square$

A typical elementary limit problem is illustrated by the following example.

Example 13: Evaluate $\lim\limits_{x \to 2} \frac{x^2 + x - 6}{x^3 - 2x^2 + x - 2}$. It's natural to try Theorem 3.21. Letting $P(x) = x^2 + x - 6$ and $Q(x) = x^3 - 2x^2 + x - 2$, we quickly find, however, that $Q(2) = 0$, so the theorem is

123

not applicable. Since $P(2) = 0$ also, $x - 2$ is a
factor of both numerator and denominator. In fact

$$\frac{x^2 + x - 6}{x^3 - 2x^2 + x - 2} = \frac{(x - 2)(x + 3)}{(x - 2)(x^2 + 1)} \quad .$$

We cannot say, without restriction, that

$$\frac{x^2 + x - 6}{x^3 - 2x^2 + x - 2} = \frac{x + 3}{x^2 + 1} \quad .$$

That is, the functions $f(x) = \dfrac{x^2 + x - 6}{x^3 - 2x^2 + x - 2}$
and $g(x) = \dfrac{x + 3}{x^2 + 1}$ are not identical, for 2 is in
the domain of g and 2 is not in the domain of f.
Where they are both defined, however, they are
equal, i.e., $f(x) = g(x)$ for all $x \neq 2$. Since
the value of the limit as x approaches 2 is independent of the value of the function at 2,

$$\lim_{x \to 2} \frac{x + 3}{x^2 + 1} = \lim_{x \to 2} \frac{x^2 + x - 6}{x^3 - 2x^2 + x - 2} \quad .$$

Applying Theorem 3.21 to the function g, we easily
conclude that

$$\lim_{x \to 2} \frac{x + 3}{x^2 + 1} = 1 = \lim_{x \to 2} \frac{x^2 + x - 6}{x^3 - 2x^2 + x - 2} \quad .$$

Theorem 3.21 enables us to find limits of
many functions. The following theorem opens the
door to even more.

Theorem 3.22: Suppose f and g are functions and
a is a limit point of the domain of f(g). Suppose
that $\lim_{x \to a} g(x) = b$, b is in the domain of f, and

lim f(x) = f(b).   Then
x→b

$$\lim_{x \to a} f(g(x)) = f(\lim_{x \to a} g(x)).$$

Proof: Denote the domains of f, g, and f(g) by
$\overline{D_f}$, $\overline{D_g}$, and $D_{f(g)}$ respectively. Suppose ε is any
positive number. There exists a positive number
δ_1 such that for all x in D_f satisfying
$0 < |x - b| < \delta_1$ we have

$$(1) \quad |f(x) - f(b)| < \varepsilon.$$

There exists a positive number δ_2 such that for
all x in D_g satisfying $0 < |x - a| < \delta_2$ we have

$$(2) \quad |g(x) - b| < \delta_1.$$

Suppose x is any number in $D_{f(g)}$ satisfying
$0 < |x - a| < \delta_2$. (Note that any number in the
domain of f(g) is automatically in the domain of
g, but not conversely.) By (1) and (2) above

$$|f(g(x)) - f(b)| < \varepsilon.$$

That is,

$$|f(g(x)) - f(\lim_{x \to a} g(x))| < \varepsilon.$$

Therefore

$$\lim_{x \to a} f(g(x)) = f(\lim_{x \to a} g(x)). \qquad \square$$

Example 14:   Evaluate $\lim\limits_{x \to -1} \sqrt{\dfrac{3x + 5}{2x^2 - 5x + 1}}$.

Let $f(x) = \sqrt{x}$, $g(x) = \dfrac{3x + 5}{2x^2 - 5x + 1}$, and a = -1.

By Theorem 3.21

$$\lim_{x \to a} g(x) = \lim_{x \to -1} \frac{3x + 5}{2x^2 - 5x + 1}$$

$$= \frac{3(-1) + 5}{2(-1)^2 - 5(-1) + 1}$$

$$= \frac{1}{4}$$

$$= b.$$

By Problem 19 of Exercise 3.1

$$\lim_{x \to b} f(x) = \lim_{x \to \frac{1}{4}} \sqrt{x} = \sqrt{\frac{1}{4}} = \frac{1}{2} = f(b).$$

By Theorem 3.22

$$\lim_{x \to -1} \sqrt{\frac{3x + 5}{2x^2 - 5x + 1}} = \sqrt{\lim_{x \to -1} \frac{3x + 5}{2x^2 - 5x + 1}} = \frac{1}{2}.$$

Theorem 3.23: Suppose the functions f and g have common domain D and a is a limit point of D. If there exists a neighborhood T of a on which g is bounded and if $\lim_{x \to a} f(x) = 0$, then $\lim_{x \to a} (fg)(x) = 0$.

Proof: Suppose $\{x_n\}$ is any sequence of elements of D converging to a, $x_n \neq a$ for all n. Since there are most finitely many elements of $\{x_n\}$ outside T, $\{g(x_n)\}$ is bounded. By Theorem 3.5 $\{f(x_n)\}$ converges to 0. By Theorem 2.17 the sequence $\{f(x_n) \cdot g(x_n)\} = \{(fg)(x_n)\}$ converges to 0. Therefore fg has the limit 0 at a by Theorem 3.6. □

126

Example 15: Evaluate $\lim\limits_{x \to 0} x \sin \frac{1}{x}$. Let $f(x) = x$
and $g(x) = \sin \frac{1}{x}$. Certainly $|g(x)| \leq 1$ for all
x in any neighborhood of 0. Since $\lim\limits_{x \to 0} f(x) = 0$,
$\lim\limits_{x \to 0} x \sin \frac{1}{x} = 0$ by Theorem 3.23. The graph is
shown in Figure 3.8. (Compare with Example 10 and
Figure 3.6.)

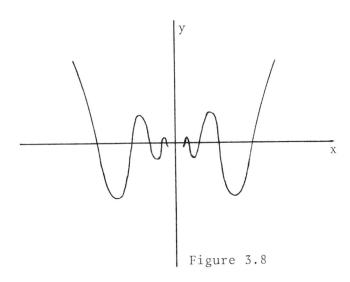

Figure 3.8

Theorem 3.24: Suppose the functions f, g, and h
have common domain D, and a is a limit point of
D. Suppose there is a positive number δ such that
for all x in D satisfying $0 < |x - a| < \delta$, we have
$g(x) \leq f(x) \leq h(x)$. If $\lim\limits_{x \to a} g(x)$ and $\lim\limits_{x \to a} h(x)$ both
exist and have the same value L, then $\lim\limits_{x \to a} f(x) = L$.

Proof: Left as an exercise.

127

This "squeeze theorem" for functions should remind you of a similar theorem for sequences. In fact that theorem can be used in proving this one.

Definition 3.25: A function f defined on a domain D is said to be increasing provided $f(x) \leq f(y)$ for all x,y in D satisfying x < y. We say that f is decreasing provided $f(x) > f(y)$ for all x,y in D satisfying x < y. A function which is either increasing or decreasing is said to be monotonic.

Our knowledge of monotonic sequences should give us a clue to the behavior of monotonic functions. Since every bounded monotonic sequence converges, one might conjecture that every bounded monotonic function has a limit at each point. This is false, however, but not very wide of the mark. Compare the following two results with Theorems 2.20 and 2.21.

Theorem 3.26: Suppose f is a bounded increasing function having domain D.

(1)   If a is a limit point of D from the left, then $\lim_{x \to a^-} f(x)$ exists.

(2)   If a is a limit point of D from the right, then $\lim_{x \to a^+} f(x)$ exists.

Proof: Suppose ε is any positive number. Let L_1 denote the least upper bound of the set

$$S_1 = \{f(x): \ x < a \text{ and } x \in D\}.$$

Hence $f(x) \leq L_1$ for all x in D such that x < a. (The existence of L_1 is guaranteed by the fact that f is bounded.) Since L_1 is the least upper bound, $L_1 - \varepsilon$ is not an upper bound for S_1. Thus there

128

exists an element y of D, y < a, such that
$L_1 - \varepsilon < f(y)$. Let δ be the positive number such
that y = a - δ. If x is any number in D satisfying a - δ < x < a, then

$$L_1 - \varepsilon < f(a - \delta) \leq f(x) \leq L_1$$

since f is increasing. Therefore $|f(x) - L_1| < \varepsilon$
for all x in D such that a - δ < x < a. By Definition 3.8, $\lim_{x \to a^-} f(x) = L_1$ and (1) is proved. The
proof of (2) is similar. If ε is any positive number, let L_2 denote the greatest lower bound of the
set

$$S_2 = \{f(x): \; x > a \text{ and } x \in D\}.$$

Hence $f(x) \geq L_2$ for all x in D such that x > a.
(The existence of L_2 is guaranteed by the fact that
f is bounded.) Since L_2 is the greatest lower
bound, $L_2 + \varepsilon$ is not a lower bound for S_2. Thus
there exists an element z of D, z > a, such that
$f(z) < L_2 + \varepsilon$. Let η be the positive number such
that z = a + η. If x is any number in D satisfying a < x < a + η, then

$$L_2 \leq f(x) \leq f(a + \eta) < L_2 + \varepsilon$$

since f is increasing. Therefore $|f(x) - L_2| < \varepsilon$
for all x in D such that a < x < a + η. By Definition 3.9, $\lim_{x \to a^+} f(x) = L_2$ and (2) is proved. □

Theorem 3.27: Suppose f is a bounded decreasing
function having domain D.

(1) If a is a limit point of D from the left, then
     $\lim_{x \to a^-} f(x)$ exists.

(2) If a is a limit point of D from the right,
     then lim f(x) exists.
         x→a+

Proof: Define the function g by g(x) = -f(x) for
every x in D. Since f is decreasing, for all x,y
in D satisfying x < y, we have

                    f(x) $\geq$ f(y)
so   -f(x) $\leq$ -f(y)
that is,   g(x) $\leq$ g(y).

Therefore g is increasing. If a is a limit point
of D from the left, lim g(x) exists by Theorem
                      x→a-
3.26. The corollary to Theorem 3.16 guarantees
the existence of lim (-1)g(x) = lim f(x). If a
                  x→a-   x→a-
is a limit point of D from the right, lim g(x)
                                        x→a+
exists by the previous theorem and so therefore
does the limit lim (-1)g(x) = lim f(x).   □
                x→a+   x→a+

     The following definition is helpful in intro-
ducing the final type of limit to be considered in
this chapter.

Definition 3.28: We say that the domain D of a
function f is unbounded to the right provided the
following is true: if M is any number, there is
an element x of D such that x > M. We say that
the domain D of a function f is unbounded to the
left provided the following is true: if M is any
number, there is an element x of D such that x < M.

Definition 3.29: Suppose f is a function whose
domain D is unbounded to the right. We say that
the limit of f as x approaches infinity is the

                        130

number L provided the following condition is satisfied:

>if ε is any positive number, there exists
>a number N such that if x is any element
>of D satisfying x > N, then
>$$|f(x) - L| < \varepsilon.$$

If the above is true, we indicate this fact by the
symbol $\lim_{x \to \infty} f(x) = L$.

Definition 3.30: Suppose f is a function whose
domain D is unbounded to the left. We say that
the limit of f as x approaches minus infinity is
the number L provided the following condition is
satisfied:

>if ε is any positive number, there exists
>a number N such that if x is any element
>of D satisfying x < N, then
>$$|f(x) - L| < \varepsilon.$$

If the above is true, we indicate this fact by
the symbol $\lim_{x \to -\infty} f(x) = L$.

The study of calculus provides many examples
of limits of this kind (sometimes called "limits
at infinity," a misleading term). Consider the
following familiar one.

Example 16: The function f(x) = Arctan x is defined for every number x. Furthermore
$$\lim_{x \to \infty} f(x) = \pi/2$$

and
$$\lim_{x \to -\infty} f(x) = -\pi/2.$$

It's not necessary for the existence of the limit in Definition 3.29 (3.30) that the domain of the function contain all numbers greater than (less than) some number. Maybe it has not occurred to you that a convergent sequence is a perfectly good example of Definition 3.29! A sequence, of course, is just a function whose domain is the set of positive integers.*

Example 17: Evaluate $\lim\limits_{x \to -\infty} (\sqrt{x^2 + x} + x)$. Some algebraic manipulation is required.

$$\sqrt{x^2 + x} + x = (\sqrt{x^2 + x} + x)\left(\frac{\sqrt{x^2 + x} - x}{\sqrt{x^2 + x} - x}\right)$$

$$= \frac{x}{\sqrt{x^2 + x} - x}$$

$$= \frac{x}{\sqrt{x^2(1 + \frac{1}{x})} - x}$$

$$= \frac{x}{|x|\sqrt{1 + \frac{1}{x}} - x} \quad \text{since } \sqrt{x^2} = |x|$$

$$= \frac{x}{-x\sqrt{1 + \frac{1}{x}} - x} \quad \text{for all } x < 0$$

$$= \frac{1}{-\sqrt{1 + \frac{1}{x}} - 1} .$$

*If $\{a_n\}$ is a sequence converging to A, we will now feel free to write $\lim\limits_{n \to \infty} a_n = A$.

132

Therefore $\lim\limits_{x \to -\infty} (\sqrt{x^2 + x} + x) = \lim\limits_{x \to -\infty} \dfrac{1}{-\sqrt{1 + \dfrac{1}{x}} - 1}$

$$= \frac{1}{-\sqrt{1} - 1}$$

$$= -\frac{1}{2} \ .$$

In evaluating $\lim\limits_{x \to -\infty} \sqrt{1 + \dfrac{1}{x}}$ we have used Problem 10 with $f(x) = \sqrt{1 + \dfrac{1}{x}}$ and $g(x) = \sqrt{1 + x}$.

1. Prove Theorem 3.15.

2. Prove Theorem 3.16.

3. Prove the corollary to Theorem 3.16.

4. Give an example of functions f and g and a number a such that both f and g fail to have a limit at a but $\lim_{x \to a} (f + g)(x)$ exists.

5. Prove or disprove: if $\lim_{x \to a} f(x)$ and $\lim_{x \to a} (fg)(x)$ both exist, then $\lim_{x \to a} g(x)$ exists.

6. Prove Theorem 3.18.

7. Prove the lemma following Theorem 3.19.

8. Prove Theorem 3.20.

9. Prove Theorem 3.24.

*10. If $g(x) = f(\frac{1}{x})$, prove that

    (a) $\lim_{x \to \infty} f(x) = L$ if and only if $\lim_{x \to 0+} g(x) = L$;

    (b) $\lim_{x \to -\infty} f(x) = L$ if and only if $\lim_{x \to 0-} g(x) = L$.

11. If a is any number prove that $\lim_{x \to a} \sqrt[3]{x} = \sqrt[3]{a}$.

In Problems 12-22, determine whether or not the limit exists, and if it does exist, evaluate it.

12. $\lim_{x \to -3} \dfrac{x + 3}{x^2 - 9}$ 13. $\lim_{x \to 0} \dfrac{\sqrt{x + 9} - 3}{x}$

14. $\displaystyle\lim_{x\to 4}\frac{x^3 - 5x^2 + 2}{x^2 - 3x + 3}$ 15. $\displaystyle\lim_{x\to\infty}\frac{\cos x}{x}$

16. (a) $\displaystyle\lim_{x\to 0}\frac{|x|}{x}$ 17. (a) $\displaystyle\lim_{x\to\infty}\frac{x}{\sqrt{x^2 + 1}}$

    (b) $\displaystyle\lim_{x\to 0-}\frac{|x|}{x}$ (b) $\displaystyle\lim_{x\to -\infty}\frac{x}{\sqrt{x^2 + 1}}$

18. $\displaystyle\lim_{x\to 4}\frac{\sqrt{x^2 + 3x + 8} - 6}{x - 4}$ 19. $\displaystyle\lim_{x\to\infty}\frac{1 - x^2}{2x^2 + 5}$

20. $\displaystyle\lim_{x\to -2}\frac{x - 2}{x^2 - 4}$ 21. $\displaystyle\lim_{x\to -1}\frac{x + 1}{\sqrt[3]{x} + 1}$

22. $\displaystyle\lim_{x\to\infty}(\sqrt{x + 1} - \sqrt{x})$

23. Prove or disprove: if f and g are monotonic functions and the range of g is a subset of the domain of f, then f(g) is a monotonic function.

*24. (a) Suppose that f has domain D and $\displaystyle\lim_{x\to\infty} f(x) = L$. Show that if L is positive [negative], there exists a positive number M such that for all x in D satisfying x > M, f(x) > 0 [f(x) < 0].
(b) Suppose that f has domain D and $\displaystyle\lim_{x\to -\infty} f(x) = L$. Show that if L is positive [negative], there exists a negative number M such that for all x in D satisfying x < M, f(x) > 0 [f(x) < 0].

25. Suppose P and Q are polynomials, a is a number, and Q(a) = 0. What statement can you make about $\displaystyle\lim_{x\to a}\frac{P}{Q}(x)$?

26. Prove that if f is increasing and bounded on the set of all numbers, then $\lim_{x \to \infty} f(x)$ exists.

27. Give an example of a monotonic function f having domain [0,1] such that f fails to have a limit at infinitely many points.

CHAPTER 4

1. Algebra of Continuous Functions

Of all properties that a function can possess, one of the most important is that of continuity. Intuitively, a function is continuous if its graph has no "breaks" or "gaps," that is, if a small change in the independent variable produces a small change in the dependent variable. Admittedly this language is very imprecise, and the formal definition is given below.

Definition 4.1: Suppose f is a function having domain D, and a is a point of D. We say that f is continuous at a provided the following condition is satisfied:

if ε is any positive number, there exists a positive number δ such that if x is any number in D satisfying $|x - a| < \delta$, then

$$|f(x) - f(a)| < \varepsilon.$$

If the above is true, we refer to a as a point of continuity of f. If f is not continuous at a, we say that f is discontinuous at a and refer to a as a point of discontinuity of f.

Definition 4.2: Suppose f is a function having domain D, and S is a subset of D. We say that f is continuous on S provided f is continuous at every point a in S. We say that f is continuous provided f is continuous on D.

The technique involved in showing continuity from Definition 4.1 is virtually the same as that used in proving the existence of a limit from

Definition 3.1. Since there are usually easier
ways than appealing to the definition, one example
of this kind should suffice.

Example 1: Let $f(x) = x^2 - 2x + 8$ for each number
x. We will show that f is continuous at every
number a. Suppose ε is any positive number. Let
δ be the smaller of 1 and $\dfrac{\varepsilon}{1 + 2|a - 1|}$, and con-
sider any number x such that $|x - a| < \delta$. From

$$x + a - 2 = (x - a) + 2(a - 1)$$

we get

$$|x + a - 2| \leq |x - a| + 2|a - 1|$$
$$< 1 + 2|a - 1| \text{ since } |x - a|$$
$$< \delta \leq 1.$$

For x satisfying $|x - a| < \delta$,

$$|f(x) - f(a)| = |(x^2 - 2x + 8) - (a^2 - 2a + 8)|$$
$$= |(x^2 - a^2) - 2(x - a)|$$
$$= |(x - a)(x + a - 2)|$$
$$= |x - a||x + a - 2|$$
$$< |x + a - 2| \, \delta$$
$$< (1 + 2|a - 1|)\delta \text{ from what was shown}$$
$$\text{above}$$
$$\leq (1 + 2|a - 1|) \frac{\varepsilon}{1 + 2|a - 1|} \text{ since}$$
$$\delta \leq \frac{\varepsilon}{1 + 2|a - 1|}$$
$$= \varepsilon.$$

The condition satisfied by a function continuous at a point is strikingly similar to the condition satisfied by a function having a limit at that

point. A comparison of Definitions 3.1 and 4.1 is in order. This discussion is facilitated by the following terminology.

Definition 4.3: Suppose a is a point of the set S. If there exists a neighborhood of a containing no point of S except a, then a is said to be an isolated point of S.

It follows easily from this definition that if a is an element of S, then a is either an isolated point of S or a limit point of S but not both.

There are two significant differences between Definitions 3.1 and 4.1. In order that f have a limit at a, it's necessary that a be a limit point of the domain D. For continuity of f at a, it's necessary that a be a point of D. Certainly either of these can be true without the other. The second difference concerns the behavior of f at a. Neither the existence nor the value of the limit of f at a is dependent on the value of f at a; indeed, f may not even be defined at a. On the other hand, the value of f at a (with one exceptional case) is important in determining continuity of f at a.

The special case mentioned above is that in which a is an isolated point of the domain D. No matter what number $f(a)$ is, f is continuous at a! For if ε is any positive number, we have only to choose δ small enough so that the inequality $|x - a| < \delta$ is satisfied by no x in D except a. Then $|f(x) - f(a)| = 0 < \varepsilon$ for all x in D such that $|x - a| < \delta$.

A function is always continuous at an isolated point of its domain. Any point of the domain which is not an isolated point is automatically a limit point. The following theorem describes the situation in this case.

Theorem 4.4: Suppose f is a function having domain D, and a is both a point of D and a limit point of D. The following two statements are equivalent:

(1)   f is continuous at a;
(2)   f has a limit at a and $\lim_{x \to a} f(x) = f(a)$.

Proof: Suppose (1) is true, and let ε be any positive number. Since f is continuous at a, there exists a positive number δ such that if x is any element of D satisfying $|x - a| < \delta$, then $|f(x) - f(a)| < \varepsilon$. Definition 3.1 is satisfied with L = f(a), and we conclude that

$$\lim_{x \to a} f(x) = f(a).$$

Suppose now that (2) is true, and let ε be any positive number. By Definition 3.1 there exists a positive number δ such that if x is any element of D satisfying $0 < |x - a| < \delta$, then $|f(x) - f(a)| < \varepsilon$ (since L = f(a)). If $0 = |x - a|$, then x = a, and certainly $|f(x) - f(a)| < \varepsilon$ for this one particular x. Therefore for each x in D such that $|x - a| < \delta$, we have $|f(x) - f(a)| < \varepsilon$, and Definition 4.1 is satisfied. □

The most likely direct use of Theorem 4.4 would be in concluding (1) from (2). The theorem could also be used to show that a function is discontinuous at a point, for if (2) is false, then so is (1). Of course (2) is false if either f fails to have a limit at a or $\lim_{x \to a} f(x) \neq f(a)$.

Example 2: Define a function f by

$$f(x) = \begin{cases} \sin \frac{1}{x} & \text{if } x \neq 0 \\ c & \text{if } x = 0 \end{cases}$$

140

where c is some number. It was shown in Example 10 of Chapter 3 that $\lim_{x \to 0} \sin \frac{1}{x}$ fails to exist. We conclude from Theorem 4.4 that for no choice of c will f be continuous at 0.

Theorem 4.5: Suppose f is a function having domain D, and a is a point of D. The following statements are equivalent.

(1) f is continuous at a;

(2) if $\{x_n\}$ is any sequence of elements of D converging to a, the sequence $\{f(x_n)\}$ converges to f(a).

Proof: Suppose (1) is true and $\{x_n\}$ is any sequence of elements of D converging to a. Let ε be any positive number. Since f is continuous at a, there exists a positive number δ such that if x is any number in D satisfying $|x - a| < \delta$, then $|f(x) - f(a)| < \varepsilon$. Since $\{x_n\}$ converges to a, there is a positive integer N such that for all $n \geq N$, $|x_n - a| < \delta$. For all $n \geq N$, then, $|f(x_n) - f(a)| < \varepsilon$. We conclude from Definition 2.3 that $\{f(x_n)\}$ converges to f(a). Suppose now that (2) is true. If a is an isolated point of D, then of course f is continuous at a, and there is nothing to prove. Suppose then that a is a limit point of D. Since (2) is true, the hypothesis of Theorem 3.6 is satisfied. The conclusion of that theorem tells us that f has the limit f(a) at a. It follows from Theorem 4.4 that f is continuous at a. □

Notice that in Theorem 4.5 we only require that a be a point of D, whereas in Theorem 4.4 a must be both a point and a limit point of D. If the requirement that a be a limit point of D is added to the hypothesis of Theorem 4.5, then of course the two conditions are still equivalent. Hence the two theorems can be combined as follows.

Corollary: Suppose f is a function having domain D, and a is both a point and a limit point of D. The following three statements are equivalent.

    (1)   f is continuous at a;

    (2)   f has a limit at a and $\lim_{x \to a} f(x) = f(a)$;

    (3)   if $\{x_n\}$ is any sequence of elements of D converging to a, the sequence $\{f(x_n)\}$ converges to $f(a)$.

    This is a good time to consider the kinds of discontinuities a function can have. Recall that a function is neither continuous nor discontinuous at a point outside its domain. Since a function is always continuous at an isolated point, a discontinuity is only possible at a point of the domain which is also a limit point of the domain.

Definition 4.6: Suppose the function f has a discontinuity at a. If $\lim_{x \to a} f(x)$ exists but $\lim_{x \to a} f(x) \neq f(a)$, we say that f has a removable discontinuity at a. Otherwise f is said to have an essential discontinuity at a.

Example 3: Define a function f by

$$f(x) = \begin{cases} x \sin \frac{1}{x} & \text{if } x \neq 0 \\ 1 & \text{if } x = 0 \end{cases}.$$

It was shown in Example 15 of Chapter 3 that
$\lim\limits_{x \to 0} x \sin \frac{1}{x} = 0$. Since $\lim\limits_{x \to 0} f(x) \neq f(0)$, f is
discontinuous at 0 by Theorem 4.4. This is a re-
movable discontinuity according to the definition
above. If we let $f(0) = 0$, then 0 is a point of
continuity. (Strictly speaking, of course, we
now have a different function which should not
have the same name, f, as the old one.)

Definition 4.7: Suppose the function f has an
essential discontinuity at a. If $\lim\limits_{x \to a-} f(x)$ and
$\lim\limits_{x \to a+} f(x)$ both exist but have different values,
we say that f has a jump discontinuity at a. If
f is unbounded in every neighborhood of a, we say
that f has an infinite discontinuity at a.

Example 4: Define a function f by

$$f(x) = \begin{cases} \dfrac{x^2 - 1}{|x + 1|} & \text{if } x \neq -1 \\ 0 & \text{if } x = -1 \end{cases}.$$

Since $|x + 1| = x + 1$ if $x + 1 > 0$ and $|x + 1| = -(x + 1)$ if $x + 1 < 0$, we easily find that

$$f(x) = \begin{cases} x - 1 & \text{if } x > -1 \\ 0 & \text{if } x = -1 \\ 1 - x & \text{if } x < -1 \end{cases}.$$

It's clear that f has a jump discontinuity at -1
since $\lim\limits_{x \to -1-} f(x) = 2$ and $\lim\limits_{x \to -1+} f(x) = -2$. The graph
is shown on the next page in figure 4.1.

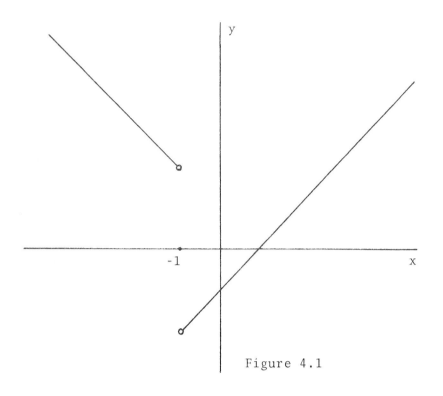

Figure 4.1

Example 5: Define a function f by

$$f(x) = \begin{cases} \dfrac{x}{x - 2} & \text{if } x < 2 \\ 1 & \text{if } x = 2 \end{cases}.$$

If M is any negative number it's not hard to see that $2 - \dfrac{2}{1 - M}$ is in the domain of f, and $f(2 - \dfrac{2}{1 - M}) = M$. Furthermore, $\lim\limits_{M \to -\infty} (2 - \dfrac{2}{1 - M}) = 2$. From this we conclude that f is unbounded in every neighborhood of 2 and thus has an infinite discontinuity at 2. The graph is shown in Figure 4.2.

144

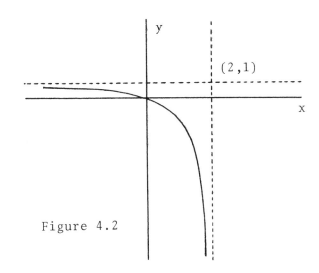

Figure 4.2

There are essential discontinuities which do not fall into either of the categories mentioned in Definition 4.7. For instance, the discontinuity at 0 in Example 2 is essential but is neither a jump nor an infinite discontinuity. We might be inclined to call it an "oscillatory discontinuity," though this term is not widely used.

If continuous functions are combined by any of the four arithmetic operations, the result is a continuous function. The following group of theorems establishes this.

Theorem 4.8: If both of the functions f and g are continuous at a, then f + g is continuous at a.

Proof: Let D denote the domain of f + g. If a is an isolated point of D, then f + g is continuous at a and there is nothing to prove. Suppose, therefore, that a is a limit point of D (of course a is a point of D since both f and g are defined at a). Then a is a limit point of the common domain of f and g. Since f is continuous at a, $\lim_{x \to a} f(x)$ exists

145

and $\lim_{x \to a} f(x) = f(a)$ by Theorem 4.4. Similarly, $\lim_{x \to a} g(x)$ exists and $\lim_{x \to a} g(x) = g(a)$. By Theorem 3.14 $\lim_{x \to a} (f + g)(x) = \lim_{x \to a} f(x) + \lim_{x \to a} g(x) = f(a) + g(a) = (f + g)(a)$. Using Theorem 4.4 once again we conclude that $f + g$ is continuous at a. $\qquad\square$

Notice that Theorem 4.4 has been used "going both ways." The first time, knowing f and g to be continuous, we concluded (2) from (1). The second time, knowing $\lim_{x \to a} (f + g)(x) = (f + g)(a)$, we concluded (1) from (2).

Theorem 4.9: If both of the functions f and g are continuous at a, then f - g is continuous at a.

Proof: Left as an exercise.

Theorem 4.10: If both of the functions f and g are continuous at a, then fg is continuous at a.

Proof: Left as an exercise.

Corollary: If f is continuous at a and c is any number, then cf is continuous at a.

Proof: Left as an exercise.

Theorem 4.11: If both of the functions f and g are continuous at a and $g(a) \neq 0$, then $\frac{f}{g}$ is continuous at a.

146

Proof: Left as an exercise.

The method of proof used in the case of the
sum will succeed for the difference, product, and
quotient. As you write down the proof of Theorem
4.11, notice that even the quotient causes no special problems. If a direct proof (using Definition
4.1) of this theorem were attempted, it would be
necessary to know that a continuous function which
is non-zero at a point is "bounded away from zero."
This result is stated precisely in the following
two theorems, which will be needed later.

Theorem 4.12: Suppose the function f having domain
D is continuous at a and $f(a) > 0$. There exist
positive numbers c and δ such that if x is any ele-
ment of D satisfying $|x - a| < \delta$, then $f(x) \geq c$.

Proof: If a is an isolated point of D, let δ be a
positive number such that $(a - \delta, a + \delta)$ contains
no point of D except a. Then the conclusion follows
immediately with $c = f(a)$. If a is a limit point
of D, $\lim_{x \to a} f(x)$ exists and $\lim_{x \to a} f(x) = f(a)$ by Theorem 4.4. By Theorem 3.17 there exist positive num-
bers c' and δ such that if x is any element of D
satisfying $0 < |x - a| < \delta$, then $f(x) > c'$. Let
c be the smaller of c' and $f(a)$. Then $f(x) \geq c$
for all x in D such that $|x - a| < \delta$. □

Theorem 4.13: Suppose the function f having domain
D is continuous at a and $f(a) < 0$. There exist
positive numbers c and δ such that if x is any ele-
ment of D satisfying $|x - a| < \delta$, then $f(x) \leq -c$.

Proof: Left as an exercise.

Theorem 4.14: Every polynomial is continuous.

Proof: The domain of every polynomial, unless restricted, is the set of all numbers. If P is any
polynomial and a is any number, $\lim_{x \to a} P(x) = P(a)$ by

Theorem 3.20 and P is continuous at a by Theorem
4.4.   □

Theorem 4.15: If P and Q are any polynomials and
a is any number such that $Q(a) \neq 0$, then $\frac{P}{Q}$ is continuous at a.

Proof: Left as an exercise.

Theorem 4.16: If the function g is continuous at
a and the function f is continuous at g(a), then
f(g) is continuous at a.

Proof: Let D denote the domain f(g). If a is an
isolated point of D, f(g) is continuous at a automatically, so suppose a is a limit point of D. We
can conclude from Theorem 4.4 that f(g) is continuous at a if we can show that $\lim_{x \to a} f(g(x)) = f(g(a))$.

This will be done by using Theorem 3.22. At this
time you need to turn back to that theorem, for the
four-part hypothesis is not easy to remember. Let's
consider these conditions one at a time. (1) We
certainly know that a is a limit point of the domain of f(g). (2) Since g is continuous at a,
$\lim_{x \to a} g(x)$ exists and $\lim_{x \to a} g(x) = g(a)$ (= b in the

theorem). (3) This number g(a) is in the domain
of f by hypothesis. (4) Since f is continuous at
g(a), $\lim_{x \to g(a)} f(x)$ exists and $\lim_{x \to g(a)} f(x) = f(g(a))$. The

hypothesis of Theorem 3.22 is satisfied, so

$$\lim_{x \to a} f(g(x)) = f(\lim_{x \to a} g(x)) = f(g(a))$$

and the proof is complete. □

You can see how easy it is to prove these continuity theorems, for most of the work was done in
proving the corresponding theorems on limits. Many
of these in turn were proved using the results on
sequences, and the mathematical structure grows
ever higher.

Example 6: Let $h(x) = \sqrt{\dfrac{x + 1}{3 - x}}$. We will show that
h is continuous wherever it is defined. It's a
routine exercise in inequalities to show that x
is in the domain of h if and only if $-1 \le x < 3$.
If functions f and g are defined by

$$f(x) = \sqrt{x} \text{ and } g(x) = \frac{x + 1}{3 - x}$$

then $h(x) = f(g(x))$. Let a be any number satisfying $-1 < a < 3$. Then g is continuous at a by Theorem 4.15. For such a number a, $g(a) \ge 0$. By
Problem 19 of Exercise 3.1 $\lim_{x \to g(a)} f(x) = f(g(a))$, and
therefore f is continuous at $g(a)$ by Theorem 4.4.
Now Theorem 4.16 tells us that $h = f(g)$ is continuous at a.

Example 7: Define a function f on the interval
$(0,1)$ in the following way. If $0 < x < 1$ and x is
irrational, let $f(x) = 0$. If $0 < x < 1$ and x is
rational, express x in the form $\dfrac{p}{q}$, where p and q
are relatively prime positive integers, and let
$f(x) = \dfrac{1}{q}$. Does f have any points of continuity,
and if so, what are they? Figure 4.3 gives a rough
idea of what the graph of f looks like. The points
plotted are those corresponding to rational
$x = \dfrac{p}{q}$ for which $q \le 12$. Suppose a is any rational

number in $(0,1)$. Then $a = \frac{p}{q}$, p and q relatively prime, and $f(a) = \frac{1}{q}$. Let ε be a positive number such that $\varepsilon < \frac{1}{q}$. For any positive number δ there is always an irrational number x satisfying $a - \delta < x < a + \delta$ and of course $f(x) = 0$. Hence $|f(x) - f(a)| = f(a) = \frac{1}{q} > \varepsilon$ and Definition 4.1 cannot be satisfied. Therefore f is discontinuous at every rational number in $(0,1)$. Suppose now that a is any irrational number in $(0,1)$. Let ε be any positive number. Observe that the inequality $f(x) \geq \varepsilon$ is satisfied by at most finitely many values of x. (Convince yourself that this is true before going on.) Since a is irrational and $f(a) = 0$, there exists a positive number δ such that for every x satisfying $a - \delta < x < a + \delta$, $f(x) < \varepsilon$. Of course $f(x) > 0$ for all x, so $|f(x) - f(a)| = f(x) < \varepsilon$ for all x such that $|x - a| < \delta$, and consequently f is continuous at every irrational number in $(0,1)$.

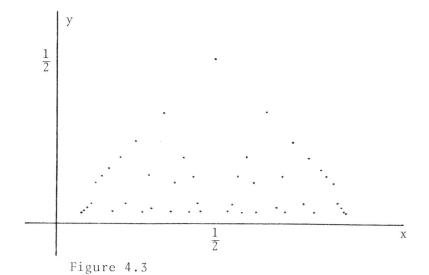

Figure 4.3

150

This example should make us aware that some of our intuitive ideas about continuity may have to be modified. A function which is continuous at the irrationals and discontinuous at the rationals is certainly not a simple function. It turns out, incidentally, that there does not exist a function continuous at the rationals and discontinuous at the irrationals.

Theorem 4.17: The function $f(x) = \sin x$ is continuous at every number a.

Proof: The trigonometric identity $\sin \alpha - \sin \beta = 2 \cos \frac{1}{2}(\alpha + \beta) \sin \frac{1}{2}(\alpha - \beta)$ is needed. Also needed is the fact that $|\sin x| \leq |x|$ for every x. Suppose ε is any positive number. Let $\delta = \varepsilon$. If $|x - a| < \delta$, then

$$
\begin{aligned}
|f(x) - f(a)| &= |\sin x - \sin a| \\[1ex]
&= |2 \cos \tfrac{1}{2}(x + a) \sin \tfrac{1}{2}(x - a)| \\[1ex]
&= 2|\cos \tfrac{1}{2}(x + a)||\sin \tfrac{1}{2}(x - a)| \\[1ex]
&\leq 2|\sin \tfrac{1}{2}(x - a)| \quad \text{since } |\cos x| \leq 1 \text{ for every } x \\[1ex]
&\leq 2|\tfrac{1}{2}(x - a)| \\[1ex]
&= |x - a| \\[1ex]
&< \varepsilon \quad \text{since } \delta = \varepsilon. \qquad \square
\end{aligned}
$$

Theorem 4.18: The function $f(x) = \cos x$ is continuous at every number a.

<u>Proof</u>: Left as an exercise.

<u>Theorem 4.19</u>: The tangent, cotangent, secant, and cosecant functions are continuous wherever they are defined.

<u>Proof</u>: Left as an exercise.

Exercise 4.1

1. Prove Theorem 4.9.

2. Prove Theorem 4.10.

3. Prove the corollary to Theorem 4.10.

4. Prove Theorem 4.11.

5. Define a function f by $f(x) = \dfrac{1 - 2x}{x + 3}$ for every $x \neq -3$. Prove directly from Definition 4.1 that f is continuous at -2.

6. Show directly from Definition 4.1 that the function f defined by $f(x) = 3x^2 - x + 2$ is continuous at every number a.

In Problems 7-12 a function f is given by means of a formula (with the understanding that there are no restrictions on the values of x except those imposed by the formula itself). Do the following in each case: (a) identify all discontinuities of f and classify each as removable, jump, infinite, or neither; (b) identify every number a not in the domain of f, and determine whether f can be defined at a in such a way as to make it continuous there.

7. $f(x) = \dfrac{x^2 - 4}{x^3 - 8}$

8. $f(x) = \dfrac{x}{x^3 + 1}$

9. $f(x) = \dfrac{x^2 - 2x - 1}{x^4 - 6x^2 + 1}$

10. $f(x) = \begin{cases} \dfrac{|x|}{x} & \text{if } x \neq 0 \\ 1 & \text{if } x = 0 \end{cases}$

11. $f(x) = \dfrac{x + 1}{\sqrt[3]{1 - x^2}}$

12. $f(x) = \begin{cases} 2x - 5 & \text{if } x \le 1 \\ 4 - x & \text{if } x \ge 1 \end{cases}$

13. Prove that $f(x) = \sqrt{x}$ is continuous for all $x \ge 0$.

14. Prove Theorem 4.13

15. Let $f(x) = -x^3 + 7x - 7$ and $a = \dfrac{3}{2}$. Find numbers c and δ satisfying Theorem 4.12. How can you be sure your answer is correct?

16. Prove or disprove: if f is continuous at a and g is discontinuous at a, then f + g is discontinuous at a.

17. Give an example of a function having at 1 a discontinuity which is neither removable, jump, nor infinite.

18. Prove Theorem 4.15.

19. Show that if f is continuous at a, then $|f|$ is continuous at a. Is the converse true?

20. Given an example of a function having domain [0,1] and continuous at only one point.

21. Prove or disprove: the only type of discontinuity possible for a monotonic function is a jump discontinuity.

22. Prove Theorem 4.18.

23. Prove Theorem 4.19.

154

24. What theorems are needed to conclude that $f(x) = \sqrt{1 + \sin x}$ is continuous for all x?

25. Suppose f is continuous at a and ε is any positive number. Prove that there exists a neighborhood of a such that if x and y are any two numbers of the domain of f in this neighborhood, then $|f(x) - f(y)| < \varepsilon$.

26. Prove the following theorem. Suppose f and g are functions and a is a limit point of the domain of $f(g)$. If $\lim_{x \to a} g(x) = b$ and f is continuous at b, then $\lim_{x \to a} f(g(x)) = f(\lim_{x \to a} g(x))$.

27. Would the statement of Problem 26 be true if each of the expressions "$\lim_{x \to a}$" is replaced by "$\lim_{x \to \infty}$?" Justify your answer.

28. If f is a function and a is a number, give a reasonable definition of "f is continuous from the left at a" and "f is continuous from the right at a."

2. Continuous Functions on Closed Intervals

We now come to an extremely important group of results concerning continuous functions. You are strongly urged to try to construct proofs of these theorems yourself before reading the ones in the book. Even if you don't always succeed, you will have a much better idea of what continuity is all about.

Theorem 4.20: If f is a continuous function on the closed interval [a,b], then f is bounded on [a,b].

Proof: A little reflection should convince you that an indirect proof is indicated. Thus we assume: there does not exist a number M such that $|f(x)| < M$ for all x in [a,b]. This assumption can be interpreted as follows:

(1)   for each positive integer n there exists a number x_n in [a,b] such that $|f(x_n)| > n$.

Two sequences have been defined--the sequence $\{x_n\}$ of elements of [a,b] and the unbounded sequence $\{f(x_n)\}$. Clearly $\{x_n\}$ is bounded, though not necessarily convergent. However, by Theorem 2.29 $\{x_n\}$ has a convergent subsequence $\{x_{i_n}\}$. Denote the limit of $\{x_{i_n}\}$ by z. Certainly z is an element of [a,b], so f(z) is a uniquely determined number. Since f is continuous at z, Theorem 4.5 tells us that the sequence $\{f(x_{i_n})\}$ converges to f(z). Every convergent sequence is bounded, so there exists a number K such that

$$|f(x_{i_n})| \leq K$$

for every positive integer n. We know from (1), however, that

$$|f(x_{i_n})| > i_n$$

for each n. This contradiction proves that f is bounded on [a,b]. □

The conclusion of the theorem above does not hold if the requirement of continuity is dropped. Neither does it hold for any kind of interval except a closed interval. Consider, for example, $f(x) = \frac{1}{x}$ on (0,1]. Can you see where the proof breaks down in such a case?

Definition 4.21: Suppose f is a function having domain D. We say that f has a maximum (or absolute maximum) on D provided there exists a number y in D such that $f(x) \leq f(y)$ for every x in D. We say that f has a minimum (or absolute minimum) on D provided there exists a number z in D such that $f(z) \leq f(x)$ for every x in D.

In Theorem 4.20 it was shown that a continuous function on a closed interval is necessarily bounded. In fact, much more than that is true.

Theorem 4.22: If f is a continuous function on the closed interval [a,b], then f has a maximum on [a,b].

Proof: Theorem 4.20 tells us that f is bounded on [a,b]. Let M denote the least upper bound of the set

$$S = \{f(x): \quad a \le x \le b\}.$$

Thus, $f(x) \le M$ for all x in [a,b]. Assume that $f(x) < M$ for all x in [a,b]. Define a function g on [a,b] by

$$g(x) = \frac{1}{M - f(x)}.$$

Note that $M - f(x) > 0$ for all x in [a,b]. We conclude from Theorem 4.11 that g is continuous on [a,b]. Hence g is bounded, so there exists a (positive) number K such that

$$g(x) = \frac{1}{M - f(x)} \le K$$

for every x in [a,b]. It follows that

$$f(x) \le M - \frac{1}{K}$$

for every x in [a,b]. This contradicts the fact that M is the least upper bound of S. We are forced to conclude that there exists at least one number y in the interval such that $f(y) = M$. Since $f(x) \le M = f(y)$ for all x in [a,b], f has a maximum. □

The proof given is certainly not the only one possible. In fact, you should be able to give an argument similar to the one in Theorem 4.20. If $f(x) < M$ for all x in the interval, with M defined as before, there exists a sequence $\{x_n\}$ of elements of [a,b] such that the terms of $\{f(x_n)\}$ get arbitrarily close to M. The continuity of f comes into play in much the same way as in the proof of Theorem 4.20.

Theorem 4.23: If f is a continuous function on the closed interval [a,b], then f has a minimum on [a,b].

158

Proof: Left as an exercise.

The following theorem expresses one of the more "intuitively obvious" properties of continuous functions. The proof, however, is far from obvious. Make a conscientious effort to prove this one yourself before looking at the argument given.

Theorem 4.24 (Bolzano's Theorem): Suppose f is a continuous function on the closed interval [a,b]. If f(a) and f(b) have opposite signs, there exists at least one number z, a < z < b, such that f(z) = 0.

Proof: Suppose that f(a) < 0 and f(b) > 0. (The case f(a) > 0 and f(b) < 0 can be handled in an entirely analogous manner.) Let z denote the greatest lower bound of the set

$$S = \{x: \ a \leq x \leq b \text{ and } f(x) \geq 0\}.$$

(The set S contains at least one element, namely b.) Thus, for all x in [a,b] such that f(x) ≥ 0, we must have x ≥ z. Also, for all x in [a,b] satisfying x < z (if such exist), we have f(x) < 0. It will be proved that f(z) = 0 by showing that both f(z) > 0 and f(z) < 0 are impossible. Assume f(z) > 0. By Theorem 4.12 there exist positive numbers c and δ such that f(x) ≥ c > 0 for all x in [a,b] satisfying |x - z| < δ. There must exist x in [a,b] such that z - δ < x < z, for z > a (since f(z) > 0). For such x, f(x) > 0, so x is in S, contradicting the fact that z is a lower bound for S. Hence f(z) > 0 is impossible. Assume f(z) < 0. By Theorem 4.13 there exist positive numbers c and δ such that f(x) ≤ -c < 0 for all x in [a,b] satisfying |x - z| < δ. There must exist x in [a,b] such that z < x < z + δ, for z < b (since f(z) < 0). Hence there is no element of S less than z + δ. That is, z + δ is a lower bound for S, contradicting the fact that z is the greatest lower bound for S. So f(z) < 0 is impossible and consequently f(z) = 0. □

Although there may be many values of x in [a,b] for which f(x) = 0, the proof just given identifies only one. In fact it's the smallest one. The difficulty in proving this theorem is virtually the same as that involved in the Bolzano-Weierstrass Theorem. In both cases we are trying to show the existence of a point (having a certain property) whose exact location is unknown. Actually, the same kind of "bisection" proof used in that theorem will also work here. Perhaps you found another proof altogether.

Before looking at the theoretical consequences of Bolzano's Theorem, it might be mentioned here that this theorem is the basis of an elementary algorithm for approximating roots of certain equations. Any equation can be put in the form $f(x) = 0$. If f is continuous, we seek numbers a and b such that f(a) and f(b) have opposite signs, for there must be at least one root of the equation between a and b. Of course it is desirable that a and b be as close together as possible.

Example 8: Find, correct to four decimal places, the only positive root of the equation $x^2 = \cos x$. We have $f(x) = x^2 - \cos x = 0$ and certainly f is continuous everywhere. The following calculations can be verified. (All decimals are correct to five places.) $f(0) = -1$ and $f(1) = .45970$, so the root is between 0 and 1. $f(.8) = -.05671$ and $f(.9) = .18839$, so the root is between .8 and .9. $f(.82) = -.00982$ and $f(.83) = .01402$, so the root is between .82 and .83. $f(.824) = -.00032$ and $f(.825) = .00207$, so the root is between .824 and .825. $f(.8241) = -.00008$ and $f(.8242) = .00016$, so the root is between .8241 and .8242. Finally, $f(.82415) = .00004$, so the root is between .8241 and .82415. Therefore, correct to four places, the root is .8241.

The principal disadvantage of this method is that much trial and error is involved. For instance, having found (quite easily) that the root is between 0 and 1, it is not obvious that we should next look around .8 and .9. Thus we might waste much time evaluating f(.5), f(.6), f(.7), etc. Still, it is a very simple method and one that always works provided, of course, the functions involved are continuous.

Theorem 4.24 says that if f is continuous and 0 is between f(a) and f(b), then f(x) = 0 for some x between a and b. What is significant about the number zero in this situation? A little reflection should indicate that any other number between f(a) and f(b) would do just as well. Hence we have the following generalization, a corollary of Bolzano's Theorem.

Theorem 4.25 (Intermediate Value Theorem): Suppose f is a continuous function on the closed interval [a,b]. If f(a) ≠ f(b) and c is any number between f(a) and f(b), there exists at least one number z, a < z < b, such that f(z) = c.

Proof: Left as an exercise.

The following statement is even stronger.

Theorem 4.26: Suppose f is a continuous function on the closed interval [a,b]. Let M and m denote the least upper bound and greatest lower bound, respectively, of the set {f(x): a < x < b}. If c is any number satisfying m < c < M, there exists at least one number z in [a,b] such that f(z) = c.

Proof: If m = M, then f is constant, and there is nothing to prove. Suppose, then, that m < M. By Theorem 4.22 and the proof of that theorem there exists a number s in [a,b] such that f(s) = M. From Theorem 4.23 and its proof we know there exists a number t in [a,b] such that f(t) = m. Assume, with no loss of generality, that s < t. Since f is continuous on [a,b], f is certainly continuous on [s,t]. The Intermediate Value Theorem applied to f on the interval [s,t] now gives the desired conclusion.   □

Corollary: Suppose f is a non-constant continuous function on the closed interval [a,b]. Let M and m denote the least upper bound and greatest lower bound, respectively, of the set {f(x): a ≤ x ≤ b}. The range of f is the closed interval [m,M].

Theorem 4.27: If P is any polynomial of odd degree, the equation $P(x) = 0$ has at least one root.

Proof: Throughout this book we work exclusively with real numbers, so it should be understood that the coefficients of the polynomial as well as the asserted root are real numbers. Let

$$P(x) = a_n x^n + a_{n-1} x^{n-1} + \ldots + a_1 x + a_0$$

where $a_n \neq 0$ and n is odd. For non-zero x we can write

$$P(x) = x^n (a_n + \frac{a_{n-1}}{x} + \frac{a_{n-2}}{x^2}$$

$$+ \ldots + \frac{a_1}{x^{n-1}} + \frac{a_0}{x^n})$$

$$= x^n Q(x)$$

162

where

$$Q(x) = a_n + \frac{a_{n-1}}{x} + \frac{a_{n-2}}{x^2} + \ldots + \frac{a_1}{x^{n-1}} + \frac{a_0}{x^n} .$$

We know that $\lim_{x \to \infty} Q(x) = a_n$ and $\lim_{x \to -\infty} Q(x) = a_n$.
Suppose $a_n > 0$. By Problem 24 of Exercise 3.2
there exists a negative number s such that $Q(s) > 0$
and a positive number t such that $Q(t) > 0$. Recalling that n is odd we see that $s^n < 0$ and $t^n > 0$.
Therefore $P(s) = s^n Q(s) < 0$ and $P(t) = t^n Q(t) > 0$.
By Bolzano's Theorem there exists a number z,
$s < z < t$, such that $P(z) = 0$. If $a_n < 0$ there
exists a negative number s such that $Q(s) < 0$ and
a positive number t such that $Q(t) < 0$. Then
$s^n < 0$ so $P(s) = s^n Q(s) > 0$ and $t^n > 0$ so $P(t) =$
$t^n Q(t) < 0$. The conclusion again follows from
Theorem 4.24. □

If the previous result is an unexpected consequence of Bolzano's Theorem, so is the following.

Theorem 4.28: Suppose n is a positive integer and
a is a number.

(1) If n is odd, there exists a number b
such that $b^n = a$.

(2) If n is even and $a > 0$, there exists
a number b such that $b^n = a$.

Proof: Define a function f by $f(x) = x^n - a$ for
every number x. To prove (1) we simply observe
that f is a polynomial of odd degree and conclude
by the previous theorem that $f(b) = 0$ for some

163

number b. Hence $b^n - a = 0$ and $b^n = a$. The
proof of (2) is somewhat different. Note that

$f(0) = 0^n - a = -a < 0$ (since $a > 0$). Also

$f(a + 1) = (a + 1)^n - a > 0$. (The last inequality
can be obtained by Bernoulli's Inequality or mathematical induction.) Since f is continuous and $f(0)$
and $f(a + 1)$ have opposite signs, Bolzano's Theorem tells us that $f(b) = 0$ for some b satisfying

$0 < b < a + 1$. Again this means that $b^n = a$.
(Note that in the proof of (2) n can either be
even or odd; however, it is necessary that a be
positive.)   □

     The following result, in quite a different
vein, is also a corollary of Bolzano's Theorem.
With a little thought you should be able to find
a simple proof.

Theorem 4.29 (Fixed Point Theorem): Suppose f is
a continuous function on the closed interval [a,b],
and suppose that the range of f is the closed interval [a,b]. There exists at least one number z,
$a \le z \le b$, such that $f(z) = z$.

Proof: Left as an exercise.

Definition 4.30: A function f defined on a domain
D is said to be strictly increasing provided
$f(x) < f(y)$ for all x,y in D satisfying $x < y$.
We say that f is strictly decreasing provided
$f(x) > f(y)$ for all x,y in D satisfying $x < y$. A
function which is either strictly increasing or
strictly decreasing is said to be strictly monotonic.

Definition 4.31: Suppose f is a function having
domain D and range R, and suppose that f is one-
to-one (i.e., for all x_1, x_2 in D such that

$x_1 \neq x_2$ we have $f(x_1) \neq f(x_2)$). Define a function g as follows: for each y in R, let g(y) = x where x is that (unique) number in D such that f(x) = y. We call g the <u>inverse function</u> of f and denote it by f^{-1}.

Be sure you understand the last definition thoroughly. Since R is the range of f, R = {f(x): x ∈ D}. For any y in R, therefore, y = f(x) for at least one x in D. There cannot be two such x's, however. For if y = $f(x_1)$ and y = $f(x_2)$, where $x_1 \neq x_2$, we have a contradiction of the fact that f is one-to-one. Note that the inverse function of f has domain R and range D, just the opposite of f. Also, since g(y) = x whenever f(x) = y, it follows that

$g(f(x)) = g(y) = x$ and $f(g(y)) = f(x) = y.$

Or, using our alternate notation,

$f^{-1}(f(x)) = x$ for every x in D

and

$f(f^{-1}(x)) = x$ for every x in R.

Example 9: Consider the function f defined by

$$f(x) = y = \frac{3 - 2x}{x + 1}$$

for all $x \neq -1$. Assume that f is not one-to-one. Then there exist numbers x_1 and x_2 such that $x_1 \neq x_2$ but $f(x_1) = f(x_2)$. This means that

$$\frac{3 - 2x_1}{x_1 + 1} = \frac{3 - 2x_2}{x_2 + 1}$$

so that

$$3x_2 + 3 - 2x_1 x_2 - 2x_1 = 3x_1 + 3 - 2x_1 x_2 - 2x_2$$

165

which reduces to $5x_1 = 5x_2$

or $$x_1 = x_2.$$

From this contradiction we conclude that f is
indeed one-to-one. The inverse of f is the function g such that $g(y) = x$ whenever $f(x) = y$. To
find the formula for g we simply solve the equation

$$y = \frac{3 - 2x}{x + 1}$$

for x in terms of y. This produces

$$x = \frac{3 - y}{y + 2}$$

and the formula for g is therefore

$$g(y) = x = \frac{3 - y}{y + 2} .$$

Since we usually prefer that the independent
variable be x instead of y, it's customary to
interchange x and y. The inverse of f is given
by

$$f^{-1}(x) = \frac{3 - x}{x + 2} .$$

Figure 4.4 shows the graphs of both functions on
the same set of axes. Can you describe the sym-
metry between these two graphs?

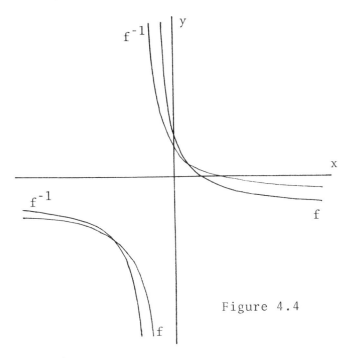

Figure 4.4

From our discussion so far it's clear that a function f has an inverse (denoted f^{-1} from now on) if and only if f is one-to-one on its domain. The fact that a function is one-to-one can sometimes be inferred from another condition, as in the following result.

Theorem 4.32: Suppose f is a strictly monotonic function on its domain D. Then f has an inverse f^{-1}. Furthermore, f^{-1} is strictly increasing if f is strictly increasing, and f^{-1} is strictly decreasing if f is strictly decreasing.

Proof: Suppose f is strictly increasing. Let x_1 and x_2 be any elements of D such that $x_1 \neq x_2$.

167

Assume, without loss of generality, that $x_1 < x_2$. Then $f(x_1) < f(x_2)$, so obviously $f(x_1) \neq f(x_2)$. Consequently f is one-to-one and therefore has an inverse f^{-1}. Denote the range of f by R, and assume that f^{-1} is not strictly increasing. Then there exist y_1, y_2 in R satisfying $y_2 < y_1$ such that $f^{-1}(y_2) \geq f^{-1}(y_1)$. Let x_1 and x_2 be those elements of D such that $f(x_1) = y_1$ and $f(x_2) = y_2$. Then $f^{-1}(y_1) = x_1$ and $f^{-1}(y_2) = x_2$. Hence

$$x_1 = f^{-1}(y_1) \leq f^{-1}(y_2) = x_2$$

and $$f(x_1) = y_1 > y_2 = f(x_2),$$

contradicting the fact that f is strictly increasing. Therefore f^{-1} is strictly increasing. The proof for a strictly decreasing function is similar. $\square$

Any one-to-one function has an inverse. If the function is continuous, is the inverse continuous? The following theorem answers that question in the affirmative, provided the domain is a closed interval.

Theorem 4.33: If f is continuous and one-to-one on the closed interval [a,b], then f^{-1} is continuous.

Proof: Let R denote the range of f. We will use Theorem 4.5 to prove that f^{-1} is continuous on R. Suppose y is any point of R and $\{y_n\}$ is any sequence

168

of elements of R converging to y. We must show that the sequence $\{f^{-1}(y_n)\}$ converges to $f^{-1}(y)$. Let $f^{-1}(y) = x$ and $f^{-1}(y_n) = x_n$ for each positive integer n. Then $f(x) = y$ and $f(x_n) = y_n$ for each n. With this new notation we must show that the sequence $\{x_n\}$ converges to x. Let $\{x_{i_n}\}$ be any convergent subsequence of $\{x_n\}$. (There exists such a subsequence since $\{x_n\}$ is bounded.) The limit of $\{x_{i_n}\}$, call it z, must be in [a,b]. Since f is continuous at z, $\{f(x_{i_n})\} = \{y_{i_n}\}$ converges to $f(z)$ (by Theorem 4.5). But $\{y_{i_n}\}$ is a subsequence of the convergent sequence $\{y_n\}$. Hence $\{y_{i_n}\}$ converges to $f(x)$ (=y), for that is the limit of $\{y_n\}$. The limit of a convergent sequence is unique, so $f(z) = f(x)$. Since f is one-to-one, $z = x$. Hence $\{x_{i_n}\}$ converges to x. The sequence $\{x_n\}$ converges to x by Problem 18 of Exercise 2.4. $\square$

Corollary: (1) If f is continuous and strictly increasing on the closed interval [a,b], f^{-1} exists and is continuous and strictly increasing on the closed interval [f(a),f(b)].

(2) If f is continuous and strictly decreasing on the closed interval [a,b], f^{-1} exists and is continuous and strictly decreasing on the closed interval [f(b),f(a)].

Proof: Left as an exercise.

Example 10: Suppose n is a positive integer. On any closed interval [a,b], where $0 \leq a < b$, the function $f(x) = x^n$ is continuous and strictly increasing. Continuity follows from the fact that f is a polynomial, and you are asked to verify the strictly increasing assertion in Problem 9 of the exercises. The inverse of f is the function $f^{-1}(x) = x^{\frac{1}{n}}$, which is continuous and strictly increasing by the corollary above.

170

Exercise 4.2

1. Prove Theorem 4.23.

2. Give an example of a function f and an interval [a,b] such that f has both a maximum and minimum on [a,b], but f is not continuous on [a,b].

3. Prove Theorem 4.25.

4. Use the Intermediate Value Theorem to conclude that the equation $x^4 - 5x^3 + 2x^2 + x + 7 = 0$ has a root between 4 and 5.

5. A function f is said to have the Intermediate Value Property on the interval [a,b] provided the following is true: if s and t are any numbers in [a,b] and c is any number between f(s) and f(t), there exists at least one number z in (s,t) such that f(z) = c. Prove or disprove: if f has the Intermediate Value Property on [a,b], then f is continuous on [a,b].

6. Prove Theorem 4.29.

7. Using Bolzano's Theorem repeatedly find, correct to two decimal places, the only real root of $x^3 - x^2 = 1$.

8. Prove the corollary to Theorem 4.33.

*9. If n is a positive integer and a and b are numbers satisfying $0 \leq a < b$, show that the function $f(x) = x^n$ is strictly increasing on [a,b].

10. Prove that if f is continuous and one-to-one on [a,b], then f is strictly monotonic on [a,b].

In each of Problems 11 through 16 determine if the given function has an inverse. If it does, find a formula for the inverse, and identify its domain and range.

11. $f(x) = 5x + 3$

12. $f(x) = 4 - x^2$

13. $f(x) = \dfrac{2}{x + 3}$

14. $f(x) = (x - 1)^3$

15. $f(x) = \dfrac{x^2 + 1}{x}, \ x \leq -1$

16. $f(x) = |x|$

17. If n is a positive integer and a is a positive number, prove that there is only one positive number b such that $b^n = a$.

18. The equation $x^4 - 4x^3 + x^2 + 6x + 2 = 0$ has four real roots. Isolate the roots; that is, find four intervals, each interval containing only one root.

19. Give an example of a one-to-one function f defined on $[0,1]$ such that the range of f is $[0,1]$ and f is not continuous at any point.

20. If r is any rational number, prove that the function $f(x) = x^r$ is continuous.

21. Define a function f by

$$f(x) = \begin{cases} x^3 - 3x^2 + 4 & \text{if } 0 \leq x < 2 \\ -x^2 + 6x - 8 & \text{if } 2 \leq x \leq 4 \end{cases}.$$

Show that the hypothesis of the Intermediate

Value Theorem is satisfied on $[0,4]$ with $c = 2$, and find every number z in $[0,4]$ such that $f(z) = 2$.

22. Prove or disprove: if f is one-to-one on $[a,b]$ and has at least one point of discontinuity, then f^{-1} has at least one point of discontinuity.

23. Give an example of a bounded, continuous function, having domain the set of all numbers, which has neither a maximum nor a minimum.

24. Suppose f and g are continuous functions on $[a,b]$ such that $f(a) \leq g(a)$ and $f(b) \geq g(b)$. Prove that $f(x) = g(x)$ for at least one x in $[a,b]$.

25. If f is any one-to-one function, explain geometrically how it is possible to sketch the graph of f^{-1}, knowing what the graph of f looks like.

26. Suppose f is bounded, continuous, and strictly increasing on the open interval (a,b). Prove that f can be defined at a and b in such a way as to make f bounded, continuous, and strictly increasing on $[a,b]$.

27. Suppose f and g are functions having domain D. Define two new functions M and m on D as follows:

$$M(x) = \max \{f(x), g(x)\}$$
$$m(x) = \min \{f(x), g(x)\}.$$

Prove that if f and g are both continuous at a point a in D, then M and m are both continuous at a.

3. Uniform Continuity

You've no doubt noticed how many theorems of the previous section involved a continuous function on a closed interval. Since we are not always fortunate enough to have our continuous functions defined on closed intervals, it would be nice if some of these results could be generalized. To get an idea what is involved here, consider the proof of Theorem 4.20 (every continuous function on a closed interval is bounded). Precisely where in the proof do we use the fact that the function's domain is a closed interval? Before reading any further, study the proof closely and see if you can answer this question.

Having analyzed the proof, you should have found two places where the characteristics of a closed interval were used. The first was in the assertion that $\{x_n\}$ is bounded, for a closed interval is bounded by definition. The second is more subtle. The sequence $\{x_{i_n}\}$ converges to a number z. Now z belongs to the interval [a,b] since every term of $\{x_{i_n}\}$ is in [a,b] (you can quickly derive a contradiction by assuming that z is not in [a,b]). Thus from any sequence of elements of the domain of f we have inferred the existence of a subsequence converging to an element in the domain. In order that the proof be valid for a more general domain D, therefore, two things must be true: (1) D must be bounded, and (2) every sequence of elements of D must contain a subsequence converging to an element of D. Although it is not obvious now, it will be shown later that (1) is true whenever (2) is true.

Before continuing with our generalization, it is convenient at this time to introduce some new terminology.

174

Definition 4.34: A set S is said to be closed provided every limit point of S is an element of S.

Recall that x is said to be a limit point of S provided every neighborhood of x contains infinitely many elements of S (Definition 2.22). If a set S has no limit points, it's understood that Definition 4.34 is satisfied automatically. In other words, the definition as given is equivalent to the following: a set S is closed provided there is no limit point of S that fails to belong to S.

Example 11: You are asked to prove in the exercises that each of the following is a closed set.

  (a) Any set having only finitely many elements.

  (b) Any closed interval.

  (c) Any set which is the intersection of a collection of closed sets.

  (d) Any set which is the union of a finite number of closed sets.

Definition 4.35: A set S is said to be open provided the following is true:

  if x is any element of S, there exists a neighborhood of x which is a subset of S.

Example 12: You are asked to prove in the exercises that each of the following is an open set.

  (a) Any open interval.

  (b) Any set which is the union of a collection of open sets.

  (c) Any set which is the intersection of a finite number of open sets.

Since the words "open" and "closed" are anto-
nyms in everyday language, we might expect the
same relationship here. This is not the case, however, for it is possible for a set to be both open
and closed at the same time! (There is only one
such non-empty set; can you think of it?) The
precise relationship between open and closed sets
is given in the following theorem.

Theorem 4.36: A set is closed if and only if its
complement is open.

Proof: Suppose S is a closed set. Let x be any
element of C(S). Since S contains all of its limit points, x is not a limit point of S. Hence
there exists a neighborhood T of x containing no
point of S. That is, T is a subset of C(S). This
means that C(S) is open.

Suppose next that C(S) is an open set. If x
is any limit point of S, every neighborhood of x
contains a point of S distinct from x. Hence no
neighborhood of x is a subset of C(S). Since C(S)
is open, x does not belong to C(S). Therefore x
is in S, and so S is closed. □

Definition 4.37: A set is said to be compact provided it is both closed and bounded.*

Theorem 4.38: A set S is compact if and only if
every sequence of elements of S has a subsequence
converging to an element of S.

*Though this definition is perfectly proper for sets
of real numbers, a different definition is usually
used in more abstract mathematical spaces. In this
development a set is said to be compact provided it
satisfies the condition given in Theorem 4.46.

176

Proof: Suppose first that S is compact, and let $\overline{\{x_n\}}$ be any sequence of elements of S. Since S is bounded, $\{x_n\}$ is bounded and so has a convergent subsequence $\{x_{i_n}\}$. Let z denote the limit of $\{x_{i_n}\}$. We must show that z is actually in S. It is convenient to consider two cases.

Case 1: the range of $\{x_{i_n}\}$ is finite. In this situation z must be one of the terms of the sequence (in reality, there exists a positive integer N such that $z = x_{i_n}$ for all $n \geq N$). Since every term of $\{x_{i_n}\}$ is in S, z is in S.

Case 2: the range of $\{x_{i_n}\}$ is infinite. Since every neighborhood of z contains all terms of the sequence from some point on, every neighborhood of z contains infinitely many elements of S. This makes z a limit point of S, and z belongs to S since S is closed.

For the other half of the proof we assume that if $\{x_n\}$ is any sequence of elements of S there exists a subsequence $\{x_{i_n}\}$ of $\{x_n\}$ which converges to an element of S. Let z be any limit point of S. By Theorem 2.23 there exists a sequence $\{x_n\}$ of elements of S converging to z. By our hypothesis $\{x_n\}$ has a subsequence $\{x_{i_n}\}$ converging to an element of S. Since every subsequence of a convergent sequence must have the same limit, $\{x_{i_n}\}$ converges to z. Therefore z is in S, proving that S is closed. Assume that S is not

177

bounded. Then for each positive integer n there exists an element x_n of S such that $|x_n| > n$. The sequence $\{x_n\}$ has no convergent subsequence, contradicting the hypothesis. Hence S is both closed and bounded, that is, compact. □

The discussion which opened this section concerned an attempt to generalize Theorem 4.20. Taking into account our new terminology and the result of the preceding theorem, that discussion indicates that every function continuous on a compact set is bounded. We can, in fact, prove an even stronger statement.

Theorem 4.39: If f is a continuous function on the compact set D, the range of f is a compact set.

Proof: Let R denote the range of f. Suppose $\{y_n\}$ is any sequence of elements of R. Then for each n there exists x_n in D such that $f(x_n) = y_n$. Since D is compact, the sequence $\{x_n\}$ has a subsequence $\{x_{i_n}\}$ converging to an element of D, call it z. Since f is continuous at z, Theorem 4.5 tells us that the sequence $\{f(x_{i_n})\}$ converges to $f(z)$ in R. Therefore the sequence $\{y_n\}$ ($= \{f(x_n)\}$) has a subsequence converging to an element of R. Hence R is compact by Theorem 4.38. □

Corollary: If f is a continuous function on the compact set D, then f is bounded.

Theorems 4.22 and 4.23 have an easy generalization to compact sets.

178

Theorem 4.40:   If f is a continuous function on
the compact set D, then f has both a maximum and
minimum on D.

Proof: By the previous result the range R of f
is bounded.   Let M denote the least upper bound
of R.   Then $f(x) \leq M$ for every x in D.   From
Problem 15 of Exercise 2.3 we know that M is
either a point or a limit point of R.   But R is
compact and therefore closed, so M is certainly
a point of R.   That is, $f(x) = M$ for at least
one x in D, so f has a maximum on D.   The proof
for the minimum is similar.   □

Theorem 4.41:   If f is continuous and one-to-one
on the compact set D, then f^{-1} is continuous.

Proof: Left as an exercise.

We need to consider one further aspect of
continuity.   Definition 4.1 can be paraphrased as
follows: if a is a number and ε is a positive
number, there exists a positive number δ such that
$|f(x) - f(a)| < \varepsilon$ for all x satisfying $|x - a| < \delta$
(provided, of course, a and x are in the domain
of f).   It should be emphasized that δ depends on
both ε and a.   If δ depended on ε only, we might
expect this to be a "stronger" type of continuity.

Definition 4.42:   Suppose f is a function having
domain D and S is a subset of D.   We say that f is
uniformly continuous on S provided the following
condition is satisfied:

    if ε is any positive number, there exists a
    positive number δ such that if x and y are
    any elements of S satisfying $|x - y| < \delta$,
    then $|f(x) - f(y)| < \varepsilon$.

We say that <u>f is uniformly continuous</u> provided f is uniformly continuous on D.

Example 13: Define a function f by $f(x) = x^2$ for every x in (-3,1]. If ε is any positive number, let $\delta = \varepsilon/6$. Then for any x and y in (-3,1] satisfying $|x - y| < \delta$ we have

$$|f(x) - f(y)| = |x^2 - y^2|$$

$$= |x + y||x - y|$$

$$< |x + y| \, \delta$$

$$\leq (|x| + |y|) \, \delta$$

$$< 6\delta$$

$$= \varepsilon.$$

Therefore f is uniformly continuous on (-3,1].

Probably the last example is not surprising. After all, the function $f(x) = x^2$ is regarded as a very well-behaved function. The next example sheds some more light on the matter.

Example 14: Define a function f by $f(x) = x^2$ for every number x, and let ε be any positive number. Suppose δ is an arbitrary (fixed) positive number. Let x and y be defined by

$$x = \frac{6\varepsilon + \delta^2}{4\delta} \quad \text{and} \quad y = \frac{6\varepsilon - \delta^2}{4\delta}.$$

Since all numbers are in the domain of f, this is certainly possible. It follows that

$$x + y = \frac{6\varepsilon + \delta^2}{4\delta} + \frac{6\varepsilon - \delta^2}{4\delta} = \frac{3\varepsilon}{\delta}$$

and $\quad x - y = \dfrac{6\varepsilon + \delta^2}{4\delta} - \dfrac{6\varepsilon - \delta^2}{4\delta} = \dfrac{\delta}{2}$.

Since both quantities are positive, $|x + y| = \dfrac{3\varepsilon}{\delta}$ and $|x - y| = \dfrac{\delta}{2}$. Note that $|x - y| < \delta$. Then

$$|f(x) - f(y)| = |x^2 - y^2|$$

$$= |x + y||x - y|$$

$$= \frac{3\varepsilon}{\delta} \cdot \frac{\delta}{2}$$

$$= \frac{3}{2}\varepsilon > \varepsilon.$$

In other words, for any $\delta > 0$ an x and y can be found satisfying $|x - y| < \delta$ such that $|f(x) - f(y)| > \varepsilon$. No δ "works" for every pair x,y so f is not uniformly continuous on its domain.

It's apparent from the last two examples that the existence of uniform continuity depends not only on the function but also its domain. If it appears that uniform continuity failed in Example 14 because both the function and its domain were unbounded, consider the following example.

Example 15: Define a function f on $(0,1)$ by $f(x) = \cos \dfrac{1}{x}$, and let $\varepsilon = 1$. Suppose δ is an arbitrary (fixed) positive number. Let n be a positive integer satisfying

$$\frac{1}{2n(2n - 1)\pi} < \delta$$

181

and define numbers x and y by

$$x = \frac{1}{(2n - 1)\pi} \text{ and } y = \frac{1}{2n\pi} .$$

Then

$$|x - y| = \left| \frac{1}{(2n - 1)\pi} - \frac{1}{2n\pi} \right| = \frac{1}{2n(2n - 1)\pi} < \delta.$$

Furthermore

$$|f(x) - f(y)| = |\cos(2n - 1)\pi - \cos 2n\pi|$$

$$= 2 > \varepsilon .$$

Therefore, for $\varepsilon = 1$ there does not exist a positive number δ having the required property, so f is not uniformly continuous.

An additional example of uniform continuity can be found in Theorem 4.17. Review the proof at this time and convince yourself that Definition 4.42 is indeed satisfied.

We have seen that the four arithmetic operations applied to continuous functions always yield continuous functions. What can be said about uniform continuity in this regard? You are asked to prove in the exercises that the sum of two uniformly continuous functions is uniformly continuous. Uniform continuity is not preserved under multiplication of functions, however, as the following example shows.

Example 16: If $f(x) = x$ for every number x, then f is uniformly continuous, for if $\varepsilon > 0$ is given, we need only choose $\delta = \varepsilon$, and then $|f(x) - f(y)| = |x - y| < \varepsilon$ for all x and y satisfying $|x - y| < \delta$. The product $f(x) \cdot f(x) = x^2$ fails to be uniformly continuous by Example 14.

It's obvious that uniform continuity implies ordinary continuity. On the other hand, a function can be continuous on its domain without being uniformly continuous. What additional property or properties should a continuous function have in order to be uniformly continuous? One of our goals is to give an answer to this question. Before achieving this goal, however, we pause to consider two theorems giving necessary conditions for uniform continuity.

Theorem 4.43: If f is a uniformly continuous function on the bounded set D, then f is bounded.

Proof: Left as an exercise.

Note that this theorem in its contrapositive form can be used to prove that a function is not uniformly continuous. If f is unbounded on the bounded set D, then f is not uniformly continuous on D. By this reasoning we can conclude, for example, that the function $f(x) = \frac{1}{x}$ is not uniformly continuous on $(0,1]$.

Theorem 4.44: Suppose f is a uniformly continuous function on the set D. If a is a limit point of D, then f has a limit at a.

Proof: The existence of the limit will be shown by using Theorem 3.6 and by using the fact that a sequence is convergent if and only if it is a Cauchy Sequence. Let $\{x_n\}$ be any sequence of elements of D converging to a, each $x_n \neq a$. Suppose ε is any positive number. Since f is uniformly continuous on D, there exists a positive number δ such that for every x and y in D satisfying $|x - y| < \delta$ we have $|f(x) - f(y)| < \varepsilon$. Now $\{x_n\}$

is a Cauchy Sequence since it converges, so there is a positive integer N such that if m > N and n ≥ N then $|x_m - x_n| < \delta$. It follows that $|f(x_m) - f(x_n)| < \varepsilon$ for such m and n. This means that $\{f(x_n)\}$ is a Cauchy Sequence, hence a convergent one, so f has a limit at a. □

Again the contrapositive can be used to show the non-existence of uniform continuity. If f fails to have a limit at some limit point of its domain, it cannot be uniformly continuous. Knowing that the function $f(x) = \cos \frac{1}{x}$ fails to have a limit at 0, we can conclude immediately that it is not uniformly continuous on (0,1) and avoid the calculations of Example 15.

Suppose f is a continuous function on the set D. If $\varepsilon > 0$ is given, there exists for each x in D a number $\delta_x > 0$ such that $|f(x) - f(y)| < \varepsilon$ for all y in D satisfying $|x - y| < \delta_x$. The subscript is used to indicate that δ_x depends on x (as well as ε). For uniform continuity there must exist a single δ that works for every x in D. One's first impulse is to try the smallest of all the δ_x's, or if there is no smallest, the greatest lower bound of all the δ_x's. This number may be zero, however, in which case uniform continuity is impossible. In order to find a sufficient condition that this greatest lower bound is actually positive, we must now consider a new idea.

Definition 4.45: If S is a set and 𝒴 is a collection of sets such that every element of S belongs to at least one of the sets of 𝒴 , then 𝒴 is said to be a cover of S. (We also say that 𝒴 covers S.) If all of the sets of 𝒴 are open sets, 𝒴 is said to be an open cover of S. Any subcollection of 𝒴

which covers S is said to be a <u>subcover</u> of S. A
<u>finite subcover</u> of S is any sub<u>collection</u> of $\mathcal{U}$
<u>which covers S</u> and contains only finitely many
sets.

<u>Theorem 4.46 (Heine-Borel Theorem)</u>: Suppose S is
a set. The following two statements are equivalent.

   (1)   S is compact.
   (2)   Every open cover of S has a finite
         subcover.

<u>Proof</u>: We first show that $(2) \Rightarrow (1)$. Our hypoth-
esis is that if $\mathcal{U}$ is any open cover of S whatsoever,
then some finite subcollection of $\mathcal{U}$ cover S. We
must show that S is both closed and bounded. Assume this is not true. Then either S fails to be
closed or S fails to be bounded, so we consider
two cases.

      Assume that S is not closed. Then there ex-
ists a limit point a of S which does not belong
to S. For each positive integer n let I_n =
$[a - \frac{1}{n}, a + \frac{1}{n}]$ and let $G_n = C(I_n)$. Now I_n is a
closed set since it is a closed interval, so G_n
is open by Theorem 4.36. Since every number except a belongs to one of the G_n's (infinitely
many of them, actually), the collection $\mathcal{U}$ =
$\{G_1, G_2, G_3, \ldots\}$ is an open cover of S. By
hypothesis there exists a finite subcover of S,
$\mathcal{U}' = \{G_{i_1}, G_{i_2}, G_{i_3}, \ldots, G_{i_N}\}$. Since a is
a limit point of S, I_{i_N} contains an element x of
S distinct from a. Consequently x does not belong
to G_{i_N} and therefore not to any set in $\mathcal{U}'$. This
is a contradiction since $\mathcal{U}'$ covers S. Hence S is

185

closed.

Assume that S is not bounded. For each positive integer n let $G_n = (-n, n)$. Then $\mathcal{Y} =$ $\{G_1, G_2, G_3, \ldots\}$ is an open cover of S (actually $\mathcal{Y}$ covers the set of all numbers). By hypothesis some finite subcollection of $\mathcal{Y}$ covers S, say $\mathcal{Y}' = \{G_{i_1}, G_{i_2}, G_{i_3}, \ldots, G_{i_N}\}$. Therefore $|x| < i_N$ for every x in S, contradicting the fact that S is unbounded. Hence S is bounded.

Now we must show that $(1) \Rightarrow (2)$. Assume that this is not true. Then there exists a compact set S and an open cover $\mathcal{Y}$ of S such that no finite subcollection of $\mathcal{Y}$ covers S. Since S is bounded, S is contained in some closed interval $I_1 = [a_1, b_1]$. If m_1 denotes the midpoint of I_1, let $I_2' = [a_1, m_1]$ and $I_2'' = [m_1, b_1]$. Either $S \cap I_2'$ or $S \cap I_2''$ cannot be covered by a finite subcollection of $\mathcal{Y}$, for if this were not so, then S could be covered by a finite subcollection of $\mathcal{Y}$. Let $I_2 = [a_2, b_2]$ be whichever of the two intervals has this property (if they both do, let I_2 be either one). Divide I_2 into two halves and repeat the argument. Continuation of this procedure yields a sequence of intervals $\{I_n\} = \{[a_n, b_n]\}$ such that, for each positive integer n, $S \cap I_n$ cannot be covered by a finite subcollection of $\mathcal{Y}$. For each positive integer n let x_n be any element of $S \cap I_n$. By Theorem 4.38 there exists a subsequence $\{x_{i_n}\}$ of $\{x_n\}$ converging to an element of S, call it z. Since z is in S, there is an element G of $\mathcal{Y}$ which contains z. Of course G is an open set, so for some positive number ε the open interval $(z - \varepsilon, z + \varepsilon)$ is a subset of G. Since $\{x_{i_n}\}$ converges

186

to z, there is a positive integer N_1 such that $|x_{i_n} - z| < \varepsilon/2$ for all $n \geq N_1$. Also, if $\ell(I_n)$ denotes the length of I_n, there is a positive integer N_2 such that $\ell(I_{i_n}) < \varepsilon/2$ for $n \geq N_2$. Let N be the larger of N_1 and N_2. Then

$$|x_{i_N} - z| < \varepsilon/2 \text{ and } \ell(I_{i_N}) < \varepsilon/2.$$

It follows that

$$|a_{i_N} - z| \leq |a_{i_N} - x_{i_N}| + |x_{i_N} - z| < \varepsilon/2 + \varepsilon/2 = \varepsilon$$

and

$$|b_{i_N} - z| \leq |b_{i_N} - x_{i_N}| + |x_{i_N} - z| < \varepsilon/2 + \varepsilon/2 = \varepsilon,$$

proving that the interval I_{i_N} is a subset of $(z - \varepsilon, z + \varepsilon)$ and therefore a subset of G. Obviously $S \cap I_{i_N}$ is a subset of G. Hence $S \cap I_{i_N}$ is covered by a finite subcollection of $\mathcal{Y}$, namely one set. Contradiction. Therefore every open cover of S has a finite subcover. □

Theorem 4.46 is one of the fundamental theorems of analysis although its importance may be difficult to appreciate at this time. It was first proved (in a somewhat different form) by Eduard Heine, in 1872. Virtually ignored, it was rediscovered in 1895 by the French mathematician, Emile Borel.* The method of proof should look

*Carl B. Boyer, A History of Mathematics(1968), p.665.

familiar; it is almost identical with that of the Bolzano-Weierstrass Theorem. As a matter of fact, it can be shown that these two famous theorems are equivalent. Moreover, they are both equivalent to the completeness property of the real number system (every set bounded above has a least upper bound).

Our principal result on uniform continuity is the following theorem, proved by means of the Heine-Borel Theorem. Read the statement, then the paragraph preceding Definition 4.45, and see if you can provide a proof yourself before reading the one given.

Theorem 4.47: If f is a continuous function on the compact set D, then f is uniformly continuous on D.

Proof: Suppose ε is any positive number. For each x in D there exists a positive number δ_x such that for all y in D satisfying $|x - y| < \delta_x$ we have $|f(x) - f(y)| < \varepsilon/2$. For each x in D let G_x denote the open interval $(x - \frac{\delta_x}{2}, x + \frac{\delta_x}{2})$, and let $\mathcal{Y}$ denote the collection of all such intervals G_x. Now $\mathcal{Y}$ is an open covering the compact set D, so some finite subcollection $\mathcal{Y}'$ of $\mathcal{Y}$ covers D. Denote the elements of $\mathcal{Y}'$ by G_{x_1}, G_{x_2}, G_{x_3}, . . . , G_{x_N}. For every x in D, therefore, there is a positive integer i, $1 \leq i \leq N$, such that $|x - x_i| < \frac{\delta_{x_i}}{2}$. Let δ be the smallest number in the set

$$\{ \frac{\delta_{x_1}}{2}, \frac{\delta_{x_2}}{2}, \frac{\delta_{x_3}}{2}, . . . , \frac{\delta_{x_N}}{2} \}.$$

Suppose now that x and y are any elements of D such that $|x - y| < \delta$. It will be shown that $|f(x) - f(y)| < \varepsilon$. (This x and y will remain fixed throughout the rest of the proof.) Since $\mathcal{Y}'$ covers D, there exists $x_k (1 \leq k \leq N)$ such that $|x - x_k| < \dfrac{\delta_{x_k}}{2}$. How far away is y from this number x_k? We have

$$|y - x_k| \leq |y - x| + |x - x_k|$$

$$< \delta + \frac{\delta_{x_k}}{2}$$

$$\leq \frac{\delta_{x_k}}{2} + \frac{\delta_{x_k}}{2}$$

$$= \delta_{x_k}.$$

Since $|x - x_k| < \dfrac{\delta_{x_k}}{2} < \delta_{x_k}$, we have by the continuity of f at x_k that

$$|f(x) - f(x_k)| < \varepsilon/2.$$

Similarly, since $|y - x_k| < \delta_{x_k}$, the continuity of f at x_k implies that

$$|f(y) - f(x_k)| < \varepsilon/2.$$

Finally, then,

$$|f(x) - f(y)| \leq |f(x) - f(x_k)| + |f(x_k) - f(y)|$$

$$< \varepsilon/2 + \varepsilon/2$$

$$= \varepsilon$$

and the proof is complete. □

Exercise 4.3

1. Prove, as stated in Example 11, that

   (a) a set having only finitely many elements is closed;

   (b) a closed interval is closed.

2. Prove, as stated in Example 11, that

   (a) a set which is the intersection of any collection of closed sets is closed;

   (b) a set which is the union of a finite number of closed sets is closed.

3. Give an example of a collection of closed sets whose union is not closed.

4. Prove, as stated in Example 12, that any open interval is open.

5. Prove, as stated in Example 12, that

   (a) a set which is the union of any collection of open sets is open;

   (b) a set which is the intersection of a finite number of open sets is open.

6. Give an example of a collection of open sets whose intersection is non-empty and not open.

7. Prove that a set S is compact if and only if every infinite subset of S has a limit point in S.

8. Prove Theorem 4.41.

9. Prove that if f and g are both uniformly continuous on a set D, then f + g is uniformly continuous on D.

10. Prove or disprove: if f and g are both bounded and uniformly continuous on a set D, then fg is uniformly continuous on D.

11. Show that if f is continuous on the set of all numbers and c is any number, the set {x: f(x) = c} is closed.

12. Show that if f is continuous on the set of all numbers and c is any number, the set {x: f(x) > c} is open.

13. Prove Theorem 4.43.

14. Give an example of an open cover of the interval (0,1] which has no finite subcover.

15. If S is any set, the set of all limit points of S is called the derived set of S and is denoted by S'. Prove that S' is closed.

16. If S is any set, the closure of S is defined to be the set $\overline{S} = S \cup S'$ (where S' is defined in Problem 15). Prove that the name is justified, that is, prove that $\overline{S}$ is a closed set.

17. Prove that $\overline{S}$ is the "smallest" closed set containing S. In other words, show that if A is any closed set containing S, then $\overline{S}$ is a subset of A. ($\overline{S}$ is defined in Problem 16).

18. Give an example of a continuous, one-to-one function whose inverse is not continuous.

19. Prove or disprove: if both f and g are uniformly continuous on a set D and g is bounded away from zero on D, then $\frac{f}{g}$ is uniformly continuous on D.

In problems 20 through 23, determine whether or not the function is uniformly continuous on its domain.

20. $f(x) = \dfrac{1}{1 + x^2},\ x \geq 0$

21. $f(x) = \sqrt{x},\ x \geq 0$

22. $f(x) = x \sin x,\ \text{all } x$

23. $f(x) = \dfrac{1}{x},\ x \geq 1$

24. Suppose f is continuous on the set D of all non-negative numbers. Prove that if $\lim_{x \to \infty} f(x)$ exists, then f is uniformly continuous on D.

25. Prove the <u>Cantor Intersection Theorem</u>. If $\{S_n\}$ is a sequence of non-empty, compact sets such that $S_{n+1} \subseteq S_n$ for every positive integer n, there exists at least one point belonging to every S_n.

26. Give examples showing that the statement in Problem 25 is false if "compact" is replaced by either "closed" or "bounded" alone.

27. Show that if f and g are both uniformly continuous on a bounded set D, then fg is uniformly continuous on D.

28. Show that if f is uniformly continuous on D, then f can be defined on D' in such a way that the extended f is uniformly continuous on $\overline{D}$. (See Problems 15 and 16 for the definitions of D' and $\overline{D}$.) Give an example showing that the conclusion is false if f is merely continuous and not uniformly continuous.

29.   Prove or disprove: if S is a closed set and
      a is a number not in S, there exists a con-
      tinuous function f such that f(a) = 0 and
      f(x) = 1 for every x in S.

CHAPTER 5

1. Algebra of Derivatives

Any student of elementary geometry knows what is meant by a "tangent line" to a circle. One of the characteristics of such a line is that it intersects the circle at only one point. To generalize the concept of tangency to curves other than circles is one of the fundamental problems of calculus, and the solution of this problem involves the notion of a derivative.

Definition 5.1: Suppose f is a function having domain D, and a is both a point and a limit point of D. Let F be the function defined by

$$F(x) = \frac{f(x) - f(a)}{x - a}$$

for each x in D different from a. We say that f is differentiable at a provided F has a limit at a, in which case the number $\lim_{x \to a} F(x)$ is called the derivative of f at a (or the slope of f at a).

Definition 5.2: Suppose f is a function having domain D, and a is both a point and a limit point of D. The derivative of f is the function f' whose value at a is given by

$$f'(a) = \lim_{x \to a} \frac{f(x) - f(a)}{x - a}$$

for every a in D where f is differentiable.

It should be pointed out that the word "derivative" has been used in two different ways. In Definition 5.1 it denotes a particular number, and

195

in Definition 5.2 it denotes a particular function. The possible ambiguity is unfortunate, but
this double usage is firmly established and usually causes no difficulty. An alternative expression, "slope," is sometimes used in the first case,
but this term has unfortunately not acquired a
large following. Since the slope of a linear function according to Definition 5.1 coincides with
the idea of slope of a line introduced in an ana-
lytic geometry, there would be no possible misunderstanding.

The definition of the derivative is sometimes
given in a slightly different form. Each number
$x \neq a$ in the domain of f can be represented $x =
a + h$ where h is some non-zero number. Since x
approaches a if and only if h approaches zero, the
following result is immediate.

Theorem 5.3: Suppose f is a function having domain
$\overline{D, \text{ and a is}}$ both a point and a limit point of D.
Then f is differentiable at a if and only if

$$\lim_{h \to 0} \frac{f(a + h) - f(a)}{h}$$

exists, with the assumption that h is a non-zero
number such that a + h is in D.

From now on it will be understood that the
statement, "f is differentiable at a" carries with
it the implication that a is both a point and a
limit point of the domain of f. It should be emphasized that the domain of f' is a subset of the
domain of f.

Definition 5.4: Suppose f is a function having
$\overline{\text{domain D, and}}$ S is a subset of D. We say that f
is differentiable on S provided f is differentiable
at every point a in S. We say that f is differentiable provided f is differentiable on D.

It sometimes happens that we have occasion to differentiate a function which is itself a derivative. This situation prompts the following terminology.

Definition 5.5: Suppose f is a differentiable function having domain D, and f' has domain D'. If f' is differentiable on some subset of D', we denote the derivative of f' by f" and call f" the second derivative of f. Similarly, the derivative of f", if it exists, is denoted by f"' and is called the third derivative of f. For completeness f' is called the first derivative of f. If n is any positive integer, the nth derivative of f is denoted by $f^{(n)}$, and we also define $f^{(0)} = f$.

Note that the first derivative of f is denoted by either f' or $f^{(1)}$, the second derivative of f by either f" or $f^{(2)}$, and the third derivative of f by either f"' or $f^{(3)}$. The prime notation becomes unwieldy beyond this point and is not used. It should be understood that the domain of $f^{(n)}$ is a subset of the domain of $f^{(n-1)}$.

Motivation for the definition of a derivative is not hard to provide. Suppose P and Q are points on the graph of a function f (see Figure 5.1). It's easy to see that the slope of the line connecting P and Q is given by $\frac{f(x) - f(a)}{x - a}$. If we think of the point Q as moving along the curve toward P, while P remains fixed, different connecting lines are obtained (the dotted lines) and therefore different slopes. In the limit, that is, as Q approaches P "arbitrarily closely," we obtain what is intuitively regarded as the line tangent to the graph at P, and the slope of this line is given by $\lim_{x \to a} \frac{f(x) - f(a)}{x - a}$, provided, of course, the limit exists.

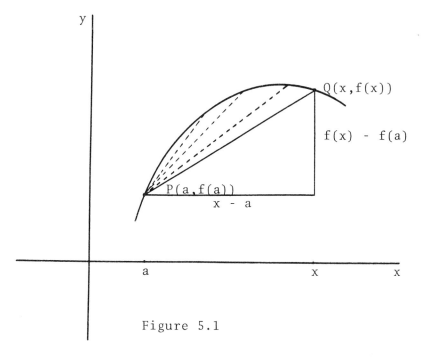

y

Q(x,f(x))

f(x) - f(a)

P(a,f(a))

x - a

a   x   x

Figure 5.1

In some cases a derivative can be found directly from the definition, though this is usually not the easiest way.

Example 1: Suppose $f(x) = \frac{3 - x}{2x + 5}$ for every $x \neq -\frac{5}{2}$. By elementary algebra we obtain

$$f(x + h) - f(x) = -\frac{11h}{(2x + 2h + 5)(2x + 5)}$$

so that

$$\frac{f(x + h) - f(x)}{h} = -\frac{11}{(2x + 2h + 5)(2x + 5)}$$

and consequently

198

$$\lim_{h \to 0} \frac{f(x + h) - f(x)}{h} = -\frac{11}{(2x + 5)^2} = f'(x).$$

It's customary in calculations of this kind to regard x as being fixed, while not actually changing the notation to reflect this fact (by setting x = a, say). In the above example it turns out that the domain of f' is the same as the domain of f since the formula for f' places no restriction on x other than that the denominator be non-zero.

Example 2: Suppose $f(x) = \sqrt{x}$ for $x \geq 0$. We have

$$\frac{f(x + h) - f(x)}{h} = \frac{\sqrt{x + h} - \sqrt{x}}{h}$$

$$= \frac{\sqrt{x + h} - \sqrt{x}}{h} \cdot \frac{\sqrt{x + h} + \sqrt{x}}{\sqrt{x + h} + \sqrt{x}}$$

$$= \frac{1}{\sqrt{x + h} + \sqrt{x}} \, .$$

It follows that

$$\lim_{h \to 0} \frac{f(x + h) - f(x)}{h} = \frac{1}{2\sqrt{x}} = f'(x).$$

The formula obtained requires x to be positive, so the domain of f' is "smaller" than the domain of f.

The definition of the derivative in elementary calculus usually requires that the domain of the function be an interval. Since our definition is not so restrictive, the following example should be illuminating.

Example 3: Suppose $f(x) = x^2$ for rational x, and f is undefined at the irrationals.   Is f

differentiable anywhere? If a is any rational
number, then a is both a point and a limit point
of the domain of f. For any rational x

$$\lim_{x \to a} \frac{f(x) - f(a)}{x - a} = \lim_{x \to a} \frac{x^2 - a^2}{x - a} = \lim_{x \to a}(x + a) = 2a$$

$$= f'(a).$$

Hence f is differentiable at every point of its
domain.

Since a derivative is a particular kind of
limit, we have from our work in Chapter 3 an
automatic necessary and sufficient condition for
differentiability. Review Theorems 3.5 and 3.6
if the next statement does not seem clear to you.

Theorem 5.6: Suppose f is a function having domain D, and a is both a point and a limit point
of D. Then f is differentiable at a if and only
if the following condition is satisfied:

if $\{x_n\}$ is any sequence of elements of D
converging to a with $x_n \neq a$ for each n, the
sequence $\left\{ \dfrac{f(x_n) - f(a)}{x_n - a} \right\}$ converges.

It should also be apparent that for each sequence $\{x_n\}$ of the type described above the common
limit of $\left\{ \dfrac{f(x_n) - f(a)}{x_n - a} \right\}$ is f'(a).

Since the study of continuity of a function
has received so much of our attention, it's natural to ask if there is any relationship between
differentiability and continuity.

Theorem 5.7: If f is differentiable at a, then f is continuous at a.

Proof: If D is the domain of f, then a must be both a point and limit point of D. Suppose $\{x_n\}$ is any sequence of elements of D converging to a, $x_n \neq a$ for each n. For each positive integer n

$$f(x_n) = \frac{f(x_n) - f(a)}{x_n - a} (x_n - a) + f(a).$$

The sequence $\left\{ \dfrac{f(x_n) - f(a)}{x_n - a} \right\}$ converges to f'(a) since f is differentiable at a. The sequences $\{x_n - a\}$ and $\{f(a)\}$ converge to 0 and f(a), respectively. Using basic results from Chapter 2 we conclude that the sequence $\{f(x_n)\}$ converges to f'(a) · 0 + f(a) = f(a). The continuity of f at a follows from Theorems 3.6 and 4.4. □

Thus differentiability at a point implies continuity at that point. The converse is not true, as the following simple example shows.

Example 4: Suppose f(x) = |x| for every number x. The fact that f is continuous at every point will be taken for granted, as this is easy to show. We will prove that f is not differentiable at 0. If a = 0, then f(a) = |0| = 0, and we have the following:

$$\lim_{x \to a+} \frac{f(x) - f(a)}{x - a} = \lim_{x \to 0+} \frac{|x| - 0}{x - 0} = \lim_{x \to 0+} \frac{x}{x} = 1$$

$$\lim_{x \to a-} \frac{f(x) - f(a)}{x - a} = \lim_{x \to 0-} \frac{|x| - 0}{x - 0} = \lim_{x \to 0-} \frac{-x}{x} = -1,$$

where we use the fact that $|x| = x$ if $x > 0$ and $|x| = -x$ if $x < 0$. By Theorem 3.10

$$\lim_{x \to a} \frac{f(x) - f(a)}{x - a}$$

does not exist for a = 0, so f is not differentiable at that point, Referring to the graph in Figure 5.2 we can see why this is the case. The derivative of a function at a point expresses the "direction" of the function's graph at that point. The graph of $f(x) = |x|$ does not have a direction at (0,0) because of the "corner" at that point. Though this function is not differentiable at 0, it is differentiable at every other point.

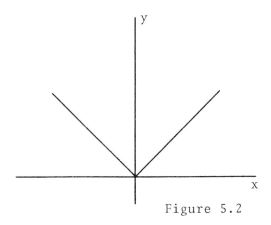

Figure 5.2

The existence of a corner (or a "cusp," as it is called when two curved lines come together, as in Figure 3.7) is not the only phenomenon which causes differentiability to fail at a point of continuity. Consider the graph of $y = \sqrt[3]{x}$.

Remembering the graph of Example 4, it is not hard to conceive of continuous functions having

202

two, three, four, or even infinitely many points where differentiability fails. To most people it would seem that any two of these points must some-how be separated. It is a remarkable fact, how-ever, that there exists a continuous function, having domain the set of all numbers, which is not differentiable at any point! Such a function is difficult to describe and impossible to sketch. The first example of a "continuous, nowhere dif-ferentiable function" was given by Bolzano in 1834.* It is functions of this kind which show that our intuition can be trusted only so far.

We next consider how to differentiate sums, differences, products, and quotients of differenti-able functions.

Theorem 5.8: Suppose f and g have common domain D, and a is both a point and a limit point of D. If f and g are both differentiable at a, then the function h = f + g is differentiable at a and h'(a) = f'(a) + g'(a).

Proof: For x in D, x ≠ a,

$$\frac{h(x) - h(a)}{x - a} = \frac{(f + g)(x) - (f + g)(a)}{x - a}$$

$$= \frac{[f(x) - f(a)] + [g(x) - g(a)]}{x - a}$$

$$= \frac{f(x) - f(a)}{x - a} + \frac{g(x) - g(a)}{x - a}.$$

Since f is differentiable at a, $\lim_{x \to a} \frac{f(x) - f(a)}{x - a} = $ f'(a), and since g is differentiable at a, $\lim_{x \to a} \frac{g(x) - g(a)}{x - a} = $ g'(a).

*Carl B. Boyer, <u>A History of Mathematics</u>, (1968), p. 565.

Using Theorem 3.14 we conclude that

$$\lim_{x \to a} \frac{h(x) - h(a)}{x - a} = h'(a) = f'(a) + g'(a). \qquad \Box$$

Theorem 5.9: Suppose f and g have common domain D, and a is both a point and a limit point of D. If f and g are both differentiable at a, then the function h = f - g is differentiable at a and h'(a) = f'(a) - g'(a).

Proof: Left as an exercise.

Theorem 5.10: Suppose f and g have common domain D, and a is both a point and a limit point of D. If f and g are both differentiable at a, then the function h = fg is differentiable at a and h'(a) = f(a)g'(a) + f'(a)g(a).

Proof: Left as an exercise.

Theorem 5.11: Suppose f and g have common domain D, and a is both a point and a limit point of D. If f and g are both differentiable at a and $g(a) \neq 0$, then the function $h = \frac{f}{g}$ is differentiable at a and $h'(a) = \dfrac{g(a)f'(a) - f(a)g'(a)}{[g(a)]^2}$.

Proof: For x in D, $x \neq a$

$$\frac{h(x) - h(a)}{x - a} = \frac{\frac{f}{g}(x) - \frac{f}{g}(a)}{x - a}$$

$$= \frac{f(x)g(a) - f(a)g(x)}{(x - a)g(x)g(a)}$$

204

$$= \frac{[f(x) - f(a)]g(a) - [g(x) - g(a)]f(a)}{(x - a)g(x)g(a)}$$

$$= \frac{f(x) - f(a)}{x - a} \cdot \frac{1}{g(x)} - \frac{g(x) - g(a)}{x - a} \cdot \frac{f(a)}{g(x)g(a)} \cdot$$

Since f is differentiable at a, $\lim\limits_{x \to a} \dfrac{f(x) - f(a)}{x - a} = $ f'(a), and since g is differentiable at a, $\lim\limits_{x \to a} \dfrac{g(x) - g(a)}{x - a} = g'(a)$. Furthermore, since $g(a) \neq 0$, $\lim\limits_{x \to a} \dfrac{1}{g(x)} = \dfrac{1}{g(a)}$ and $\lim\limits_{x \to a} \dfrac{f(a)}{g(x)g(a)} = \dfrac{f(a)}{[g(a)]^2}$. Therefore

$$\lim\limits_{x \to a} \frac{h(x) - h(a)}{x - a} = h'(a)$$

$$= f'(a) \cdot \frac{1}{g(a)} - g'(a) \cdot \frac{f(a)}{[g(a)]^2}$$

$$= \frac{g(a)f'(a) - f(a)g'(a)}{[g(a)]^2} \cdot$$

Several limit theorems from Chapter 3 have been used in the proof. □

We next consider the problem of the composition of two functions. If g is differentiable at a and f is differentiable at g(a), is f(g) differentiable at a, and if so, what is a formula for the derivative? These questions are answered by the following theorem, one of the more difficult in elementary calculus.

Theorem 5.12 (Chain Rule): Suppose g is differentiable at a and f is differentiable at g(a). Then

the function h = f(g) is differentiable at a, and
h'(a) = f'(g(a)) · g'(a).

Proof: Denote the domains of f and g by D_f and
D_g, respectively. Define a function v as follows:

$$v(x) = \frac{f(x) - f(g(a))}{x - g(a)} - f'(g(a))$$
$$\text{for all } x \text{ in } D_f, x \neq g(a).$$
$$v(x) = 0 \qquad \text{if } x = g(a)$$

Thus v has domain D_f. Since f is differentiable
at g(a),

$$\lim_{x \to g(a)} \frac{f(x) - f(g(a))}{x - g(a)} = f'(g(a)).$$

It follows from the definition of v that
$\lim_{x \to g(a)} v(x) = 0$, and since v(g(a)) = 0, v is continuous at g(a). Of course g is continuous at a
because g is differentiable there. We conclude
by Theorem 4.16 that v(g) is continuous at a. Consequently

$$\lim_{x \to a} [v(g)](x) = \lim_{x \to a} v(g(x)) = v(g(a)) = 0.$$

For each x in D_g such that g(x) ≠ g(a) we have

$$v(g(x)) = \frac{f(g(x)) - f(g(a))}{g(x) - g(a)} - f'(g(a)).$$

This follows from the definition of v where x is
replaced by g(x). For such x elementary algebra shows that

$$f(g(x)) - f(g(a))$$
$$= [v(g(x)) + f'(g(a))][g(x) - g(a)].$$

206

This relation is clearly true for all x in D_g such that $g(x) = g(a)$, so it is valid for all x in D_g. Using this expression,

$$h'(a) = \lim_{x \to a} \frac{f(g(x)) - f(g(a))}{x - a}$$

$$= \lim_{x \to a} \{v(g(x)) + f'(g(a))\}\{\frac{g(x) - g(a)}{x - a}\}$$

$$= \left[\lim_{x \to a} \{v(g(x)) + f'(g(a))\}\right] \cdot \left[\lim_{x \to a} \frac{g(x) - g(a)}{x - a}\right]$$

$$= [0 + f'(g(a))] \cdot g'(a)$$

$$= f'(g(a)) \cdot g'(a). \qquad \Box$$

It may seem that the proof above is unnecessarily complicated. Consider the following. Since

$$\frac{h(x) - h(a)}{x - a} = \frac{f(g(x)) - f(g(a))}{x - a}$$

$$= \frac{f(g(x)) - f(g(a))}{g(x) - g(a)} \cdot \frac{g(x) - g(a)}{x - a},$$

one would like to say

$$h'(a) = \lim_{x \to a} \frac{h(x) - h(a)}{x - a}$$

$$= \lim_{x \to a} \frac{f(g(x)) - f(g(a))}{g(x) - g(a)} \cdot \lim_{x \to a} \frac{g(x) - g(a)}{x - a}$$

and therefore $h'(a) = f'(g(a)) \cdot g'(a)$ since f is known to be differentiable at $g(a)$ and g is known to be differentiable at a. You are asked to explain in one of the exercises why this reasoning is invalid.

Lemma: If c is a number and $f(x) = c$ for every x, then f is differentiable and $f'(x) = 0$.

Proof: Left as an exercise.

Lemma: If $f(x) = x$ for every number x, then f is differentiable and $f'(x) = 1$.

Proof: Left as an exercise.

Theorem 5.13: Suppose n is a non-zero integer. If $f(x) = x^n$, then f is differentiable and

(i) $f'(x) = nx^{n-1}$ for all x if $n > 0$;

(ii) $f'(x) = nx^{n-1}$ for all $x \neq 0$ if $n < 0$.

Proof: We first show by mathematical induction that the formula holds for all positive integers. The case $n = 1$ is taken care of by the preceding lemma. Assume that if $f(x) = x^k$, then $f'(x) = kx^{k-1}$. We must show that if $f(x) = x^{k+1}$, then $f'(x) = (k + 1)x^k$. Now

$$f(x) = x^{k+1} = x^k \cdot x = g(x) \cdot h(x),$$

where $g(x) = x^k$ and $h(x) = x$. By Theorem 5.10

208

$$f'(x) = g(x)h'(x) + g'(x)h(x)$$

$$= x^k \cdot 1 + kx^{k-1} \cdot x$$

$$= x^k + kx^k$$

$$= (k + 1)x^k$$

and the formula is established for every positive integer n (and any number x). Suppose now that n is any negative integer. For each $x \neq 0$

$$f(x) = x^n = \frac{1}{x^{-n}} , \quad -n > 0.$$

Therefore

$$f'(x) = \frac{(x^{-n})(0) - (1)(-nx^{-n-1})}{(x^{-n})^2} = \frac{nx^{-n-1}}{x^{-2n}} = nx^{n-1}$$

where we have used Theorem 5.11 and the fact that the formula is already known for positive integers. □

Corollary: If $P(x) = \sum\limits_{k=0}^{n} a_k x^k$ is any polynomial, then P is differentiable and $P'(x) = \sum\limits_{k=1}^{n} ka_k x^{k-1}$.

Proof: Left as an exercise.

Theorem 5.14: If $f(x) = x^r$, where $x > 0$ and r is any rational number, then f is differentiable and

$$f'(x) = rx^{r-1}.$$

Proof: Left as an exercise.

In order to differentiate the trigonometric functions it is necessary to know the value of $\lim_{x \to 0} \frac{\sin x}{x}$. Anyone who has gone through a standard calculus course has seen this limit evaluated. Because of its importance and also because of its difficulty, one of the methods of evaluation is included here.

Theorem 5.15: If x is measured in radians, then $\lim_{x \to 0} \frac{\sin x}{x} = 1$.

Proof: We start with a circle of radius 1 centered at the origin. Part of this circle is shown in Figure 5.3. Suppose x is a positive angle as indicated by the graph. Both AB and CD are perpendicular to the x-axis with CD tangent to the circle at C. Using $\triangle AOB$

$$\sin x = \frac{|AB|}{|OA|} = |AB| \text{ since } |OA| = 1,$$

and using $\triangle DOC$

$$\tan x = \frac{|DC|}{|OC|} = |DC| \text{ since } |OC| = 1.$$

From these results we get

$$\text{area } \triangle AOC = \frac{1}{2} |OC||AB| = \frac{1}{2} \sin x$$

and

$$\text{area } \triangle DOC = \frac{1}{2} |OC||DC| = \frac{1}{2} \tan x.$$

210

Furthermore, the area of sector AOC = $\frac{1}{2}$ x(1)^2 = $\frac{1}{2}$ x (this formula would not be true if x were measured in degrees). From Figure 5.3 we observe that

area ΔAOC < area sector AOC < area ΔDOC.

Hence

$$\frac{1}{2} \sin x < \frac{1}{2} x < \frac{1}{2} \tan x$$

$$1 < \frac{x}{\sin x} < \frac{1}{\cos x}$$

$$\cos x < \frac{\sin x}{x} < 1.$$

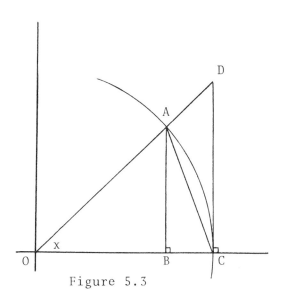

Figure 5.3

Since the cosine function is continuous everywhere (Theorem 4.18) and since cos 0 = 1, $\lim_{x \to 0} \cos x = 1$.

211

Trivially, $\lim_{x \to 0} 1 = 1$. From the inequality above and Theorem 3.24 (the "squeeze theorem") we conclude that

$$\lim_{x \to 0} \frac{\sin x}{x} = 1.$$

If the angle is negative, say $x = -y$ for $y > 0$, $\frac{\sin x}{x} = \frac{\sin(-y)}{-y} = \frac{-\sin y}{-y} = \frac{\sin y}{y}$ ($\sin(-y) =$ $-\sin y$ since the sine function is an odd function), and the limit is 1 just as it was in the positive case. $\square$

It's because of the simplicity of the previous result that radian measure of angles is preferable to degree measure. From now on it will be understood (as it is in most analysis books) that all trigonometric functions use radian measure.

<u>Theorem 5.16</u>: The sine function $f(x) = \sin x$ is differentiable and $f'(x) = \cos x$ for every number x.

<u>Proof</u>: The identity $\sin \alpha - \sin \beta = 2\cos \frac{1}{2}(\alpha + \beta)$ $\sin \frac{1}{2}(\alpha - \beta)$ is needed in the proof. Suppose a is any number. Then

$$\frac{\sin x - \sin a}{x - a} = \frac{2\cos \frac{1}{2}(x + a) \sin \frac{1}{2}(x - a)}{x - a}$$

$$= \cos \frac{1}{2}(x + a) \cdot \frac{\sin \frac{1}{2}(x - a)}{\frac{1}{2}(x - a)}.$$

Now $\lim_{x \to a} \cos \frac{1}{2}(x + a) = \cos a$

because the cosine function is continuous

212

everywhere. Since $\lim\limits_{x \to a} \frac{1}{2}(x - a) = 0$, we conclude
by Theorem 5.15 that $\lim\limits_{x \to a} \dfrac{\sin \frac{1}{2}(x - a)}{\frac{1}{2}(x - a)} = 1$.

Therefore

$$f'(a) = \lim_{x \to a} \frac{\sin x - \sin a}{x - a}$$

$$= \lim_{x \to a} \cos \tfrac{1}{2}(x + a) \cdot \lim_{x \to a} \frac{\sin \frac{1}{2}(x - a)}{\frac{1}{2}(x - a)}$$

$$= \cos a.$$

Since a was arbitrary, $f'(x) = \cos x$ for every
number x. $\qquad\qquad\square$

Theorem 5.17: The cosine function $f(x) = \cos x$
is differentiable and $f'(x) = -\sin x$ for every
number x.

Proof: Left as an exercise.

Theorem 5.18: The tangent, cotangent, secant, and
cosecant functions are differentiable wherever they
are defined. Moreover,

  (i)   if $f(x) = \tan x$, $f'(x) = \sec^2 x$;

  (ii) if $f(x) = \cot x$, $f'(x) = -\csc^2 x$;

  (iii) if $f(x) = \sec x$, $f'(x) = \sec x \tan x$;

  (iv) if $f(x) = \csc x$, $f'(x) =$
        $-\csc x \cot x$.

Proof: Left as an exercise.

Example 5: To find $h'(x)$ if $h(x) = \cos(2 + x - x^2)$, we write $h(x) = f(g(x))$, where $f(x) = \cos x$ and $g(x) = 2 + x - x^2$. Since both f and g are differentiable everywhere, the Chain Rule applies and

$$h'(x) = f'(g(x)) \cdot g'(x)$$

$$= -\sin(2 + x - x^2) \cdot (1 - 2x)$$

$$= (2x - 1) \sin(2 + x - x^2).$$

The theorems of this section simplify considerably the problem of finding derivatives. Nevertheless, there are still occasions when it's necessary to resort to the definition.

Example 6: Suppose f is defined by

$$f(x) = \begin{cases} x \sin \dfrac{1}{x} & \text{if } x \neq 0 \\ 0 & \text{if } x = 0 \end{cases}.$$

Where is f differentiable? (See Figure 3.8 for a sketch.) For all $x \neq 0$ it is a routine matter to show that $f'(x) = \sin \dfrac{1}{x} - \dfrac{1}{x} \cos \dfrac{1}{x}$. To check on differentiability at 0, we have the following:

$$\lim_{x \to 0} \frac{f(x) - f(0)}{x - 0} = \lim_{x \to 0} \frac{x \sin \dfrac{1}{x} - 0}{x} = \lim_{x \to 0} \sin \dfrac{1}{x}.$$

Since this limit does not exist, f is not differentiable at 0.

Exercise 5.1

1. Using either the definition of the derivative or Theorem 5.3 find $f'(x)$ if $f(x) = \dfrac{1}{\sqrt{1 - x^2}}$.

2. Prove Theorem 5.9.

3. Prove Theorem 5.10.

4. Sketch a graph of $f(x) = \dfrac{\sin x}{x}$.

5. Prove the two lemmas preceding Theorem 5.13.

6. Prove the corollary to Theorem 5.13.

7. Following the proof of the Chain Rule is an argument which purports to be a proof of that theorem. Find the flaw in the reasoning.

8. Determine all points at which the graph of $f(x) = x^4 - x^3 + x^2 - 3x + 1$ has a horizontal tangent.

9. Prove Theorem 5.14.

10. Prove Theorem 5.16 using Theorem 5.3.

11. Evaluate $\lim\limits_{x \to 0} \dfrac{\sin x}{x}$ if x is measured in degrees.

12. Prove or disprove: there exists a function having domain an interval which is differentiable at exactly one point.

13. Prove Theorem 5.17.

In Problems 14-17 evaluate the given limit.

14. $\lim_{x \to 0} \dfrac{\cos x - 1}{x}$
15. $\lim_{x \to 0} \dfrac{x}{\sin 5x}$

16. $\lim_{x \to 0} \dfrac{\tan x}{x}$
17. $\lim_{x \to \frac{\pi}{2}} \dfrac{\frac{\pi}{2} - x}{\cos x}$

18. Prove Theorem 5.18.

19. If each of f,g and h is differentiable, find a formula for k' if k = fgh.

In Problems 20-24 find a formula for f'(x).

20. $f(x) = x|x|$
21. $f(x) = \sqrt[3]{x^2 - 1}$

22. $f(x) = |x^2 - 3|$

23. $f(x) = \begin{cases} x^2 \sin \dfrac{1}{x} & \text{if } x \neq 0 \\ 0 & \text{if } x = 0 \end{cases}$

24. $f(x) = \cos(\sin(\cos x))$

25. State and prove a theorem describing the points at which a rational function (quotient of two polynomials) is differentiable.

26. Give an example of a function which is differentiable three times at a point but not four times.

27. Show that if f and $|f|$ are both differentiable, then $|f|'|f| = f'f$.

28. Prove or disprove: if f is differentiable at every point of a compact set D, then f is uniformly continuous on D.

216

29. Suppose f is differentiable. Show that f' is odd if f is even and even if f is odd.

30. Find two points on the graph of $f(x) = \dfrac{2 - x^2}{x + 4}$ where the tangent line is parallel to the line 5x = 2y + 6.

31. Determine whether or not the function

$$f(x) = \begin{cases} 1 + 6x - x^2 & \text{if } x \le 7 \\ 5 - 8x & \text{if } x > 7 \end{cases}$$

fails to be differentiable anywhere.

32. Suppose f is differentiable at a. Show that the limit

$$\lim_{h \to 0} \frac{f(a + h) - f(a - h)}{2h}$$

exists and equals f'(a). Is the existence of this limit sufficient to insure the differentiability of f at a?

33. Prove that if f and g are both differentiable n times, where n is a positive integer, then

$$(fg)^{(n)} = \sum_{k=0}^{n} \binom{n}{k} f^{(k)} g^{(n-k)} \ .$$

2. Properties of Differentiable Functions

Knowledge of the derivative of a function can be the key to understanding many of that function's properties. This section is devoted to a study of several interesting and useful theorems involving differentiation. As each theorem is stated, try to find a proof yourself before reading the one given.

Definition 5.19: Suppose f is a function whose domain D includes the number c. We say that f has a relative maximum at c provided there exists a positive number ε such that $f(x) \leq f(c)$ for all x in D satisfying $|x - c| < \varepsilon$. We say that f has a relative minimum at c provided there exists a positive number ε such that $f(x) \geq f(c)$ for all x in D satisfying $|x - c| < \varepsilon$.

Theorem 5.20: Suppose the function f is differentiable at a point c of its domain D, and suppose $f'(c) > 0$. There exists a positive number ε such that for all x in D satisfying $0 < |x - c| < \varepsilon$ we have $f(x) < f(c)$ if $x < c$ and $f(x) > f(c)$ if $x > c$.

Proof: The function $\dfrac{f(x) - f(c)}{x - c}$ has a limit at c since f is differentiable there, and furthermore this limit is positive. By Theorem 3.17 there exist positive numbers t and ε such that

$$\frac{f(x) - f(c)}{x - c} > t > 0$$

for all x in D satisfying $0 < |x - c| < \varepsilon$. In order that this quotient be positive, it's necessary that both numerator and denominator have the same sign. Hence, if $x < c$ then $f(x) < f(c)$, and if $x > c$ then $f(x) > f(c)$. $\square$

218

Theorem 5.21: Suppose the function f is differentiable at a point c of its domain D, and suppose
f'(c) < 0. There exists a positive number ε such
that for all x in D satisfying 0 < |x - c| < ε we
have f(x) > f(c) if x < c and f(x) < f(c) if
x > c.

An immediate corollary of the preceding pair
of theorems is the following useful result.

Theorem 5.22: Suppose the function f is differentiable at a point c of its domain D, and c is a
limit point of D from both the left and right.
If f has either a relative minimum or maximum at
c, then f'(c) = 0.

Proof: We prove the contrapositive: if f'(c) ≠
0, then f has neither a relative minimum nor maximum at c. Suppose f'(c) > 0. If ε is any positive number, there exists x in D such that
c - ε < x < c and f(x) < f(c), and there exists
y in D such that c < y < c + ε and f(y) > f(c).
Hence f has neither a relative minimum nor maximum at c. If f'(c) < 0, the argument is similar.
□

The theorem above is usually stated in the
following less general form. "If f is differentiable at an interior point c of the interval [a,b]
and f has either a relative maximum or minimum at
c, then f'(c) = 0." (To say that c is an interior
point of [a,b] means that a < c < b.)

The converse of Theorem 5.22 is easily seen
to be false. The function $f(x) = x^3$ has a zero
derivative at 0 but has neither a relative minimum nor maximum there. It should also be emphasized that a function can have a relative minimum
or maximum at a point where the derivative fails
to exist, as f(x) = |x|, for example.

The following theorem was first published by the French mathematician Michel Rolle in 1691.* It is one of those theorems that seems "intuitively obvious" but nevertheless requires a certain amount of argument.

Theorem 5.23 (Rolle's Theorem): Suppose f is continuous on the closed interval [a,b] and differentiable on the open interval (a,b). If f(a) = 0 = f(b), there exists at least one number z in (a,b) such that f'(z) = 0.

Proof: If f(x) = 0 for all x in [a,b], the conclusion is obvious. Suppose, then, that f(x) ≠ 0 for at least one x in [a,b]. Now f is continuous on [a,b] and therefore has both an absolute maximum and an absolute minimum on [a,b]. Since f is not identically zero, at least one of these two values must be non-zero. Suppose, without loss of generality, that the maximum value of f occurs at z and f(z) ≠ 0. Then a < z < b since f(a) = 0 = f(b). It's clear that f has a relative maximum at z as well as an absolute maximum. Since f is differentiable at z, the hypothesis of Theorem 5.22 is satisfied, and therefore f'(z) = 0.   □

Rolle's Theorem does not apply to many functions because of its restrictive hypothesis. Occasionally, however, the theorem can be used in an interesting way.

Example 7: Let $f(x) = x^3 - 9x^2 + 20x + 1$ for all x. We find that $f(-1) = -29$ and $f(0) = 1$. By Bolzano's Theorem there is at least one root c of $f(x) = 0$ between -1 and 0. Are there any others? Bolzano's Theorem doesn't tell us. Suppose there is another, that is, assume that $f(z) = 0$, $-1 < z < 0$, and $z \neq c$. Rolle's Theorem can be

*Carl B. Boyer, A History of Mathematics, (1968), p, 474.

applied to f on the interval $[z,c]$ or $[c,z]$, which-ever is the case, to conclude $f'(x) = 0$ for some x between c and z. Now $f'(x) = 3x^2 - 18x + 20$, and the roots of $f'(x) = 0$ are easily found to be $3 \pm \frac{1}{3} \sqrt{21}$. Since neither of these numbers is in $(-1,0)$, there is only one root of $f(x) = 0$ be-tween -1 and 0.

The principal value of Rolle's Theorem is that it enables us to prove the following extreme-ly important theorem.

Theorem 5.24 (Mean Value Theorem): If f is con-tinuous on the closed interval $[a,b]$ and differ-entiable on the open interval (a,b), there exists at least one number z in (a,b) such that

$$f'(z) = \frac{f(b) - f(a)}{b - a} .$$

Proof: The theorem has an appealing geometric interpretation (see Figure 5.4). If L is the line joining the points $(a, f(a))$ and $(b, f(b))$, the slope of L is $\frac{f(b) - f(a)}{b - a}$. According to the theorem there is a point on the graph of f at which the tangent line is parallel to L. The sketch also suggests a possible proof. If h is a function which measures the vertical distance between L and f, then h is zero at both end points since L and f intersect there. Perhaps Rolle's Theorem can be applied. The equation for L is easily found to be $y = f(a) + \frac{f(b) - f(a)}{b - a} (x - a)$. Accordingly, we define a function h by

$$h(x) = f(a) + \frac{f(b) - f(a)}{b - a} (x - a) - f(x)$$

221

for every x in [a,b]. Since the function
$f(a) + \dfrac{f(b) - f(a)}{b - a}$ (x - a) is continuous and
differentiable everywhere, h is continuous wherever f is continuous and differentiable wherever
f is differentiable. Thus h is continuous on
[a,b] and differentiable on (a,b). It's a routine
matter to verify that h(a) = 0 and h(b) = 0.

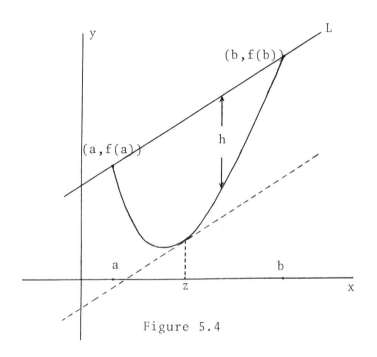

Figure 5.4

Hence Rolle's Theorem applies to h, and we conclude
that there is a number z, a < z < b, such that
h'(z) = 0. Since $h'(x) = \dfrac{f(b) - f(a)}{b - a}$ - f'(x) for
every x in (a,b), it follows that

$$f'(z) = \frac{f(b) - f(a)}{b - a}$$ □

222

Many important theorems in analysis can be easily proved using the Mean Value Theorem. In addition, the theorem can also be used to establish some interesting inequalities.

Example 8: We will prove that $\sqrt{1 + c} < \frac{1}{2} c + 1$ for every $c > 0$. Let $f(x) = \sqrt{1 + x}$ on the interval $[0,c]$. By the Mean Value Theorem (convince yourself the hypothesis is satisfied) there is a number z, $0 < z < c$, such that

$$\frac{f(c) - f(0)}{c - 0} = f'(z).$$

Simplifying,

$$\frac{\sqrt{1 + c} - 1}{c} = \frac{1}{2\sqrt{1 + z}} < \frac{1}{2\sqrt{1 + 0}} = \frac{1}{2}.$$

It follows that

$$\sqrt{1 + c} < \frac{1}{2} c + 1.$$

Theorem 5.25: Suppose f is continuous on $[a,b]$ and differentiable on (a,b).

   (a)   If $f'(x) > 0$ for all x in (a,b), then f is strictly increasing on $[a,b]$.

   (b)   If $f'(x) < 0$ for all x in (a,b), then f is strictly decreasing on $[a,b]$.

Proof: Part (a) is proved as follows. Suppose x and y are any numbers satisfying $a \le x < y \le b$. We must show that $f(x) < f(y)$. Since the hypothesis of the Mean Value Theorem is satisfied by f on $[x,y]$, there exists a number z, $x < z < y$, such that

$$\frac{f(y) - f(x)}{y - x} = f'(z)$$

223

and so $f(y) - f(x) = (y - x) f'(z)$.

Now $y - x > 0$ since $x < y$, and $f'(z) > 0$ by hypothesis. Therefore $f(y) - f(x) > 0$, from which $f(x) < f(y)$ follows. The proof of (b) is similar. $\square$

   The theorem above has the following variant: if $f'(x) \geq 0$ [$f'(x) \leq 0$] for all x in (a,b), then f is increasing [decreasing] on [a,b].

Theorem 5.26: Suppose f is continuous on the closed interval [a,b], and f is differentiable on the open interval (a,b) with the possible exception of a single point c.

   (a)   If $f'(x) > 0$ for all $x < c$ and $f'(x) < 0$ for all $x > c$, then f has a relative maximum at c.

   (b)   If $f'(x) < 0$ for all $x < c$ and $f'(x) > 0$ for all $x > c$, then f has a relative minimum at c.

Proof: Left as an exercise.

   The previous theorem is usually referred to in calculus as the "First Derivative Test."

Theorem 5.27: Suppose f is continuous on [a,b] and differentiable on (a,b). If $f'(x) = 0$ for every x in (a,b), then f is a constant function on [a,b].

Proof: Left as an exercise.

Theorem 5.28: Suppose both f and g are continuous on [a,b] and differentiable on (a,b). If

224

f'(x) = g'(x) for all x in (a,b), then there
exists a number C such that f(x) = g(x) + C for
every x in [a,b].

Proof: Define a function h by h(x) = f(x) - g(x)
for every x in [a,b]. Clearly h is continuous
on [a,b] and differentiable on (a,b). Moreover,
h'(x) = f'(x) - g'(x) = 0 for every x in (a,b).
By Theorem 5.27 there is a number C such that
h(x) = C for every x in [a,b]. It follows that
f(x) = g(x) + C for every x in [a,b].   □

     Though two functions having the same deriva-
tive need not be equal, they are "almost equal"--
one is equal to the other plus a constant. Geometrically this means that the graph of one is
obtained from the graph of the other by a transla-
tion in the vertical direction.

Definition 5.29: The function f is said to be an
antiderivative of the function g on the set S provided f'(x) = g(x) for every x in S.

Theorem 5.30: If f is any particular antiderivative of g on the set S, every antiderivative of g
on S is of the form f + C for some constant C.

Proof: Left as an exercise.

     It's natural at this point to ask which func-
tions have antiderivatives, that is, which functions
are themselves derivatives? Give some thought to
this question before continuing.

Definition 5.31: A function f defined on a set S
is said to have the intermediate value property
on S provided the following condition is satisfied:

if a and b are any numbers in S for which
f(a) ≠ f(b) and c is any number between f(a)
and f(b), there exists at least one number
z between a and b such that f(z) = c.

Theorem 5.32: Suppose f is differentiable on
(a,b). If f'(x) ≠ 0 for all x in (a,b), then
either f'(x) > 0 for all x in (a,b) or f'(x) < 0
for all x in (a,b).

Proof: Assume the statement is not true. Then
there exist numbers p and q satisfying a < p < q <
b such that f'(p) and f'(q) have opposite signs.
Now f is differentiable and therefore continuous
on [p,q], so f has a maximum at some point s and
a minimum at some point t in [p,q]. Clearly s ≠ t,
for otherwise f would be constant and have a zero
derivative. Furthermore, either s = p and t = q
or s = q and t = p, for if either s or t were an
interior point, f would have a zero derivative
there by Theorem 5.22. Suppose s = p and t = q.
Then f'(p) < 0 (assume f'(p) > 0 and get a contradiction by Theorem 5.20) and f'(q) < 0 (assume
f'(q) > 0 and get a contradiction by Theorem 5.20).
This is a contradiction since f'(p) and f'(q)
have opposite signs. If s = q and t = p, we infer
that f'(q) > 0 and f'(p) > 0, also a contradiction.
Therefore, either f'(x) > 0 for all x in (a,b) or
f'(x) < 0 for all x in (a,b).   □

Corollary: Suppose f is differentiable on (a,b).
If there exist numbers x and y in (a,b) such that
f'(x) > 0 and f'(y) < 0, then there is at least
one number z between x and y such that f'(z) = 0.

Proof: Left as an exercise.

Theorem 5.33: If f is differentiable on [a,b],
then f' has the intermediate value property on [a,b].

Proof: Suppose s and t are any numbers in [a,b] for which f'(s) ≠ f'(t), and c is any number between f'(s) and f'(t). Suppose, without loss of generality, that s < t. On the interval [s,t] define a function g by

$$g(x) = f(x) - cx.$$

Clearly g is differentiable on [s,t], and g'(x) = f'(x) - c. If f'(s) < c < f'(t), then g'(s) = f'(s) - c < 0 and g'(t) = f'(t) - c > 0. If f'(t) < c < f'(s), then g'(s) > 0 and g'(t) < 0. In either case g' has opposite signs at s and t. Using the corollary to the preceding theorem, we conclude that there is a number z between s and t such that g'(z) = 0, i.e., f'(z) = c. ☐

It can now be asserted that any function failing to have the intermediate value property cannot be a derivative. Since all continuous functions have the intermediate value property (Theorem 4.25), we might wonder if every continuous function is a derivative and, conversely, if every derivative is a continuous function. The first of these questions cannot be answered until the next chapter; the second is answered by the example below.

Example 9: Define a function f by

$$f(x) = \begin{cases} x^2 \sin \frac{1}{x} & \text{if } x \neq 0 \\ 0 & \text{if } x = 0 \end{cases}.$$

It's easy to show that $f'(x) = 2x \sin \frac{1}{x} - \cos \frac{1}{x}$ for all x ≠ 0. At 0 we have

$$f'(0) = \lim_{x \to 0} \frac{f(x) - f(0)}{x - 0}$$

$$= \lim_{x \to 0} \frac{x^2 \sin \frac{1}{x}}{x}$$

$$= \lim_{x \to 0} x \sin \frac{1}{x}$$

$$= 0$$

where the limit was evaluated in Example 15, Chapter 3. Therefore

$$f'(x) = \begin{cases} 2x \sin \frac{1}{x} - \cos \frac{1}{x} & \text{if } x \neq 0 \\ 0 & \text{if } x = 0 \end{cases}$$

and f is differentiable for all x. Since $\lim_{x \to 0} 2x \sin \frac{1}{x} = 0$ and $\lim_{x \to 0} \cos \frac{1}{x}$ does not exist, $\lim_{x \to 0} f'(x)$ does not exist, and therefore f' is not continuous at 0.

A function which is a derivative need not be continuous. In the preceding example continuity failed at only one point. It can be shown, however, that there exists a function, differentiable on a closed interval, whose derivative is discontinuous at uncountably many points!

One question which has not been considered so far is the following: if a differentiable function has an inverse, is the inverse differentiable? The following theorem answers this question for most situations that arise.

Theorem 5.34 (Inverse Function Theorem): Suppose f is differentiable on [a,b] and $f'(x) \neq 0$ for all x in (a,b). Then f has an inverse f^{-1} whose domain [c,d] is either [f(a),f(b)] or [f(b),f(a)].

228

Moreover, f^{-1} is differentiable on (c,d), and if y is any number in (c,d),

$$(f^{-1})'(y) = \frac{1}{f'(x)}$$

where x is that number in (a,b) such that $f(x) = y$.

Proof: Using Theorems 5.32 and 5.25 we conclude that f is strictly monotonic on $[a,b]$. Also, f is continuous since it is differentiable. From the corollary to Theorem 4.33 it follows that f has a continuous inverse f^{-1} whose domain $[c,d]$ is $[f(a),f(b)]$ or $[f(b),f(a)]$ according to whether f is strictly increasing or strictly decreasing. Suppose y is any number in (c,d). Then $f(x) = y$ for some (unique) x in (a,b). We want to consider the limit

$$\lim_{t \to y} \frac{f^{-1}(t) - f^{-1}(y)}{t - y} \ .$$

Since t is in the domain of f^{-1}, there is a unique s in $[a,b]$ such that $f(s) = t$. By the continuity f^{-1} at y, as t approaches y, $f^{-1}(t)$ approaches $f^{-1}(y)$, that is, s approaches x (since $f^{-1}(t) = s$ and $f^{-1}(y) = x$). Therefore

$$(f^{-1})'(y) = \lim_{t \to y} \frac{f^{-1}(t) - f^{-1}(y)}{t - y}$$

$$= \lim_{s \to x} \frac{s - x}{f(s) - f(x)}$$

$$= \frac{1}{\displaystyle\lim_{s \to x} \frac{f(s) - f(x)}{s - x}}$$

$$= \frac{1}{f'(x)}$$

where we use the fact that $f(s) \neq f(x)$ whenever $s \neq x$ (since f is one-to-one) and, of course, the fact that f is differentiable at x. $\qquad\qquad \square$

Example 10: Show that the function f given by $f(x) = x^4 - 2x^3 + 2x - 4$ on $[1,5]$ has an inverse f^{-1}, and evaluate $(f^{-1})'(0)$. We find that $f'(x) = 4x^3 - 6x^2 + 2 = 2(2x + 1)(x - 1)^2$. It follows from this equation that $f'(x) > 0$ for all $x > -\frac{1}{2}$ except $x = 1$. The hypothesis of Theorem 5.34 is satisfied by f on $[1,5]$, so f has an inverse f^{-1}. Hence

$$(f^{-1})'(0) = \frac{1}{f'(x)}$$

where x is the number in $(1,5)$ for which $f(x) = 0$. By inspection $x = 2$. Therefore $(f^{-1})'(0) = \frac{1}{10}$.

Example 11: Let f denote the restriction of the sine function to the interval $[-\pi/2, \pi/2]$, that is, $f(x) = \sin x$, $-\pi/2 \leq x \leq \pi/2$. Now $f'(x) = \cos x$ for all x, and $\cos \overline{x} > \overline{0}$ for x satisfying $-\pi/2 < x < \pi/2$. By the Inverse Function Theorem f has an inverse f^{-1} whose domain is $[\sin(-\pi/2), \sin \pi/2] = [-1,1]$. Furthermore, if y is any number in $(-1,1)$ and x is that number in $(-\pi/2, \pi/2)$ such that $f(x) = y$, then

$$(f^{-1})'(y) = \frac{1}{f'(x)} = \frac{1}{\cos x}$$

$$= \frac{1}{\sqrt{1 - \sin^2 x}}$$

$$= \frac{1}{\sqrt{1 - (f(x))^2}}$$

$$= \frac{1}{\sqrt{1 - y^2}} \quad .$$

Ordinarily, of course, we write $f^{-1}(x) = \text{Arcsin } x$ and $(f^{-1})'(x) = \dfrac{1}{\sqrt{1 - x^2}}$.

The other inverse trigonometric functions can be handled in a similar manner. Two of them are considered in the exercises. With the theory that has been developed so far we are able to handle most of the familiar functions of calculus. You many have noticed, however, that no mention has yet been made of the exponential and logarithmic functions. It would be too much of a digression to rigorously develop the properties of these functions, but they are too important to ignore completely. In the remainder of the book these functions will be used occasionally in examples and exercises, though not in the theoretical development. The standard properties established in calculus will be assumed. As usual, the natural logarithm function will be denoted by $f(x) = \ln x$, and e will denote the base of natural logarithms.

Theorem 5.35 (Generalized Mean Value Theorem): If both of the functions f and g are continuous on [a,b] and differentiable on (a,b), there exists at least one number z in (a,b) such that

231

$$[f(b) - f(a)]g'(z) = [g(b) - g(a)]f'(z).$$

Proof: Define on $[a,b]$ a function h by $h(x) =$ $[f(b) - f(a)]g(x) - [g(b) - g(a)]f(x)$. It follows from the properties of f and g that h is continuous on $[a,b]$ and differentiable on (a,b). A routine calculation shows that $h(a) = f(b)g(a) - f(a)g(b) = h(b)$. By the Mean Value Theorem there is a number z in (a,b) such that

$$h'(z) = \frac{h(b) - h(a)}{b - a} = 0.$$

Since $h'(z) = [f(b) - f(a)]g'(z) - [g(b) - g(a)]f'(z)$, the conclusion follows immediately. □

Corollary: Suppose both of the functions f and g are continuous on $[a,b]$ and differentiable on (a,b). If $g'(x) \neq 0$ for all x in (a,b), there exists at least one number z in (a,b) such that

$$\frac{f'(z)}{g'(z)} = \frac{f(b) - f(a)}{g(b) - g(a)} .$$

Proof: Left as an exercise.

Example 12: Suppose $f(x) = e^{x^2}$, $g(x) = x^2$, and c is any positive number. If the corollary is applied on the interval $[0,c]$, we conclude that there is a number z satisfying $0 < z < c$ such that

$$\frac{f(c) - f(0)}{g(c) - g(0)} = \frac{f'(z)}{g'(z)} ,$$

that is,
$$\frac{e^{c^2} - 1}{c^2} = \frac{2ze^{z^2}}{2z} .$$

Therefore $\quad e^{c^2} = 1 + c^2 e^{z^2}$.

Since $0 < z < c$, $0 < z^2 < c^2$, and consequently $1 < e^{z^2} < e^{c^2}$ since f is increasing on $[0,c]$.

Hence $\quad 1 + c^2 e^{z^2} > 1 + c^2$

and therefore $\quad e^{c^2} > 1 + c^2$,

that is, $\quad e^{x^2} > 1 + x^2$ for all $x > 0$.

Many important limits in analysis are of the form $\lim\limits_{x \to a} \dfrac{f(x)}{g(x)}$, where both $\lim\limits_{x \to a} f(x) = 0$ and $\lim\limits_{x \to a} g(x) = 0$. Assuming that algebraic manipulation fails to reduce the limit to a tractable form, it becomes necessary to seek more sophisticated techniques. Without doubt, the most useful of these techniques is what has come to be called "L'Hospital's Rule." This result bears the name of the French marquis, G. F. A. de L'Hospital, for it appeared initially in a book he wrote, the first textbook on differential calculus ever published. Historical research has shown, however, that the result was actually discovered by the Swiss mathematician, Jean Bernoulli, in 1694.*

L'Hospital's Rule is really a collection of theorems, each differing from the others by only a minor variation. The following is typical.

*Carl B. Boyer, A History of Mathematics, (1968), p. 460.

Theorem 5.36 (L'Hospital's Rule): Suppose both of the functions f and g are differentiable on (a,b) and $g'(x) \neq 0$ for all x in (a,b). If

$$\lim_{x \to a+} f(x) = 0 = \lim_{x \to a+} g(x)$$

and if

$$\lim_{x \to a+} \frac{f'(x)}{g'(x)} \text{ exists,}$$

then $\lim_{x \to a+} \frac{f(x)}{g(x)}$ exists and $\lim_{x \to a+} \frac{f(x)}{g(x)} = \lim_{x \to a+} \frac{f'(x)}{g'(x)}$.

Proof: Define functions F and G as follows:

$$F(x) = \begin{cases} f(x) & \text{if } a < x < b \\ 0 & \text{if } x = a \end{cases} \qquad G(x) = \begin{cases} g(x) & \text{if } a < x < b \\ 0 & \text{if } x = a \end{cases}$$

Since $\lim_{x \to a+} f(x) = 0$ and $\lim_{x \to a+} g(x) = 0$, both F and G are continuous at a. If x is any number satisfying $a < x < b$, then F and G are both continuous on $[a,x]$ and differentiable on (a,x). Using the corollary to Theorem 5.35, we can assert that there is a number z in (a,x) such that

$$\frac{F'(z)}{G'(z)} = \frac{F(x) - F(a)}{G(x) - G(a)} = \frac{F(x)}{G(x)} ,$$

where we have used the fact that $F(a) = 0 = G(a)$. Since $F(x) = f(x)$ and $G(x) = g(x)$ for all x in (a,b),

$$\frac{f'(z)}{g'(z)} = \frac{f(x)}{g(x)} .$$

Since $\lim\limits_{x\to a+} \dfrac{f'(x)}{g'(x)}$ is known to exist, we conclude from Problem 24 of Exercise 3.1 that $\lim\limits_{x\to a+} \dfrac{f(x)}{g(x)}$ exists and has the same value. $\square$

A similar theorem can be proved for left-hand limits at a right endpoint. These two results can then be combined to produce a similar theorem where the limit is taken without regard to direction. We will freely use these results in the future. The following variation is a little different.

Theorem 5.37 (L'Hospital's Rule): Suppose M is a number, both of the functions f and g are differentiable for all $x > M$, and $g'(x) \neq 0$ for all $x > M$. If

$$\lim_{x\to\infty} f(x) = 0 = \lim_{x\to\infty} g(x)$$

and if $\qquad \lim\limits_{x\to\infty} \dfrac{f'(x)}{g'(x)}$ exists,

then $\lim\limits_{x\to\infty} \dfrac{f(x)}{g(x)}$ exists and $\lim\limits_{x\to\infty} \dfrac{f(x)}{g(x)} = \lim\limits_{x\to\infty} \dfrac{f'(x)}{g'(x)}$.

Proof: Left as an exercise.

A variant of this theorem is obtained by considering limits of the form $\lim\limits_{x\to -\infty}$. Both of these results will be used in the future when needed.

Example 13: $\lim\limits_{x\to 1} \dfrac{\ln x}{2x^2 - x - 1} = \lim\limits_{x\to 1} \dfrac{\frac{1}{x}}{4x - 1} =$

235

$$\lim_{x \to 1} \frac{1}{x(4x - 1)} = \frac{1}{3} .$$

Example 14: It's often necessary to use L'Hospital's Rule in connection with other techniques. For instance,

$$\lim_{x \to 0} \frac{x - \sin x}{\tan^3 x} = \lim_{x \to 0} \frac{1 - \cos x}{3 \tan^2 x \sec^2 x} ,$$

and there is no reason why the rule cannot be applied to the limit on the right since the hypothesis is satisfied. The resulting expression is quite complicated, however, and can be avoided by multiplying numerator and denominator by $1 + \cos x$ instead. Thus,

$$\lim_{x \to 0} \frac{x - \sin x}{\tan^3 x} = \lim_{x \to 0} \frac{1 - \cos x}{3 \tan^2 x \sec^2 x}$$

$$= \lim_{x \to 0} \frac{\sin^2 x}{3(1 + \cos x)\tan^2 x \sec^2 x}$$

$$= \lim_{x \to 0} \frac{\cos^4 x}{3(1 + \cos x)}$$

$$= \frac{1}{6}$$

Exercise 5.2

1. Prove Theorem 5.21.

2. Prove Theorem 5.26.

3. Determine where the function $f(x) = x^2\sqrt{4 - x}$ is increasing and where it is decreasing.

4. Prove Theorem 5.27.

5. Prove or disprove: if f is differentiable and one-to-one on its domain D, then $f'(x) \neq 0$ for all x in D.

6. Prove Theorem 5.30.

7. Show that $|\sin x - \sin y| \leq |x - y|$ for all numbers x and y.

8. Define a function f by

$$f(x) = \begin{cases} x + 2x^2 \sin \dfrac{1}{x} & \text{if } x \neq 0 \\ 0 & \text{if } x = 0 \end{cases}.$$

Show that $f'(0) > 0$, and show that there is no neighborhood of 0 on which f is increasing. Does this contradict Theorem 5.20?

9. Prove the corollary to Theorem 5.32.

10. Give an example of a differentiable function f on an interval [a,b] such that f' is not bounded on [a,b].

11. Use the Mean Value Theorem to show that $3 \dfrac{1}{10} < \sqrt[3]{30} < 3 \dfrac{1}{9}$.

12. Prove the corollary to Theorem 5.35.

13. Prove or disprove: if $\lim_{x \to a} f'(x)$ does not exist, then $f'(a)$ does not exist.

14. Using the restriction of the tangent function to the interval $(-\pi/2, \pi/2)$, determine the derivative of $f(x) = \text{Arctan } x$ by means of the Inverse Function Theorem.

15. Prove Theorem 5.37.

16. Suppose f is differentiable on $[a,b]$. Show that between any two roots of $f(x) = 0$ on $[a,b]$ there is at least one root of $f'(x) = 0$.

17. If f is differentiable for all $x \geq M$, where M is some number, and if $\lim_{x \to \infty} f'(x) = 0$, prove that $\lim_{x \to \infty} \frac{f(x)}{x} = 0$.

18. Show that the equation $x^2 = x \cos x - \sin x + 2$ has exactly two roots.

19. Show that $\frac{x}{1 + x^2} < \text{Arctan } x < x$ for every $x > 0$.

20. Prove the "Second Derivative Test." Suppose f is differentiable on (a,b), c is a number in (a,b), and $f'(c) = 0$. If f' is differentiable at c, then f has a relative maximum at c if $f''(c) < 0$ and a relative minimum at c if $f''(c) > 0$.

21. Generalize the theorem in the previous problem. If $f'(c) = 0$ and $n(n \geq 2)$ is the first positive integer for which $f^{(n)}(c) \neq 0$, determine a criterion for deciding whether f has a relative minimum or a relative maximum at c.

22. Prove that if f has a bounded derivative on (a,b), then f is uniformly continuous on (a,b).

238

23. (a) Using the restriction of the secant function to the intervals $[0,\pi/2)$ and $(\pi/2,\pi]$, determine the derivative of $f(x) = $ Arcsec x by means of the Inverse Function Theorem.
(b) Using the restriction of the secant function to the intervals $[-\pi,-\pi/2)$ and $[0,\pi/2)$, determine the derivative of $f(x) = $ Arcsec x by means of the Inverse Function Theorem.

24. Prove that if f is differentiable on (a,b) and f' is monotonic on (a,b), then f' is continuous on (a,b).

25. Suppose f is differentiable on $[a,b]$ and $f'(a) = f'(b)$. Show that there exists a number c in (a,b) such that $\dfrac{f(c) - f(a)}{c - a} = f'(c)$.

26. Prove that $\dfrac{x - 1}{x} < \ln x < x - 1$ for all $x > 1$. Does the inequality hold for any other x?

27. Prove or disprove: if f is differentiable for all $x > M$, where M is some number, and if $\lim_{x\to\infty} f(\overline{x}) = 0$, then $\lim_{x\to\infty} f'(x) = 0$.

28. Evaluate $\lim_{x\to 0}(\dfrac{1}{x^2} - \dfrac{1}{\tan^2 x})$.

29. Prove that if P is a polynomial of degree n, the equation $P(x) = 0$ has at most n roots.

30. Prove that if $f'(a) > 0$ and f' is continuous at a, then there exists some neighborhood of a on which f is increasing.

*31. Define a function f by
$$f(x) = \begin{cases} e^{-\frac{1}{x^2}} & \text{if } x \neq 0 \\ 0 & \text{if } x = 0 \end{cases}.$$

(a) Show that $f'(0) = 0$. (b) Show that for every positive integer n, $f^{(n)}(0) = 0$.

CHAPTER 6

1. The Riemann Integral

One of the two main problems which prompted
the development of calculus was that of finding
"the area under a curve," that is, the area of a
region whose boundary consists of one or more line
segments and the graph of a (non-linear) function.
For a function whose graph is a parabola the problem was solved in the third century B.C. by Archimedes, one of the greatest mathematicians of all
time. The method of Archimedes was apparently
one which could be generalized to other cases,
but this did not happen. Despite the fact the
ancient Greeks were so close, integral calculus
was not developed until ninteen centuries later!

Definition 6.1: Suppose [a,b] is an interval. A
finite set of points

$$P = \{x_0, x_1, x_2, \ldots, x_n\}$$

is called a partition of [a,b] provided $a = x_0 <$
$x_1 < x_2 < \ldots < x_n = b$. If

$$Q = \{y_0, y_1, y_2, \ldots, y_m\}$$

is a partition of [a,b] such that for each integer
i, $0 \le i \le n$, there exists an integer j, $0 \le j \le m$,
such that $x_i = y_j$, then Q is said to be a refinement of P.

Definition 6.2: Suppose f is a bounded function
on [a,b], and $P = \{x_0, x_1, x_2, \ldots, x_n\}$ is a
partition of [a,b]. For each integer i, $1 \le i \le n$,

241

we define

$$M_i(f) = \text{least upper bound } \{f(x): \quad x_{i-1} \leq x \leq x_i\}$$

and

$$m_i(f) = \text{greatest lower bound } \{f(x): \quad x_{i-1} \leq x \leq x_i\}.$$

[If only one function is under discussion and there is no possibility of misunderstanding, we will write M_i instead of $M_i(f)$ and m_i instead of $m_i(f)$.] We also define

$$U(f,P) = \sum_{i=1}^{n} M_i(f)(x_i - x_{i-1})$$

and

$$L(f,P) = \sum_{i=1}^{n} m_i(f)(x_i - x_{i-1})$$

and call these, respectively, the upper sum and lower sum for f corresponding to the partition P. Note that $L(f,P) \leq U(f,P)$ for any function f and any partition P.

Theorem 6.3: Suppose f is a bounded function on [a,b], and P is a partition of [a,b]. If Q is any refinement of P, then $U(f,Q) \leq U(f,P)$.

Proof: Suppose $P = \{x_0, x_1, x_2, \ldots, x_n\}$ and $Q = \{y_0, y_1, y_2, \ldots, y_m\}$, where Q is a refinement of P. Consider the case where Q contains exactly one more point than P. Then one and only one of the points of Q, say y_k, is distinct from the points of P. Suppose y_k is in the interval $[x_{j-1}, x_j]$. Then

242

$$U(f,P) = \sum_{i=1}^{n} M_i (x_i - x_{i-1})$$

and

$$U(f,Q) = \sum_{i=1}^{j-1} M_i (x_i - x_{i-1}) + M'(y_k - x_{j-1})$$

$$+ M''(x_j - y_k) + \sum_{i=j+1}^{n} M_i (x_i - x_{i-1})$$

where M' and M'' are the least upper bounds of f on $[x_{j-1}, y_k]$ and $[y_k, x_j]$, respectively. But $M' \leq M_j$ and $M'' \leq M_j$. Hence

$$M'(y_k - x_{j-1}) + M''(x_j - y_k) \leq M_j (y_k - x_{j-1})$$

$$+ M_j (x_j - y_k) = M_j (x_j - x_{j-1}).$$

Therefore

$$U(f,Q) \leq \sum_{i=1}^{j-1} M_i (x_i - x_{i-1}) + M_j (x_j - x_{j-1})$$

$$+ \sum_{i=j+1}^{n} M_i (x_i - x_{i-1})$$

$$= \sum_{i=1}^{n} M_i (x_i - x_{i-1})$$

$$= U(f,P).$$

If Q contains s points not in P, s > 2, choose
one of these "extra" points and add it to P, obtaining a refinement Q_1 of P. Then $U(f,Q_1) \leq U(f,P)$
by the proof above. Add another "extra" point to
Q_1, obtaining a refinement Q_2 of Q_1. Then
$U(f,Q_2) \leq U(f,Q_1)$ and so $U(f,Q_2) \leq U(f,P)$. Repe-
tition of the argument shows that $U(f,Q) \leq U(f,P)$. $\square$

Theorem 6.4: Suppose f is a bounded function on
[a,b], and P is a partition of [a,b]. If Q is
any refinement of P, then $L(f,Q) \geq L(f,P)$.

Proof: Left as an exercise.

Theorem 6.5: Suppose f is a bounded function on
[a,b]. If P and Q are any partitions of [a,b]
whatsoever, $L(f,P) \leq U(f,Q)$.

Proof: Let R be the partition of [a,b] obtained
by combining all points of both P and Q. Since
R is a refinement of both P and Q,

$$L(f,P) \leq L(f,R) \text{ and } U(f,R) \leq U(f,Q)$$

by the preceding two theorems. Clearly $L(f,R) \leq$
$U(f,R)$, so

$$L(f,P) \leq L(f,R) \leq U(f,R) \leq U(f,Q). \qquad \square$$

The previous theorem can be paraphrased as,
"no lower sum can exceed any upper sum." It's
important to realize that there is no relationship assumed between the partitions P and Q; in
particular, neither need be a refinement of the
other.

244

Definition 6.6: Suppose f is a bounded function on [a,b]. We define the upper integral of f on [a,b] by

$$\overline{I} \, _a^b(f) = \text{greatest lower bound}$$

$$\{U(f,P): \; P \text{ is a partition of } [a,b]\}$$

and the lower integral of f on [a,b] by

$$\underline{I} \, _a^b(f) = \text{least upper bound}$$

$$\{L(f,P): \; P \text{ is a partition of } [a,b]\}.$$

When there is no danger of misunderstanding, $\overline{I} \, _a^b$ and $\underline{I} \, _a^b$ will be used instead of $\overline{I} \, _a^b(f)$ and $\underline{I} \, _a^b(f)$.

Theorem 6.7: If f is a bounded function on [a,b], then $\underline{I} \, _a^b \leq \overline{I} \, _a^b$.

Proof: Assume that $\underline{I} \, _a^b > \overline{I} \, _a^b$, and let $\underline{I} \, _a^b - \overline{I} \, _a^b = \varepsilon$. By definition of $\overline{I} \, _a^b$ there is a partition P of [a,b] such that $U(f,P) - \overline{I} \, _a^b < \varepsilon/2$. By definition of $\underline{I} \, _a^b$ there is a partition Q of [a,b] such that $\underline{I} \, _a^b - L(f,Q) < \varepsilon/2$. Then

$$U(f,P) - L(f,Q) = [U(f,P) - \overline{I} \, _a^b]$$

$$+ [\overline{I} \, _a^b - \underline{I} \, _a^b]$$

$$+ \ [\underline{I} \ _a^b \ - \ L(f,Q)]$$

$$< \ \varepsilon/2 \ - \ \varepsilon \ + \ \varepsilon/2$$

$$= \ 0.$$

Thus, $U(f,P) < L(f,Q)$, contradicting Theorem 6.5. $\square$

Example 1: Let f be the function defined on [0,1] by

$$f(x) = \begin{cases} 0 \text{ if } x \text{ is rational} \\ 1 \text{ if } x \text{ is irrational} \end{cases} .$$

Suppose $P = \{x_0, x_1, x_2, \ldots, x_n\}$ is any partition of [0,1]. Since every interval $[x_{i-1}, x_i]$ contains both rational and irrational numbers, $M_i = 1$ and $m_i = 0$ for $i = 1, 2, \ldots, n$. Therefore

$$U(f,P) = \sum_{i=1}^{n} 1(x_i - x_{i-1}) = x_n - x_0 = 1$$

and

$$L(f,P) = \sum_{i=1}^{n} 0(x_i - x_{i-1}) = 0$$

for every partition P. It follows that

$$\overline{I} \ _a^b(f) = 1 \text{ and } \underline{I} \ _a^b(f) = 0.$$

246

Definition 6.8: If f is a bounded function on [a,b], we say that <u>f is integrable on [a,b]</u> provided $\underline{I}\,_a^b(f) = \overline{I}\,_a^b(f)$. If this is true, the common value of $\underline{I}\,_a^b(f)$ and $\overline{I}\,_a^b(f)$ is called <u>the integral of f on [a,b]</u> and is denoted by either of the symbols

$$\int_a^b f(x)dx \quad \text{or} \quad \int_a^b f.$$

It should be emphasized that the definition above describes only one of several different kinds of "integral." Technically this is the <u>Riemann Integral</u>, named in honor of the outstanding German mathematician, Bernhard Riemann. It is probably the easiest integral to define and the only one considered in this text. Other important integrals are the Stieltjes Integral and the Lebesgue Integral (to mention only two). When consulting different books it is necessary to see which integral is being used.

A word about notation is in order here. In most cases a mathematical symbol should convey certain information in the simplest possible way. On this basis the symbol $\int_a^b f$ for the integral would be preferable to $\int_a^b f(x)dx$. The latter symbol, however, turns out to be more useful in several important instances and, in addition, has behind it the weight of tradition. In using the notation $\int_a^b f(x)dx$ it should be clearly understood that x is a "dummy variable," and any other symbol could be used in its place. For instance,

$$\int_a^b f(x)dx = \int_a^b f(y)dy = \int_a^b f(t)dt = \int_a^b f(\alpha)d\alpha.$$

It's sometimes possible to prove a function f integrable on an interval [a,b] without actually

considering all of the partitions of [a,b]. If $\mathcal{J}$
is a collection of partitions of [a,b], let

$$\overline{J}_{\mathcal{J}} = \text{greatest lower bound}$$

$$\{U(f,P): \quad P \text{ a partition of } \mathcal{J} \}$$

and

$$\underline{J}_{\mathcal{J}} = \text{least upper bound}$$

$$\{L(f,P): \quad P \text{ a partition of } \mathcal{J} \}.$$

By the definitions of $\overline{I}_a^b$ and $\underline{I}_a^b$, it follows
that $\overline{I}_a^b \leq \overline{J}_{\mathcal{J}}$ and $\underline{I}_a^b \geq \underline{J}_{\mathcal{J}}$. If $\overline{J}_{\mathcal{J}} = \underline{J}_{\mathcal{J}}$, it
inevitably follows that $\overline{I}_a^b = \underline{I}_a^b$ - and hence f
is integrable - since $\underline{I}_a^b > \overline{I}_a^b$ is impossible.

Example 2: We will show that the function $f(x) = x$
is integrable on any interval [a,b]. For each
positive integer n let $\delta_n = \dfrac{b - a}{n}$, and let P_n
be the partition of [a,b] defined by $P_n = \{a,$
$a + \delta_n, a + 2\delta_n, \ldots, a + n\delta_n\}$. Denote by $\mathcal{J}$
the collection of all the P_n's. Since f is con-
tinuous, f attains its least upper bound and
greatest lower bound on each interval. Furthermore f is increasing, so the least upper bound
occurs at the right end point and the greatest
lower bound occurs at the left end point of each
interval. Therefore

$$U(f,P_n) = \sum_{i=1}^{n} f(a + i\delta_n)\delta_n$$

$$= \delta_n \sum_{i=1}^{n} (a + i\delta_n)$$

248

$$= \delta_n [na + \delta_n \sum_{i=1}^{n} i]$$

$$= \frac{b - a}{n} [na + \frac{b - a}{n} \cdot \frac{n(n + 1)}{2}]$$

$$= a(b - a) + \frac{1}{2}(b - a)^2 (1 + \frac{1}{n})$$

and

$$L(f,P_n) = \sum_{i=0}^{n-1} f(a + i\delta_n)\delta_n$$

$$= \delta_n \sum_{i=0}^{n-1} (a + i\delta_n)$$

$$= \delta_n [na + \delta_n \sum_{i=0}^{n-1} i]$$

$$= \frac{b - a}{n} [na + \frac{b - a}{n} \cdot \frac{(n - 1)n}{2}]$$

$$= a(b - a) + \frac{1}{2}(b - a)^2 (1 - \frac{1}{n}).$$

It follows that

$$\overline{J}_* = \lim_{n \to \infty} U(f,P_n)$$

$$= a(b - a) + \frac{1}{2}(b - a)^2$$

$$= \frac{1}{2}(b^2 - a^2)$$

249

and

$$\underline{J}_{f} = \lim_{n \to \infty} L(f, P_n)$$

$$= a(b - a) + \frac{1}{2}(b - a)^2$$

$$= \frac{1}{2}(b^2 - a^2).$$

Therefore f is integrable on [a,b] and $\int_a^b x\ dx = \frac{1}{2}(b^2 - a^2)$.

Though this method is easier than using the definition of the integral, there is still considerable computation involved. We would certainly hope for a shorter method.

Theorem 6.9: If f is a bounded function on [a,b], then f is integrable on [a,b] if and only if the following condition is satisfied:

if ε is any positive number, there exists a partition P of [a,b] such that $U(f,P) - L(f,P) < \varepsilon$.

Proof: Suppose that for each $\varepsilon > 0$ there is a partition P such that $U(f,P) - L(f,P) < \varepsilon$. Assume that f is not integrable on [a,b]. Then $\underline{I}_a^b < \overline{I}_a^b$. Suppose ε is the positive number such that $\overline{I}_a^b - \underline{I}_a^b = \varepsilon$. Let P be a partition of [a,b] such that $U(f,P) - L(f,P) < \varepsilon$. Since $\overline{I}_a^b \le U(f,P)$ and $\underline{I}_a^b \ge L(f,P)$,

$$\overline{I}_a^b - \underline{I}_a^b \le U(f,P) - L(f,P) < \varepsilon,$$

250

a contradiction. Hence f is integrable on [a,b].
Suppose now that f is integrable on [a,b], and
let ε be any positive number. Let P be a partition of [a,b] such that

$$U(f,P) < \overline{I} \,_a^b + \varepsilon/2,$$

and let Q be a partition of [a,b] such that

$$\underline{I} \,_a^b - \varepsilon/2 < L(f,Q).$$

Adding, and using the fact that $\underline{I} \,_a^b = \overline{I} \,_a^b$,

$$U(f,P) - \varepsilon/2 < L(f,Q) + \varepsilon/2$$

or

$$U(f,P) - L(f,Q) < \varepsilon.$$

Let R be the partition formed by combining the
points of both P and Q. Using Theorems 6.3 and
6.4,

$$U(f,R) - L(f,R) \leq U(f,P) - L(f,Q) < \varepsilon. \qquad \square$$

Theorem 6.9 turns out to be almost indispensable in establishing the basic properties of the
integral. It usefulness lies in the fact that
least upper bounds and greatest lower bounds are
not involved.

In several of the theorems that follow a
function is assumed to be integrable on some interval. Since the definition of integral was
only given for bounded functions, the assumption
of integrability tacitly carries with it the
assumption of boundedness.

Theorem 6.10: If f is integrable on [a,b] and c is any number satisfying a < c < b, then f is integrable on both [a,c] and [c,b], and furthermore,

$$\int_a^c f(x)\ dx + \int_c^b f(x)\ dx = \int_a^b f(x)\ dx.$$

Proof: Suppose ε is any positive number. Since f is integrable on [a,b], there is, by Theorem 6.9, a partition P of [a,b] such that $U(f,P) - L(f,P) < \varepsilon$. Let Q be the partition obtained by adding the point c to P. (If c was already a point of P, then Q = P). Let Q_1 be that part of Q belonging to [a,c], and let Q_2 be that part of Q belonging to [c,b]. It follows that

$$\varepsilon > U(f,Q) - L(f,Q) = U(f,Q_1) + U(f,Q_2)$$

$$- L(f,Q_1) - L(f,Q_2)$$

$$= [U(f,Q_1) - L(f,Q_1)]$$

$$+ [U(f,Q_2) - L(f,Q_2)].$$

Both of the expressions in brackets are non-negative. Hence

$$U(f,Q_1) - L(f,Q_1) < \varepsilon$$

and

$$U(f,Q_2) - L(f,Q_2) < \varepsilon.$$

The integrability of f on both [a,c] and [c,b] follows from Theorem 6.9. □

252

Corollary: If f is integrable on [a,b], then f is integrable on every subinterval of [a,b].

Proof: Left as an exercise.

Theorem 6.11: If f is integrable on both [a,c] and [c,b], then f is integrable on [a,b].

Proof: Suppose ε is any positive number. There exists a partition P_1 of [a,c] such that

$$U(f,P_1) - L(f,P_1) < \varepsilon/2,$$

and there exists a partition P_2 of [c,b] such that

$$U(f,P_2) - L(f,P_2) < \varepsilon/2.$$

Let P be the partition of [a,b] obtained by combining the points of both P_1 and P_2. Then

$$U(f,P) - L(f,P) = U(f,P_1) + U(f,P_2)$$

$$- L(f,P_1) - L(f,P_2)$$

$$= [U(f,P_1) - L(f,P_1)]$$

$$+ [U(f,P_2) - L(f,P_2)]$$

$$< \varepsilon/2 + \varepsilon/2$$

$$= \varepsilon$$

253

and f is integrable on [a,b] by Theorem 6.9.   □

Definition 6.12:   If f is integrable on [a,b], we
define $\int_b^a f(x)\ dx = -\int_a^b f(x)\ dx$.   We also define
$\int_a^a f(x)\ dx = 0$.

Theorem 6.13:   Suppose f is integrable on [p,q],
and a,b,c are any numbers (not necessarily dis-
tinct) in [p,q].   Then $\int_a^c f(x)\ dx + \int_c^b f(x)\ dx = \int_a^b f(x)\ dx$.

Proof: Left as an exercise.

Theorem 6.14:   If f is integrable on [a,b] and k
is any number, the function kf is integrable on
[a,b] and $\int_a^b (kf)(x)\ dx = k \int_a^b f(x)\ dx$.

Proof: Consider first the trivial case k = 0.
It's easy to see that $\underline{I}\ _a^b\ (kf) = 0 = \overline{I}\ _a^b\ (kf)$, kf
is integrable on [a,b], and the conclusion is
clearly true.

    Suppose next that k > 0, and let ε be any
positive number.   There exists a partition P =
$\{x_0,\ x_1,\ x_2,\ .\ .,\ x_n\}$ of [a,b] such that
$U(f,P) - L(f,P) < \frac{\varepsilon}{k}$.   We find that

$$U(fk,P) = \sum_{i=1}^{n} M_i(kf)(x_i - x_{i-1})$$

254

$$= \sum_{i=1}^{n} kM_i(f)(x_i - x_{i-1})$$

$$= k \sum_{i=1}^{n} M_i(f)(x_i - x_{i-1})$$

$$= k \; U(f,P)$$

and

$$L(kf,P) = \sum_{i=1}^{n} m_i(kf)(x_i - x_{i-1})$$

$$= \sum_{i=1}^{n} km_i(f)(x_i - x_{i-1})$$

$$= k \sum_{i=1}^{n} m_i(f)(x_i - x_{i-1})$$

$$= k \; L(f,P).$$

Consequently

$$U(kf,P) - L(kf,P) = k \; U(f,P) - k \; L(f,P)$$
$$= k[U(f,P) - L(f,P)]$$
$$< k(\frac{\varepsilon}{k})$$
$$= \varepsilon$$

and the integrability of kf follows from Theorem 6.9. Finally, consider the case where $k < 0$. Notice the properties of least upper bound and greatest lower bound used in this situation. If

255

ε is any positive number, there is a partition $P = \{x_0,\ x_1,\ x_2,\ .\ .\ .,\ x_n\}$ of $[a,b]$ such that $U(f,P) - L(f,P) < -\dfrac{\varepsilon}{k}$. (This is positive of course, since $k < 0$.) Then

$$U(kf,P) = \sum_{i=1}^{n} M_i(kf)(x_i - x_{i-1})$$

$$= \sum_{i=1}^{n} km_i(f)(x_i - x_{i-1})$$

$$= k \sum_{i=1}^{n} m_i(f)(x_i - x_{i-1})$$

$$= kL(f,P)$$

and

$$L(kf,P) = \sum_{i=1}^{n} m_i(kf)(x_i - x_{i-1})$$

$$= \sum_{i=1}^{n} kM_i(f)(x_i - x_{i-1})$$

$$= k \sum_{i=1}^{n} M_i(f)(x_i - x_{i-1})$$

$$= kU(f,P).$$

Therefore

$$U(kf,P) - L(kf,P) = kL(f,P) - kU(f,P)$$

$$= -k[U(f,P) - L(f,P)]$$

$$< -k\left(-\dfrac{\varepsilon}{k}\right) = \varepsilon$$

256

and kf is again integrable by Theorem 6.9.   □

Theorem 6.15: If both f and g are integrable on
[a,b], then the function f + g is integrable on
[a,b], and $\int_a^b (f + g)(x)dx = \int_a^b f(x)dx + \int_a^b g(x)dx$.

Proof: Left as an exercise.

Corollary: If both f and g are integrable on [a,b],
then the function f - g is integrable on [a,b],
and $\int_a^b (f - g)(x)dx = \int_a^b f(x)dx - \int_a^b g(x)dx$.

Proof: Since g is integrable on [a,b], -g is integrable on [a,b] by Theorem 6.14, and $\int_a^b (-g)(x)dx =$
$-\int_a^b g(x)dx$. Therefore f - g = f + (-g) is integrable on [a,b] by Theorem 6.15, and $\int_a^b (f - g)(x)dx=$
$\int_a^b f(x)dx - \int_a^b g(x)dx$.   □

One might expect the next theorem to state
that the product of two integrable functions is
integrable. We could, in fact, state and prove
such a theorem at this time, but the proof would
be quite long. The following group of theorems
will make the proof trivial, though their usefulness extends far beyond obtaining this one result.

Theorem 6.16: If f is integrable on [a,b] and
f(x) $\geq$ 0 for all x in [a,b], then $\int_a^b f(x)dx \geq 0$.

Proof: If P is any partition of [a,b], L(f,P) $\geq$ 0.
Since $\underline{I}\,_a^{\,b} \geq L(f,P)$, $\underline{I}\,_a^{\,b} \geq 0$, and since f is

257

integrable, $\int_a^b f(x)dx = \underline{I} \, {}_a^b \geq 0.$ □

Corollary: If both f and g are integrable on [a,b] and $f(x) \leq g(x)$ for all x in [a,b], then $\int_a^b f(x)dx \leq \int_a^b g(x)dx.$

Proof: Left as an exercise.

Theorem 6.17: If f is integrable on [a,b], then $|f|$ is integrable on [a,b] and $|\int_a^b f(x)dx| \leq \int_a^b |f|(x)dx.$

Proof: Suppose ε is any positive number. Since f is integrable on [a,b], there exists a partition $P = \{x_0, x_1, x_2, \ldots, x_n\}$ of [a,b] such that $U(f,P) - L(f,P) < \varepsilon$. Note the following: for each integer i, $1 \leq i \leq n$, $M_i(f) - m_i(f) =$ least upper bound $\{|f(x) - f(y)|: x,y$ in $[x_{i-1},x_i]\}$ and likewise

$$M_i(|f|) - m_i(|f|) = \text{least upper bound}$$

$$\left\{\left||f(x)| - |f(y)|\right|: x,y \text{ in } [x_{i-1},x_i]\right\}.$$

Using the inequality $\left||f(x)| - |f(y)|\right| \leq |f(x) - f(y)|$, we see that

$$M_i(|f|) - m_i(|f|) \leq M_i(f) - m_i(f).$$

Consequently

258

$$U(|f|,P) - L(|f|,P)$$

$$= \sum_{i=1}^{n} [M_i(|f|) - m_i(|f|)](x_i - x_{i-1})$$

$$\leq \sum_{i=1}^{n} [M_i(f) - m_i(f)](x_i - x_{i-1})$$

$$= U(f,P) - L(f,P)$$

$$< \varepsilon,$$

and therefore $|f|$ is integrable by Theorem 6.9. To establish the inequality we use the corollary to the preceding theorem. Since $f(x) \leq |f|(x)$ and $-f(x) \leq |f|(x)$ for all x in $[a,b]$, and since $|f|$ is now known to be integrable on $[a,b]$, we get

$$\int_a^b f(x)dx \leq \int_a^b |f|(x)dx$$

and

$$-\int_a^b f(x)dx \leq \int_a^b |f|(x)dx.$$

That is,

$$-\int_a^b |f|(x)dx \leq \int_a^b f(x)dx \leq \int_a^b |f|(x)dx$$

and therefore

$$\left|\int_a^b f(x)dx\right| \leq \int_a^b |f|(x)dx. \qquad \square$$

Theorem 6.18: If f is integrable on $[a,b]$, then f^2 is integrable on $[a,b]$.

Proof: Suppose ε is any positive number. Since f is integrable on $[a,b]$, f is bounded there. Let M be a positive number such that $|f(x)| < M$ for all x in $[a,b]$. By Theorem 6.17 $|f|$ is integrable on $[a,b]$, so there is a partition $P = \{x_0, x_1, x_2, \ldots, x_n\}$ of $[a,b]$ such that $U(|f|,P) - L(|f|,P) < \frac{\varepsilon}{2M}$. Note that

$$M_i(f^2) = [M_i(|f|)]^2 \text{ and } m_i(f^2) = [m_i(|f|)]^2$$

for each i, $1 \leq i \leq n$. Therefore

$U(f^2,P) - L(f^2,P)$

$$= \sum_{i=1}^{n} [M_i(f^2) - m_i(f^2)](x_i - x_{i-1})$$

$$= \sum_{i=1}^{n} \{[M_i(|f|)]^2 - [m_i(|f|)]^2\}(x_i - x_{i-1})$$

$$= \sum_{i=1}^{n} [M_i(|f|) + m_i(|f|)][M_i(|f|) - m_i(|f|)](x_i - x_{i-1})$$

$$\leq 2M \sum_{i=1}^{n} [M_i(|f|) - m_i(|f|)](x_i - x_{i-1})$$

$$= 2M[U(|f|,P) - L(|f|,P)]$$

$$< 2M(\frac{\varepsilon}{2M})$$

$$= \varepsilon$$

and integrability of f^2 follows from the very useful Theorem 6.9. □

Theorem 6.19: If both f and g are integrable on
[a,b], then the function fg is integrable on [a,b].

Proof: From $fg = \frac{1}{4}[(f + g)^2 - (f - g)^2]$ we conclude that fg is integrable by the use of Theorems
6.15, 6.18, 6.14 and the corollary to Theorem
6.15. □

Exercise 6.1

1. Prove Theorem 6.4.

*2. Prove that any constant function $f(x) = k$ is integrable on any interval $[a,b]$ and that $\int_a^b f(x)dx = k(b - a)$.

3. Define f on $[0,1]$ by
$$f(x) = \begin{cases} x \text{ if } x \text{ is rational} \\ 1 - x \text{ if } x \text{ is irrational} \end{cases}.$$ Evaluate the upper and lower integrals of f on $[0,1]$.

4. Prove the corollary to Theorem 6.10.

5. Use the method of Example 2 to evaluate $\int_0^2 x^2 dx$.

6. Prove Theorem 6.13.

7. Use the method of Example 2 to evaluate $\int_1^4 (x - 2)^2 dx$.

8. Prove Theorem 6.15.

9. Use Theorem 6.9 to prove that the function $f(x) = e^x$ is integrable on $[0,1]$.

10. Prove the corollary to Theorem 6.16.

*11. If f is integrable on $[a,b]$ and $m \leq f(x) \leq M$ for all x in $[a,b]$, show that $m(b - a) \leq \int_a^b f(x)dx \leq M(b - a)$.

12. Suppose both f and g are integrable on $[a,b]$, c is a number in $[a,b]$, and $f(x) = g(x)$ for all x in $[a,b]$ except $x = c$. Show that

262

$$\int_a^b f(x)\,dx = \int_a^b g(x)\,dx.$$

13. Suppose f is integrable on [a,b], c is a number in [a,b], and g is a function such that $f(x) = g(x)$ for all x in [a,b] except $x = c$. Show that g is integrable on [a,b] and
$$\int_a^b f(x)\,dx = \int_a^b g(x)\,dx.$$

14. Generalize the previous problem to the case where f and g fail to be equal at only n points, where n is any positive integer.

15. Prove or disprove: if f is a function such that $|f|$ is integrable on an interval [a,b], then f is integrable on [a,b].

16. If [a,b] is any interval, show that any polynomial P, with domain restricted to [a,b], is integrable on that interval.

17. Define a function f on [0,2] by $f(x) = \dfrac{x^2}{\sqrt{4 + x^5}}$. Given that f is integrable on [0,2], show that
$$\frac{4}{9} \le \int_0^2 \frac{x^2}{\sqrt{4 + x^5}}\,dx \le \frac{4}{3}.$$

18. A function f is said to be a step function on [a,b] provided there is a partition $\{x_0, x_1, x_2, \ldots, x_n\}$ of [a,b] and constants $c_1, c_2, \ldots, c_n$ such that for each i, $1 \le i \le n$, $f(x) = c_i$ if $x_{i-1} < x < x_i$ (the values of f at the partition points are not specified). Show that every step function is integrable and find a formula for the value of the integral.

19. Prove that if both f and g are integrable on [a,b] and there exists a positive number c such that $|g(x)| > c$ for all x in [a,b], then $\frac{f}{g}$ is integrable on [a,b].

20. Suppose f is defined on [0,1]. For each positive integer n let $P_n = \{\frac{0}{n}, \frac{1}{n}, \frac{2}{n}, \ldots, \frac{n}{n}\}$. Show that if $\lim_{n \to \infty} L(f,P_n) = \lim_{n \to \infty} U(f,P_n)$, then f is integrable on [0,1], and the value of the integral is this common limit.

21. Suppose f is integrable on [0,1]. For each positive integer n let

$$s_n = \frac{1}{n} \sum_{i=1}^{n} f(\frac{i}{n}).$$

Show that $\lim_{n \to \infty} s_n = \int_0^1 f(x)dx$.

22. If each of $f_1, f_2, \ldots, f_n$ is integrable on [a,b], show that the function $\sum_{i=1}^{n} f_i$ is integrable on [a,b], and $\int_a^b (\sum_{i=1}^{n} f_i)(x)dx = \sum_{i=1}^{n} \int_a^b f_i(x)dx$.

23. Give an example of a function f and an interval [a,b] such that f^2 is integrable on [a,b], but f is not integrable on [a,b].

24. Prove or disprove: if both f and h are integrable on [a,b], $\int_a^b f(x)dx = \int_a^b h(x)dx$, and g is a function such that $f(x) \leq g(x) \leq h(x)$ for all x in [a,b], then g is integrable on [a,b].

264

25. Prove the Cauchy-Schwarz Inequality for Integrals. If both f and g are integrable on [a,b], then

$$[\int_a^b f(x)g(x)dx]^2 \leq [\int_a^b f^2(x)dx][\int_a^b g^2(x)dx].$$

26. Define a function f on [0,1] as follows. If x is irrational, let $f(x) = 0$, and also let $f(0) = 0$. If x is a positive rational number, express x (uniquely) in the form $x = \frac{p}{q}$, where p and q are relatively prime positive integers, and let $f(x) = \frac{1}{q}$. Show that f is integrable on [0,1] and, in fact, $\int_0^1 f(x)dx = 0$.

2.   Properties of Integrable Functions

All of our results so far have been concerned with functions which are known to be integrable. Sooner or later we must face the question, "Which functions are integrable?" The ideal answer to a question of this kind is a condition on a function which is both necessary and sufficient for integrability. Such conditions are hard to find, and we will consider only those which are sufficient.

Theorem 6.20: If f is monotonic on [a,b], then f is integrable on [a,b].

Proof: Suppose f is increasing on [a,b]. If f is constant, we know that f is integrable by Problem 2 of Exercise 6.1, so suppose f is not constant. Then $f(a) < f(b)$. If ε is any positive number, define δ by

$$\delta = \frac{\varepsilon}{f(b) - f(a)},$$

and let $P = \{x_0, x_1, x_2, \ldots, x_n\}$ be a partition of [a,b] such that $x_i - x_{i-1} < \delta$ for $i = 1, 2, \ldots, n$. On each subinterval $[x_{i-1}, x_i]$ we have $M_i(f) = f(x_i)$ and $m_i(f) = f(x_{i-1})$ since f is increasing on [a,b]. Therefore

$$U(f,P) - L(f,P) = \sum_{i=1}^{n} f(x_i)(x_i - x_{i-1})$$

$$- \sum_{i=1}^{n} f(x_{i-1})(x_i - x_{i-1})$$

$$= \sum_{i=1}^{n} [f(x_i) - f(x_{i-1})](x_i - x_{i-1})$$

$$< \delta \sum_{i=1}^{n} [f(x_i) - f(x_{i-1})]$$

$$= \delta [f(b) - f(a)]$$

$$= \varepsilon$$

so f is integrable on [a,b] by Theorem 6.9. If
f is decreasing on [a,b], then -f is increasing
and therefore integrable on [a,b]. Hence f =
(-1)(-f) is integrable on [a,b] by Theorem 6.14. $\square$

The next theorem states that all continuous
functions are integrable. Recall that a continuous function on a closed interval is uniformly
continuous, and see if you can provide a proof
yourself before reading the one given.

Theorem 6.21: If f is continuous on [a,b], then
f is integrable in [a,b].

Proof: Note that f is bounded on [a,b] by Theorem
4.20. Suppose ε is any positive number. By Theorem 4.47 f is uniformly continuous on [a,b], so
there exists a positive number δ such that for
any x and y in [a,b] satisfying $|x - y| < \delta$ we
have $|f(x) - f(y)| < \frac{\varepsilon}{b - a}$. Let $P = \{x_0, x_1,$
$x_2, \ldots , x_n\}$ be any partition of [a,b] such
that $x_i - x_{i-1} < \delta$ for $i = 1, 2, \ldots , n$. By
Theorems 4.22 and 4.23 f attains its least upper
bound and greatest lower bound on each subinterval. Thus there exists for each i, $1 \leq i \leq n$,
numbers s_i and t_i in $[x_{i-1}, x_i]$ such that $f(s_i) =$
$m_i(f)$ and $f(t_i) = M_i(f)$. Therefore

$$U(f,P) - L(f,P) = \sum_{i=1}^{n} [f(t_i) - f(s_i)](x_i - x_{i-1}]$$

$$< \frac{\varepsilon}{b - a} \sum_{i=1}^{n} (x_i - x_{i-1})$$

$$= \frac{\varepsilon}{b - a}(b - a)$$

$$= \varepsilon$$

and the integrability of f again follows from
Theorem 6.9.   □

The last two theorems guarantee the integrability of many functions. Note that some functions are known to be integrable by one of the two
theorems but not the other. A continuous function
need not be monotonic, and a monotonic function
can have infinitely many points of discontinuity.
On the other hand there are integrable functions
which are neither monotonic nor continuous. Consider, for example, the function f defined on
[0,2] by $f(x) = 1 - x$ if $0 < x < 1$ and $f(x) = 1$
if $1 < x < 2$. The integrability of this function
follows from Theorems 6.20 and 6.11. To summarize,
we have two sufficient conditions for integrability
(monotonicity and continuity), neither of which is
necessary, and one necessary condition for integrability (boundedness) which is not sufficient.

Definition 6.22: Suppose f is integrable on [a,b],
and c is any (fixed) number in [a,b]. A function
F defined by $f(x) = \int_{c}^{x} f(t)dt$, x in [a,b], is called
an indefinite integral of f on [a,b].

Make sure you understand the definition.
Since f is integrable on [a,b], f is integrable
on every subinterval [c,x] of [a,b] by the corollary to Theorem 6.10. Associated with each number x in [a,b] is the unique number $\int_{c}^{x} f(t)dt$.
Thus a function is defined on [a,b], and the name
of this function is F. Since the definition of F
involves f, it's not surprising that there should

be a non-trivial relationship between the two functions. The nature of this relationship is extremely important and will be investigated in the next group of theorems.

Theorem 6.23: Suppose f is integrable on [a,b]. If F, defined by

$$F(x) = \int_c^x f(t)dt,$$

is any indefinite integral of f on [a,b], then F is uniformly continuous on [a,b].

Proof: Let M denote a positive number such that $|f(x)| \leq M$ for every x in [a,b]. If ε is any positive number, let $\delta = \frac{\varepsilon}{M}$. For any two numbers x and y in [a,b] satisfying $|x - y| < \delta$, we have

$$|F(x) - F(y)| = \left| \int_c^x f(t)dt - \int_c^y f(t)dt \right|$$

$$= \left| \int_y^x f(t)dt \right| \quad \text{by Theorem 6.13}$$

$$\leq \int_y^x |f(t)|dt \quad \text{by Theorem 6.17}$$

$$\leq M|x - y| \quad \text{by Problem 11 of Exercise 6.1}$$

$$< M\delta$$

$$= \varepsilon. \qquad \qquad \Box$$

It's interesting that F is continuous at every point, even points of discontinuity of f. The next theorem shows that F is not only continuous but also differentiable at all points where f is continuous. But there is something much more surprising than this!

269

Theorem 6.24 (First Fundamental Theorem of Calculus): Suppose f is integrable on [a,b]. If F, defined by

$$F(x) = \int_c^x f(t)dt,$$

is any indefinite integral of f on [a,b], then F is differentiable at every point z of [a,b] where f is continuous, and $F'(z) = f(z)$.

Proof: Suppose ε is any positive number. Since f is continuous at z, there exists a positive number δ such that if x is in [a,b] and $|x - z| < \delta$, then $|f(x) - f(z)| < \varepsilon$. For any such x we have

$$\left| \frac{F(x) - F(z)}{x - z} - f(z) \right|$$

$$= \left| \frac{1}{x - z} \left[\int_c^x f(t)dt - \int_c^z f(t)dt \right] - f(z) \right|$$

$$= \left| \frac{1}{x - z} \int_z^x f(t)dt - f(z) \right|$$

$$= \left| \frac{1}{x - z} \int_z^x f(t)dt - \frac{1}{x - z} \int_z^x f(z)dt \right|$$

$$\text{since } f(z) \text{ is a constant}$$

$$= \left| \frac{1}{x - z} \int_z^x [f(t) - f(z)]dt \right|$$

$$\leq \frac{1}{|x - z|} \int_z^x |f(t) - f(z)|dt$$

$$< \frac{1}{|x - z|} \varepsilon |x - z| \quad \text{since t is}$$

$$\text{between z and x, that is, } |t - z| < \delta$$

$$= \varepsilon$$

270

and the desired result is established directly from Definition 5.1. An immediate consequence is the following. □

Corollary: If f is continuous on [a,b] and F, defined by

$$F(x) = \int_c^x f(t)\,dt,$$

is any indefinite integral of f on [a,b], then F is differentiable and $F'(x) = f(x)$ for every x in [a,b].

This theorem is important, of course, because it shows that differentiation and integration are related. Differentiation came about in an effort to solve the problem of finding a tangent to a curve. The theory of integration, on the other hand, owes its existence to the problem of finding the area under a curve. These two processes were developed to solve completely different problems, and the fact that they are intimately related is truly remarkable.

You might wonder how Theorem 6.24 or its corollary would be discovered in the first place. Suppose the function f of Figure 6.1 is continuous. Since F(u) can be thought of as the area under the graph of f from c to u, $F(x) - F(z)$

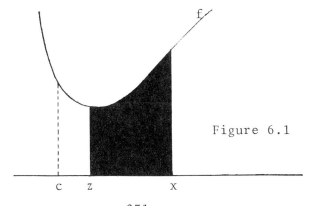

Figure 6.1

271

represents the shaded area. If x is close to z, one could expect the shaded area to be approximately that of the rectangle having width x - z and length f(z). That is,

$$F(x) - F(z) \approx (x - z)f(z),$$

or

$$\frac{F(x) - F(z)}{x - z} \approx f(z).$$

The closer x is to z, the better this approximation should be. So it's not unreasonable to expect F'(z) = f(z) since the limit of the left side is the derivative of F at z.

Incidentally, the corollary to Theorem 6.24 settles an unanswered question from the last chapter--every continuous function is the derivative of some function.

The following theorem, an easy consequence of our last result, provides a most useful method for evaluating integrals.

Theorem 6.25: If f is continuous on [a,b] and g is any antiderivative of f on [a,b], then

$$\int_a^b f(x)dx = g(b) - g(a).$$

Proof: Recall (Definition 5.29) that an antiderivative of f is simply any function whose derivative is f. If we define F on [a,b] by

$$F(x) = \int_a^x f(t)dt,$$

we know by the corollary to Theorem 6.24 that F is an antiderivative of f on [a,b]. Furthermore, by Theorem 5.30 there exists a constant C such that F(x) = g(x) + C for every x in [a,b]. Therefore F(b) - F(a) = [g(b) + C] - [g(a) + C] = g(b) - g(a). Since

272

$$F(b) = \int_a^b f(t)dt \text{ and } F(a) = \int_a^a f(t)dt = 0,$$

it follows that

$$\int_a^b f(t)dt = F(b) - F(a) = g(b) - g(a). \qquad \square$$

Example 3: Suppose $\int_{\sqrt{2}}^3 \dfrac{1}{\sqrt{(x^2 - 1)^3}}\, dx$ is to be

evaluated. If $g(x) = -\dfrac{x}{\sqrt{x^2 - 1}}$, it is easily

shown that $g'(x) = \dfrac{1}{\sqrt{(x^2 - 1)^3}}$. Therefore

$$\int_{\sqrt{2}}^3 \frac{1}{\sqrt{(x^2 - 1)^3}}\, dx = g(3) - g(\sqrt{2}) = -\frac{3}{\sqrt{8}} + \sqrt{2} = \frac{\sqrt{2}}{4}.$$

If we form an indefinite integral of a continuous function f and differentiate the result, we
wind up with the original function f. Thus, differentiation and integration are inverse processes,
at least if the integration is performed first
(on a continuous function). What about revers-
ing the order? If we differentiate a differentiable function f and form an indefinite integral
of f', do we get the original function f? Not
necessarily, for the simple reason that f' may
not be integrable. Consider the following example.

Example 4: Define a function f by

$$f(x) = \begin{cases} x^2 \sin \dfrac{1}{x^2} & \text{if } x \neq 0 \\[2mm] 0 & \text{if } x = 0 \end{cases}.$$

By a routine calculation for $x \neq 0$ and the definition of derivative for $x = 0$ we find that

$$f'(x) = \begin{cases} 2x \sin \dfrac{1}{x^2} - \dfrac{2}{x} \cos \dfrac{1}{x^2} & \text{if } x \neq 0 \\ 0 & \text{if } x = 0 \end{cases}.$$

Since $\lim\limits_{x \to 0} 2x \sin \dfrac{1}{x^2} = 0$ and $\dfrac{2}{x} \cos \dfrac{1}{x^2}$ is unbounded in every neighborhood of zero, f' is unbounded and therefore not integrable on any interval containing zero.

In order to prove that differentiation followed by integration leads back to the original function, we must simply assume that the derivative is integrable. The desired result is obtained in the following theorem and its corollaries.

Theorem 6.26 (Second Fundamental Theorem of Calculus): If f is differentiable on [a,b] and f' is integrable on [a,b], then

$$\int_a^b f'(x)\,dx = f(b) - f(a).$$

Proof: Suppose $P = \{x_0, x_1, x_2, \ldots, x_n\}$ is any partition of [a,b]. Applying the Mean Value Theorem to each of the n subintervals $[x_{i-1}, x_i]$ we assert the existence of numbers z_i, $x_{i-1} < z_i < x_i$, such that $f(x_i) - f(x_{i-1}) = f'(z_i)(x_i - x_{i-1})$. If, for each i,

m_i = greatest lower bound $\{f'(x): \ x_{i-1} \leq x \leq x_i\}$

and

M_i = least upper bound $\{f'(x): \ x_{i-1} \leq x \leq x_i\}$,

274

then

$$m_i(x_i - x_{i-1}) \leq f'(z_i)(x_i - x_{i-1}) \leq M_i(x_i - x_{i-1})$$

and therefore

$$m_i(x_i - x_{i-1}) \leq f(x_i) - f(x_{i-1}) \leq M_i(x_i - x_{i-1}).$$

Consequently

$$\sum_{i=1}^{n} m_i(x_i - x_{i-1}) \leq \sum_{i=1}^{n} [f(x_i) - f(x_{i-1})]$$

$$\leq \sum_{i=1}^{n} M_i(x_i - x_{i-1})$$

and so

$$L(f',P) \leq f(b) - f(a) \leq U(f',P).$$

Since the last inequality holds for any partition P whatsoever,

$$\underline{I}\,_a^b(f') \leq f(b) - f(a) \leq \overline{I}\,_a^b(f').$$

But f' is integrable by hypothesis, so the upper and lower integrals are equal. Hence

$$\int_a^b f'(x)dx = f(b) - f(a). \qquad \square$$

Corollary: Suppose f is differentiable and f' is integrable on [a,b]. If c is any (fixed) number in [a,b] and x is any number in [a,b], then

$$f(x) = f(c) + \int_c^x f'(t)dt.$$

Proof: Left as an exercise.

Corollary: If f is integrable on [a,b] and g is any antiderivative of f on [a,b], then

$$\int_a^b f(x)dx = g(b) - g(a).$$

Proof: Since $g'(x) = f(x)$ for every x in [a,b],

$$\int_a^b f(x)dx = \int_a^b g'(x)dx = g(b) - g(a). \qquad \square$$

This corollary is seen to be a strengthening of Theorem 6.25. In practice, however, the gain is slight. Try to think of an example where the former applies and the latter does not.

Theorem 6.27 (Integration by Parts): If both f and g are differentiable on [a,b] and f' and g' are integrable on [a,b], then

$$\int_a^b (fg')(x)dx = f(b)g(b) - f(a)g(a) - \int_a^b (f'g)(x)dx.$$

Proof: Both f and g are differentiable, therefore continuous, and therefore integrable on [a,b]. Hence fg' and f'g are integrable on [a,b]. Since $(fg)' = fg' + f'g$, $(fg)'$ is also integrable by Theorem 6.15. Certainly

$$\int_a^b (fg)'(x)dx = \int_a^b (fg')(x)dx + \int_a^b (f'g)(x)dx.$$

But by Theorem 6.26

$$\int_a^b (fg)'(x)dx = (fg)(b) - (fg)(a).$$

Therefore

$$\int_a^b (fg')(x)dx + \int_a^b (f'g)(x)dx = (fg)(b) - (fg)(a)$$

and consequently

276

$$\int_a^b (fg')(x)dx = f(b)g(b) - f(a)g(a) - \int_a^b (f'g)(x)dx.$$

Example 5: To evaluate $\int_0^{\sqrt{3}} \dfrac{x^3 dx}{\sqrt{4 - x^2}}$ we can define

f by $f(x) = x^2$ and g' by $g'(x) = \dfrac{x}{\sqrt{4 - x^2}}$. It

can be shown that $f'(x) = 2x$ and $g(x) = -\sqrt{4 - x^2}$.
Using Theorem 6.27

$$\int_0^{\sqrt{3}} \dfrac{x^3 dx}{\sqrt{4 - x^2}} = (fg)(\sqrt{3}) - (fg)(0) + \int_0^{\sqrt{3}} 2x\sqrt{4 - x^2} \, dx$$

$$= -3 + \frac{14}{3} = \frac{5}{3} .$$

Theorem 6.25 has been used to evaluate the second

integral, where an antiderivative of $2x\sqrt{4 - x^2}$

can be shown to be $-\frac{2}{3}\sqrt{(4 - x^2)^3}$.

The previous theorem is valuable for evaluating integrals of a certain kind. The following
theorem is even more useful, for it applies to
a larger class of integrals.

Theorem 6.28 (Change of Variable): Suppose g is
differentiable on [c,d] and g' is integrable on
[c,d]. If f is defined and continuous on the
range of g, if $g(c) = a$, and $g(d) = b$, then

$$\int_c^d f(g(x))g'(x)dx = \int_a^b f(x)dx.$$

Proof: Define a function F by

$$F(x) = \int_a^x f(t)dt, \quad x \text{ in the range of g.}$$

277

By Theorem 6.24 F is differentiable and F' = f.
Define a function h on [c,d] by

$$h(x) = F(g(x)).$$

By Theorem 5.12 h is differentiable for every x
in [c,d] and h'(x) = F'(g(x))g'(x) = f(g(x))g'(x).
Furthermore, f(g) is continuous on [c,d] by Theorem 4.16 and therefore integrable on [c,d]. Finally, h' is integrable on [c,d], for it is the product of the two integrable functions f(g) and g'.
Using Theorems 6.26 and 6.25

$$\int_c^d h'(x)dx = h(d) - h(c)$$

$$= F(g(d)) - F(g(c))$$

$$= F(b) - F(a)$$

$$= \int_a^b f(x)dx.$$

Since h' = f(g)g', $\int_c^d f(g(x))g'(x)dx = \int_a^b f(x)dx.$ □

Note that in the theorem above the interval
[a,b] may be a proper subset of the domain of f
since f must be defined on the entire range of g.
Notice also that the theorem covers the case
where g(c) = g(d).

Example 6:   To evaluate

$$\int_{\frac{\pi}{6}}^{\frac{\pi}{2}} \frac{\cos x}{(1 + \sin x)^2} \, dx$$

we let $f(x) = \frac{1}{x^2}$ and g(x) = 1 + sin x. Then g'(x) =
cos x and $f(g(x))g'(x) = \frac{\cos x}{(1 + \sin x)^2}$. Since
$c = \frac{\pi}{6}$ and $d = \frac{\pi}{2}$, $a = \frac{3}{2}$ and b = 2. Therefore

$$\int_{\frac{\pi}{6}}^{\frac{\pi}{2}} \frac{\cos x}{(1 + \sin x)^2} \, dx = \int_{\frac{3}{2}}^{2} \frac{1}{x^2} \, dx = \frac{1}{6} \, .$$

In some circumstances it may be necessary to approximate the value of an integral if it cannot be determined exactly. There are several "mean value theorems for integrals" that can be helpful in this regard. Problem 11 of Exercise 6.1 can be considered in this category, but the approximation given there is often too crude to be of any value.

Theorem 6.29 (First Mean Value Theorem for Integrals): Suppose both f and g are integrable on [a,b] and g never changes sign on [a,b]. If m and M denote, respectively, the greatest lower bound and least upper bound of $\{f(x): a \le x \le b\}$, there exists a number c satisfying $m \le c \le M$ such that

$$\int_a^b f(x)g(x)dx = c\int_a^b g(x)dx.$$

Moreover, if f is continuous on [a,b], there exists a number z satisfying $a \le z \le b$ such that
$\int_a^b f(x)g(x)dx = f(z)\int_a^b g(x)dx.$

Proof: Either $g(x) \ge 0$ for all x in [a,b] or $g(x) \le 0$ for all x in [a,b]. Suppose the former. From

$$m \le f(x) \le M$$

we get

$$mg(x) \le f(x)g(x) \le Mg(x)$$

and therefore

$$m\int_a^b g(x)dx \le \int_a^b f(x)g(x)dx \le M\int_a^b f(x)dx$$

by the corollary to Theorem 6.16. If $\int_a^b g(x)dx = 0$, the last step shows that $\int_a^b f(x)g(x)dx = 0$, and the first part of the conclusion follows for any choice of c. If $\int_a^b g(x)dx \neq 0$, let

$$c = \frac{\int_a^b f(x)g(x)dx}{\int_a^b g(x)dx} .$$

Then $m \leq c \leq M$ by the inequality above and the desired equality follows immediately. If f is continuous on [a,b], then, by Theorem 4.26, f(z) = c for some z satisfying $a \leq z \leq b$, and the second part of the conclusion is established. Suppose now that $g(x) \leq 0$ for all x in [a,b]. Then $(-g)(x) \geq 0$ for all x in [a,b] so there is a number c, $m \leq c \leq M$, such that

$$\int_a^b f(x)(-g)(x)dx = c\int_a^b (-g)(x)dx$$

from which we get

$$\int_a^b f(x)g(x)dx = c\int_a^b g(x)dx. \qquad \square$$

The following special case is sometimes called "The Mean Value Theorem for Integrals."

Corollary: If f is continuous on [a,b], there exists a number z in [a,b] such that

$$\int_a^b f(x)dx = f(z)(b - a).$$

Proof: Define g by g(x) = 1 for every x in [a,b], and apply the theorem. $\qquad \square$

The corollary has a simple geometric interpretation if f is non-negative (see Figure 6.2).

280

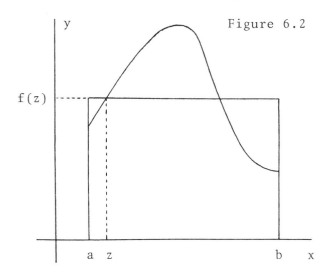

Figure 6.2

There is a number z in [a,b] such that the area
under the graph of f is equal to the area of a
rectangle with dimensions b - a and f(z).

<u>Example 7</u>: The integral $\int_0^1 \dfrac{x}{\sqrt{x^3 + 8}} \, dx$ cannot
be evaluated by the method of finding an antideri-
vative. We can approximate its value as follows.
Let $f(x) = \dfrac{1}{\sqrt{x^3 + 8}}$ and $g(x) = x$. Then

$$\int_a^b g(x)\,dx = \int_0^1 x\,dx = \frac{1}{2}$$

and, for any x in [0,1],

$$\frac{1}{3} \leq f(x) = \frac{1}{\sqrt{x^3 + 8}} \leq \frac{1}{2\sqrt{2}} \ .$$

281

Therefore

$$\frac{1}{6} = \frac{1}{3}(\frac{1}{2}) \leq \int_0^1 \frac{x}{\sqrt{x^3 + 8}} \, dx \leq \frac{1}{2\sqrt{2}} \, (\frac{1}{2}) = \frac{\sqrt{2}}{8} \, ,$$

so

$$0.166 < \int_0^1 \frac{x}{\sqrt{x^3 + 8}} \, dx < 0.177.$$

This inequality is valuable, of course, since the upper and lower bounds are close together.

Exercise 6.2

1. Evaluate $\int_0^1 |3x - 2| dx$.

2. Prove the first corollary to Theorem 6.26.

3. Suppose f is continuous on [a,b], c is any number in [a,b], and G is defined by

$$G(x) = \int_x^c f(t)dt, \quad x \text{ in } [a,b].$$

   Show that G is differentiable and evaluate $G'(x)$.

4. Evaluate $\int_{-1}^3 \dfrac{1 - x}{\sqrt[3]{x^2 - 2x + 5}} \, dx$ by Theorem 6.28.
   Identify the functions f and g.

5. Give an example of a function f and an interval [a,b] such that f has an antiderivative on [a,b] but f is not integrable on [a,b].

6. Prove that if f is continuous on [a,b] and $\int_a^b f(x)dx = 0$, there is at least one number z in [a,b] such that $f(z) = 0$.

7. If f denotes the function of Example 4 and a and b are any numbers satisfying $0 < a < b$, show that $\lim\limits_{a \to 0+} \int_a^b f'(x)dx = f(b) - f(0)$.

8. Evaluate $\int_1^2 \dfrac{x - 1}{x^2} e^x dx$.

9. Suppose f is continuous on [a,b]. Suppose u and v are differentiable on a set D, and the ranges of u and v are in [a,b]. If, for each x in D,
$$G(x) = \int_{u(x)}^{v(x)} f(t)dt,$$

283

prove that G is differentiable and $G'(x) =$
$f(v(x))v'(x) - f(u(x))u'(x)$.

In Problems 10 - 15 find a formula for the derivative of the given function.

10. $f(x) = \int_1^x \sqrt[3]{t^2 + 5}\, dt$

11. $f(x) = \int_x^0 \dfrac{t}{t^3 + 1}\, dt$

12. $f(x) = \int_1^{x^2} \sqrt[3]{t^2 + 5}\, dt$

13. $f(x) = \int_x^{x^2} \cos t^2 dt$

14. $f(x) = \int_{x^2}^{\cos x^2} \cos t^2 dt$

15. $f(x) = \int_0^x x e^{t^2} dt$

16. Prove that if f is bounded on [a,b] and f has at most finitely many points of discontinuity, then f is integrable on [a,b].

17. Prove or disprove: if f is continuous and non-negative on [a,b] and $f(x) > 0$ for at least one x in [a,b], then $\int_a^b f(x)dx > 0$.

In Problems 18 - 20 use Theorem 6.29 to establish the given inequality.

18. $\dfrac{6}{\pi} \leq \int_1^{\sqrt{3}} \dfrac{x^3}{\text{Arctan } x}\, dx \leq \dfrac{8}{\pi}$

19. $\dfrac{1}{3e} \leq \int_0^1 \dfrac{x^2}{e^{x^2}}\, dx \leq \dfrac{1}{\sqrt{8e}}$

20. $\frac{4}{3} \leq \int_0^2 \frac{x^3}{\sqrt{x^3 + 1}} \, dx \leq \frac{8}{3}$

21. Without trying to evaluate the integral, obtain the best upper and lower bounds you can for

$$\int_{\frac{\pi}{6}}^{\frac{\pi}{2}} \frac{\sin x}{x} \, dx.$$

22. Prove the corollary to Theorem 6.29 by applying Theorem 5.24 to the function

$$F(x) = \int_a^x f(t) dt.$$

23. Prove or disprove: if f is integrable and non-negative on [a,b], then $\sqrt{f}$ is integrable on [a,b].

24. Prove the Minkowski Inequality for Integrals. If both f and g are integrable on [a,b], then

$$\sqrt{\int_a^b [f(x) + g(x)]^2 dx} \leq \sqrt{\int_a^b [f(x)]^2 dx}$$

$$+ \sqrt{\int_a^b [g(x)]^2 dx} \ .$$

25. Give an example of a function f integrable on an interval [a,b] such that for some z in [a,b] F is differentiable and $F'(z) \neq f(z)$ (where $F(x) = \int_a^x f(t) dt$).

26. Prove the "Second Mean Value Theorem for Integrals." Suppose g is integrable and never changes sign on [a,b]. If f is monotonic on [a,b], there exists a number z, $a \leq z \leq b$, such that

$$\int_a^b f(x)g(x)dx = f(a)\int_a^z g(x)dx + f(b)\int_z^b g(x)dx.$$

Chapter 7

1. Algebra of Convergent Series and Convergence Tests for Positive Term Series

Many important concepts in mathematics arise from attempts to generalize commonplace ideas. The notion of infinite series is a good example of this. It's a known fact that any finite collection of numbers has a unique sum. Indeed, the sum may be obtained by adding the numbers in any order whatsoever. Is there any reasonable way of defining the "sum" of an infinite collection of numbers? The study of infinite series answers this question and investigates consequences of the definition.

Definition 7.1: An <u>infinite series</u> is an ordered pair of sequences $(\{a_n\}, \{s_n\})$, where $s_n = \sum\limits_{i=1}^{n} a_i$ for each positive integer n. For each positive integer n, a_n is said to be the nth <u>term</u> of the series, and s_n is said to be the nth <u>partial sum</u> of the series. The series is said to <u>converge</u> if the sequence $\{s_n\}$ converges and to <u>diverge</u> if $\{s_n\}$ diverges. In the case of convergence the limit of $\{s_n\}$ is called the <u>sum</u> of the series.

The ordered pair notation above is rarely used in practice. Instead, we use $a_1 + a_2 + a_3 + \ldots$ or $a_1 + a_2 + \ldots + a_n + \ldots$ or $\sum\limits_{n=1}^{\infty} a_n$ to represent a series. (From now on, "series" is used interchangeably with "infinite series.") The last of the three notations above is perhaps the best, for it's quite compact and is an obvious generalization of the symbol for a finite sum.

287

Using the notation of the definition, if $\{s_n\}$ converges to s, s is called the sum of the series, and it's customary to write $\sum_{n=1}^{\infty} a_n = s$. This is a notational inconsistency, for it means that the symbol " $\sum_{n=1}^{\infty} a_n$ " represents a series and, in the case of convergence, a number. It's awkward to avoid this problem, so we will follow tradition and allow the inconsistency to stand.

Since convergence of a series is defined in terms of convergence of a sequence, it seems clear that the study of series will involve some of our results on sequences. In fact, part of the work has already been done and merely has to be recast in a new notation.

Example 1: (a) The sequence of partial sums for the series

$$1 - 1 + 1 - 1 + 1 - 1 + \ldots$$

is $\{s_n\} = \{1, 0, 1, 0, 1, 0, \ldots\}$. Since the sequence diverges, the series diverges. (b) The sequence of partial sums for the series

$$2 + 2 + 2 + \ldots + 2 + \ldots$$

is $\{s_n\} = \{2, 4, 6, \ldots, 2n, \ldots\}$. Since the sequence diverges, the series diverges. (c) The sequence of partial sums for the series

$$\frac{1}{2} + \frac{1}{4} + \frac{1}{8} + \ldots + \frac{1}{2^n} + \ldots$$

is $\{s_n\} = \{\frac{1}{2}, \frac{3}{4}, \frac{7}{8}, \ldots, 1 - (\frac{1}{2})^n, \ldots\}$. Since the sequence converges to 1, the series converges, and, in fact,

$$\sum_{n=1}^{\infty} \frac{1}{2^n} = 1.$$

Example 2: Consider the series

$$\sum_{n=1}^{\infty} \frac{1}{4n^2 - 1} .$$

It's easy to show that

$$\frac{1}{4n^2 - 1} = \frac{1}{2} \left(\frac{1}{2n - 1} - \frac{1}{2n + 1} \right).$$

Concerning the sequence of partial sums we find that

$$s_1 = \frac{1}{2} \left(\frac{1}{1} - \frac{1}{3} \right)$$

$$s_2 = \frac{1}{2} \left(\frac{1}{1} - \frac{1}{3} + \frac{1}{3} - \frac{1}{5} \right)$$

$$s_3 = \frac{1}{2} \left(\frac{1}{1} - \frac{1}{3} + \frac{1}{3} - \frac{1}{5} + \frac{1}{5} - \frac{1}{7} \right)$$

and, in general,

$$s_n = \frac{1}{2} \left(\frac{1}{1} - \frac{1}{3} + \frac{1}{3} - \frac{1}{5} + \cdots \right.$$

$$\left. + \frac{1}{2n - 3} - \frac{1}{2n - 1} + \frac{1}{2n - 1} - \frac{1}{2n + 1} \right).$$

Therefore

$$s_n = \frac{1}{2} \left(1 - \frac{1}{2n + 1} \right) = \frac{n}{2n + 1} .$$

Since $\{s_n\}$ converges to $\frac{1}{2}$, the series converges, and

289

$$\sum_{n=1}^{\infty} \frac{1}{4n^2 - 1} = \frac{1}{2}.$$

It's apparent from the last example that determination of convergence or divergence of a series directly from the definition is not always easy. In fact, in most cases it's impossible. The only reason Example 2 succeeds, for instance, is because of the "collapsing sum" involved, a very rare occurrence.

<u>Theorem 7.2</u>: Suppose c is any number. If $\sum_{n=1}^{\infty} a_n$ converges and has sum s, then $\sum_{n=1}^{\infty} ca_n$ converges and has sum cs.

<u>Proof</u>: For each positive integer n let $s_n = \sum_{i=1}^{n} a_i$ and $t_n = \sum_{i=1}^{n} ca_i$. Clearly $t_n = c \sum_{i=1}^{n} a_i = cs_n$. Since $\sum_{n=1}^{\infty} a_n = s$, $\{s_n\}$ converges to s. By the corollary to Theorem 2.11 $\{cs_n\} = \{t_n\}$ converges to cs. Hence $\sum_{n=1}^{\infty} ca_n = cs$. □

<u>Corollary</u>: Suppose c is any non-zero number. If $\sum_{n=1}^{\infty} a_n$ diverges, then $\sum_{n=1}^{\infty} ca_n$ diverges.

<u>Proof</u>: Assume that $\sum_{n=1}^{\infty} ca_n$ converges for some $c \neq 0$. Then $\sum_{n=1}^{\infty} (\frac{1}{c}) ca_n = \sum_{n=1}^{\infty} a_n$ converges by the theorem, a contradiction. □

Theorem 7.3: If $\sum_{n=1}^{\infty} a_n$ converges and has sum s and $\sum_{n=1}^{\infty} b_n$ converges and has sum t, then $\sum_{n=1}^{\infty} (a_n + b_n)$ converges and has sum s + t.

Proof: For each positive integer n let $s_n = \sum_{i=1}^{n} a_i$, $t_n = \sum_{i=1}^{n} b_i$, and $u_n = \sum_{i=1}^{n} (a_i + b_i)$. Then $u_n = s_n + t_n$. By hypothesis $\{s_n\}$ converges to s and $\{t_n\}$ converges to t. It follows from Theorem 2.10 that $\{u_n\} = \{s_n + t_n\}$ converges to s + t. Hence $\sum_{n=1}^{\infty} (a_n + b_n) = s + t$. $\qquad\qquad$ ☐

Corollary: If $\sum_{n=1}^{\infty} a_n$ converges and has sum s and $\sum_{n=1}^{\infty} b_n$ converges and has sum t, then $\sum_{n=1}^{\infty} (a_n - b_n)$ converges and has sum s - t.

Proof: Left as an exercise.

Corollary: If $\sum_{n=1}^{\infty} a_n$ converges and $\sum_{n=1}^{\infty} b_n$ diverges, then $\sum_{n=1}^{\infty} (a_n + b_n)$ diverges.

Proof: Left as an exercise.

Concerning a particular series there are two basic questions that can be asked: "does it converge or diverge? and if it converges, what is the sum?" One of our main goals is to establish several

291

criteria which will enable us to answer the first
question, at least for many series. The second
question is more difficult and can only be answered
in special cases.

Ideally we seek conditions both necessary and
sufficient for convergence. Although the following theorem provides such a condition, it is usually
difficult to apply in practice. There are many
theorems, so-called "convergence tests," involving
conditions which fall into one category or the other, and we will consider several of these. Most
have names for easy reference.

Theorem 7.4 (Cauchy Criterion for Series): The

series $\sum\limits_{n=1}^{\infty} a_n$ converges if and only if the follow-

ing is true:

if ε is any positive number, there exists
a positive integer N such that for any integer $n \geq N$ and any positive integer k,

$$|a_{n+1} + a_{n+2} + \cdots + a_{n+k}| < \varepsilon.$$

Proof: Left as an exercise.

The proof is a simple application of the
Cauchy Criterion for sequences. A useful special
case of the theorem is the following.

Corollary (nth Term Test): If $\{a_n\}$ is not a null

sequence, then $\sum\limits_{n=1}^{\infty} a_n$ diverges.

Proof: We prove the contrapositive: if $\sum\limits_{n=1}^{\infty} a_n$
converges, then $\{a_n\}$ is a null sequence. Suppose
$\sum\limits_{n=1}^{\infty} a_n$ converges and ε is any positive number.
By the theorem there exists a positive integer N
such that $|a_{n+1}| < \varepsilon$ for all $n \geq N$. Thus $\{a_n\}$
converges to zero by Definition 2.3. $\qquad\qquad\square$

Example 3: The series $\sum\limits_{n=1}^{\infty} \cos \frac{1}{n}$ diverges since
$\{\cos \frac{1}{n}\}$ converges to 1.

The nth term test says that $\sum\limits_{n=1}^{\infty} a_n$ diverges
if either: (1) $\{a_n\}$ converges to a non-zero num-
ber, or (2) $\{a_n\}$ diverges. Let it be clearly
stated that the converse of the nth term test is
false--if $\{a_n\}$ converges to zero, we can conclude
neither convergence nor divergence of $\sum\limits_{n=1}^{\infty} a_n$.
Note the following important example.

Example 4: Consider the harmonic series

$$\sum\limits_{n=1}^{\infty} \frac{1}{n} = 1 + \frac{1}{2} + \frac{1}{3} + \frac{1}{4} + \ldots \;.$$

The sequence of partial sums is $\{s_n\} = \{1 + \frac{1}{2} +$
$\ldots + \frac{1}{n}\}$. By Example 22 of Chapter 2 $\{s_n\}$ diverges and therefore $\sum\limits_{n=1}^{\infty} \frac{1}{n}$ diverges.

There are other ways of proving the harmonic
series divergent, as we will find later. Remember

that this is a divergent series $\sum_{n=1}^{\infty} a_n$ for which
$\{a_n\}$ converges to zero. Many people have had their
intuition shattered by this example, and it's
worthwhile to consider it a little longer. The
sequence $\{s_n\} = \{1 + \frac{1}{2} + \frac{1}{3} + \ldots + \frac{1}{n}\}$ is clearly
an increasing sequence since all terms of the se-
ries are positive. Since $\{s_n\}$ diverges, it must
be unbounded above. That is, if M is any number
whatsoever, there exists a positive integer N such
that $s_N > M$. For example, there is a positive
integer N such that

$$1 + \frac{1}{2} + \frac{1}{3} + \frac{1}{4} + \ldots + \frac{1}{N} > 1,000,000.$$

When considered in this light, the divergence of
the harmonic series is truly remarkable. Even
though each individual term has a negligible effect
on the sum, the cumulative effect of a large number of such terms is enormous.

Definition 7.5: If a is a number and r is a number, a series of the form

$$a + ar + ar^2 + ar^3 + \ldots$$

is called a geometric series with ratio r.

Geometric series are extremely important.
For one reason, the sum of a convergent geometric
series can be found by a simple formula.

Theorem 7.6: For $a \neq 0$ the geometric series a +
$ar + ar^2 + \ldots$ converges if $|r| < 1$ and diverges
if $|r| \geq 1$. If $|r| < 1$, then

$$a + ar + ar^2 + \ldots = \frac{a}{1 - r}.$$

Proof: If $r = 1$ the series is $a + a + a + a \ldots$, and if $r = -1$ the series is $a - a + a - a + \ldots$, both of which diverge by the nth term test. If $|r| > 1$, we know from our work on sequences that $\{ar^n\}$ diverges, so the series again diverges by the nth term test. Suppose now that $|r| < 1$. In this case $\{r^n\}$ converges to zero. If

$$s_n = a + ar + ar^2 + \ldots + ar^{n-1},$$

by Problem 20 of Exercise 1.1 we have

$$s_n = \frac{a}{1 - r} (1 - r^n).$$

Since $\{r^n\}$ converges to zero, $\{s_n\}$ converges to $\frac{a}{1 - r}$, that is,

$$a + ar + ar^2 + \ldots = \frac{a}{1 - r}. \qquad \square$$

Example 5: The series $\sum\limits_{n=1}^{\infty} (-\frac{2}{3})^{n-1}$ is a geometric series with $a = 1$ and $r = -\frac{2}{3}$. Therefore

$$\sum_{n=1}^{\infty} (-\frac{2}{3})^{n-1} = 1 - \frac{2}{3} + \frac{4}{9} - \frac{8}{27} + \ldots$$

$$= \frac{1}{1 - (-\frac{2}{3})}$$

$$= \frac{3}{5}.$$

Definition 7.7: The series $\sum\limits_{n=1}^{\infty} a_n$ is said to be a positive term series provided there is a positive

295

integer N such that $a_n \geq 0$ for all $n \geq N$.

It should be clear from the definition and from your knowledge of sequences that convergence or divergence of a series is independent of the behavior of any finite number of terms of the series. That is why properties such as the one above need not hold for all terms of the series but only "from some point on." In this vein the following theorem is included.

Theorem 7.8: Suppose $\sum_{n=1}^{\infty} a_n$ is a series and N is a positive integer. Either $\sum_{n=1}^{\infty} a_n$ and $\sum_{n=N}^{\infty} a_n$ both converge or they both diverge.

Proof: Left as an exercise.

Theorem 7.9: A positive term series converges if and only if its sequence of partial sums is bounded above.

Proof: Suppose $\sum_{n=1}^{\infty} a_n$ is a positive term series whose sequence of partial sums is $\{s_n\}$. If $\sum_{n=1}^{\infty} a_n$ converges then $\{s_n\}$ converges, and every convergent sequence is bounded above (and below). Suppose, on the other hand, that $\{s_n\}$ is bounded above. There is a positive integer N such that $a_n \geq 0$ for all $n \geq N$. Hence

$$s_n - s_{n-1} = a_n \geq 0 \text{ for } n \geq N,$$

proving that $\{s_n\}$ is increasing. By Theorem 2.20 $\{s_n\}$ converges, and consequently $\sum_{n=1}^{\infty} a_n$ con-verges. □

Theorem 7.10 (Direct Comparison Test for Conver-gence): Suppose $\sum\limits_{n=1}^{\infty} a_n$ is a positive term series and $\sum\limits_{n=1}^{\infty} b_n$ is a convergent positive term series. If there exists a positive integer N such that $a_n \leq b_n$ for all $n \geq N$, then $\sum\limits_{n=1}^{\infty} a_n$ converges.

Proof: For each positive integer n let $s_n = \sum\limits_{i=1}^{n} a_i$ and $t_n = \sum\limits_{i=1}^{n} b_i$. By Theorem 7.9 there is a number T such that, for every positive integer n,

$$\sum_{i=1}^{n} b_i = t_n \leq T.$$

By hypothesis

$$\sum_{i=N+1}^{n} a_i \leq \sum_{i=N+1}^{n} b_i \text{ for } n \geq N + 1.$$

(The last inequality is actually true for $n \geq N$.) Adding $\sum\limits_{i=1}^{N} a_i$ to both sides,

$$s_n = \sum_{i=1}^{n} a_i \leq \sum_{i=1}^{N} a_i + \sum_{i=N+1}^{n} b_i$$

$$= \sum_{i=1}^{N} a_i + t_n - \sum_{i=1}^{N} b_i$$

$$\leq T + \sum_{i=1}^{N} (a_i - b_i) \text{ for } n \geq N + 1.$$

If M denotes the largest number of the set $\{s_1,$ $s_2, \ldots, s_N, T + \sum_{i=1}^{N} (a_i - b_i)\}$, then $s_n \leq M$ for all n, and $\sum_{n=1}^{\infty} a_n$ converges by Theorem 7.9. $\square$

Example 6: Consider the series $\sum_{n=1}^{\infty} \frac{1}{n!}$. It was shown in Example 6 of Chapter 1 that $2^n \leq n!$ for $n \geq 4$. Therefore

$$\frac{1}{n!} \leq \frac{1}{2^n} \text{ for } n \geq 4.$$

Since $\sum_{n=1}^{\infty} \frac{1}{2^n}$ converges (it's a geometric series with ratio $\frac{1}{2}$), $\sum_{n=1}^{\infty} \frac{1}{n!}$ converges by the previous theorem.

Theorem 7.11 (Direct Comparison Test for Divergence): Suppose $\sum_{n=1}^{\infty} a_n$ is a positive term series and $\sum_{n=1}^{\infty} b_n$ is a divergent positive term series. If there exists a positive integer N such that $a_n \geq b_n$ for all $n \geq N$, then $\sum_{n=1}^{\infty} a_n$ diverges.

Proof: Left as an exercise.

Example 7: Consider the series $\sum_{n=1}^{\infty} \frac{2n}{n^2 + 5}$. It's a routine matter to show that $\frac{2n}{n^2 + 5} > \frac{1}{n}$ for $n \geq 3$. Since $\sum_{n=1}^{\infty} \frac{1}{n}$ diverges, $\sum_{n=1}^{\infty} \frac{2n}{n^2 + 5}$ must also diverge.

In some cases convergence or divergence of a series can be determined easily by one of the two preceding theorems. Many times, however, the relevant inequality is difficult if not impossible to establish. Note that a series cannot be proved divergent by Theorem 7.10 nor convergent by Theorem 7.11.

Theorem 7.12 (Integral Test)*: Suppose $\sum_{n=1}^{\infty} a_n$ is a positive term series. Suppose there is a function f and a positive integer N such that f is non-negative and decreasing for all $x \geq N$, and $f(n) = a_n$ for $n \geq N$. The series $\sum_{n=1}^{\infty} a_n$ converges if and only if the sequence $\{\int_{N}^{N+n} f(x)dx\}$ converges.

Proof: By Theorem 7.8 it suffices to prove the theorem for $\sum_{n=N+1}^{\infty} a_n$ instead of $\sum_{n=1}^{\infty} a_n$. For each positive integer n let $s_n = \sum_{i=N+1}^{N+n} a_i$ and $t_n = \int_{N}^{N+n} f(x)dx$. Note that $\{s_n\}$ is increasing since $a_n \geq 0$ for $n \geq N$, and $\{t_n\}$ is increasing since $f(x) \geq 0$ for $x \geq N$. For any integer $n \geq N$ we have

$$a_{n+1} = f(n + 1) \leq f(x) \leq f(n) = a_n$$

for all x satisfying $n \leq x \leq n + 1$. By the corollary to Theorem 6.16

$$a_{n+1} \leq \int_{n}^{n+1} f(x)dx \leq a_n, \quad n \geq N$$

*This test was first proved by Colin Maclaurin in 1742 and later rediscovered by Cauchy.

299

and therefore

$$(1) \quad \sum_{i=N+1}^{N+n} a_i \leq \int_N^{N+n} f(x)\,dx \leq \sum_{i=N}^{N+n-1} a_i, \quad n \geq 1.$$

(Note that the integrals exist since f is monotonic.) Suppose $\{t_n\}$ converges, and denote the limit by T. Then $t_n \leq T$ for all n since $\{t_n\}$ is increasing. Using the left half of (1),

$$s_n \leq t_n \leq T, \quad n \geq 1$$

and $\sum_{n=N+1}^{\infty} a_n$ converges by Theorem 7.9. Suppose, on the other hand, that the series converges, and let S denote the limit of $\{s_n\}$. Then $s_n \leq S$ for $n \geq 1$. Using the right half of (1),

$$t_n \leq a_N + s_{n-1} \leq a_N + S, \quad n \geq 2$$

and $\{t_n\}$ converges by Theorem 2.20. $\quad\square$

Example 8: If p is a number, any series of the form $\sum_{n=1}^{\infty} \dfrac{1}{n^p}$ is called a p-series. We see that the function $f(x) = \dfrac{1}{x^p}$ satisfies all conditions of the integral test. It's a routine matter to show that

$$\int_1^n \frac{dx}{x^p} = \begin{cases} \dfrac{1 - n^{1-p}}{p - 1} & \text{if } p \neq 1 \\[2mm] \ln n & \text{if } p = 1 \end{cases}.$$

For the first of the two possibilities, we consider two cases: $p > 1$ and $p < 1$. If $p > 1$ the sequence

$\left\{\dfrac{1 - n^{1 - p}}{p - 1}\right\}$ converges to $\dfrac{1}{p - 1}$, and if $p < 1$
the sequence $\left\{\dfrac{1 - n^{1 - p}}{p - 1}\right\}$ diverges. Also $\{\ln n\}$
diverges. Therefore $\sum\limits_{n=1}^{\infty} \dfrac{1}{n^p}$ converges if and only
if $p > 1$. Note that this result contains the divergence of the harmonic series as a special case.

Theorem 7.13 (Limit Comparison Test): Suppose
$\sum\limits_{n=1}^{\infty} a_n$ and $\sum\limits_{n=1}^{\infty} b_n$ are positive term series and
$b_n > 0$ for all n. If the sequence $\left\{\dfrac{a_n}{b_n}\right\}$ converges
to a positive number L, then the series $\sum\limits_{n=1}^{\infty} a_n$
and $\sum\limits_{n=1}^{\infty} b_n$ both converge or both diverge.

Proof: By hypothesis there is a positive integer
N such that for all $n \geq N$

$$\left|\dfrac{a_n}{b_n} - L\right| < \dfrac{L}{2} .$$

Therefore

$$(1) \quad \dfrac{L}{2} < \dfrac{a_n}{b_n} < \dfrac{3L}{2} , \quad n \geq N.$$

From the left half of (1),

$$(2) \quad b_n < \dfrac{2}{L} a_n, \quad n \geq N$$

and from the right half of (1),

$$(3) \quad a_n < \dfrac{3L}{2} b_n, \quad n \geq N.$$

Using (2), if $\sum_{n=1}^{\infty} a_n$ converges then $\sum_{n=1}^{\infty} \frac{2}{L} a_n$ converges, and $\sum_{n=1}^{\infty} b_n$ converges by Theorem 7.10.

Using (3), if $\sum_{n=1}^{\infty} b_n$ converges then $\sum_{n=1}^{\infty} \frac{3L}{2} b_n$ converges, and $\sum_{n=1}^{\infty} a_n$ converges by Theorem 7.10.

The contrapositives of the statements just proved show that if either series diverges the other diverges also. ☐

The following variations of the limit comparison test are sometimes useful, though care must be exercised in applying them.

Theorem 7.14: Suppose $\sum_{n=1}^{\infty} a_n$ is a positive term series and $\sum_{n=1}^{\infty} b_n$ is a convergent positive term series such that $b_n > 0$ for all n. If the sequence $\left\{ \dfrac{a_n}{b_n} \right\}$ converges to zero, then $\sum_{n=1}^{\infty} a_n$ converges.

Proof: Left as an exercise.

Theorem 7.15: Suppose $\sum_{n=1}^{\infty} b_n$ is a divergent positive term series and $\sum_{n=1}^{\infty} a_n$ is a positive term series such that $a_n > 0$ for all n. If the sequence $\left\{ \dfrac{b_n}{a_n} \right\}$ converges to zero, then $\sum_{n=1}^{\infty} a_n$ diverges.

Proof: Left as an exercise.

302

There are several important facts to be noted about the five comparison tests presented. (1) All five tests apply only to positive term series. (2) In order that these tests be effective, it's important to have at hand a large collection of series whose convergence or divergence is known. (3) When investigating an unknown series, one must conjecture whether or not the series converges in order to know if a convergent or a divergent series should be chosen for comparison. If the wrong type is used, the test will be inconclusive.

Example 9: To investigate convergence of $\sum\limits_{n=1}^{\infty} \dfrac{1}{(2n + 1)\sqrt{n + 3}}$ we can use the series $\sum\limits_{n=1}^{\infty} \dfrac{1}{n^{3/2}}$ in the limit comparison test. If $a_n = \dfrac{1}{(2n + 1)\sqrt{n + 3}}$ and $b_n = \dfrac{1}{n^{3/2}}$, it's a routine matter to show that

$$\frac{a_n}{b_n} = \sqrt{\frac{n^3}{4n^3 + 16n^2 + 13n + 3}} .$$

Therefore $\left\{\dfrac{a_n}{b_n}\right\}$ converges to $\sqrt{\dfrac{1}{4}} = \dfrac{1}{2}$. The series $\sum\limits_{n=1}^{\infty} \dfrac{1}{n^{3/2}}$ converges since it's a p-series with $p > 1$. Hence $\sum\limits_{n=1}^{\infty} \dfrac{1}{(2n + 1)\sqrt{n + 3}}$ converges by Theorem 7.13.

Theorem 7.16 (Polynomial Test): Suppose P(n) is a polynomial of degree p and Q(n) is a polynomial of degree q. The series $\sum\limits_{n=1}^{\infty} \dfrac{P(n)}{Q(n)}$ converges if and only if $p + 2 \le q$.

303

Proof: Left as an exercise.

Example 10: The series $\displaystyle\sum_{n=1}^{\infty} \frac{(n-1)^2}{n^3 + 2n}$ diverges since $p = 2$, $q = 3$, and $p + 2 > q$.

We close this section with the following interesting result on positive term series.

Theorem 7.17: Suppose $\{a_n\}$ is a decreasing null sequence. If $\{na_n\}$ is not a null sequence, then $\displaystyle\sum_{n=1}^{\infty} a_n$ diverges.

Proof: We prove the contrapositive: if $\displaystyle\sum_{n=1}^{\infty} a_n$ converges, then $\{na_n\}$ is a null sequence. Suppose ε is any positive number. Since $\displaystyle\sum_{n=1}^{\infty} a_n$ converges and $\{a_n\}$ is decreasing, there is a positive integer N such that for all $n > N$, $a_{n-1} \geq a_n$ and

$$a_{N+1} + a_{N+2} + \cdots + a_n < \frac{\varepsilon}{2}.$$

Therefore

$$a_n + a_n + \cdots + a_n \leq a_{N+1} + a_{N+2} + \cdots + a_n < \frac{\varepsilon}{2}$$

for all $n > N$, i.e.,

$$(n - N)a_n < \frac{\varepsilon}{2}.$$

Since $\{a_n\}$ is a null sequence, there exists an

304

integer $M > N$ such that $a_n < \frac{\varepsilon}{2N}$ for all $n \geq M$. For all $n \geq M$, therefore,

$$(n - N)a_n < \frac{\varepsilon}{2}$$

$$na_n < Na_n + \frac{\varepsilon}{2}$$

$$< N(\frac{\varepsilon}{2N}) + \frac{\varepsilon}{2}$$

$$= \varepsilon,$$

and $\{na_n\}$ is a null sequence by Definition 2.3. $\square$

Example 11: Consider the series $\sum\limits_{n=1}^{\infty} \frac{1}{n \text{ Arctan } n}$. For $n \geq 1$, $n + 1 > n$ and Arctan $(n + 1) > $ Arctan n. Therefore $(n + 1)$ Arctan $(n + 1) > n$ Arctan n, so $\frac{1}{(n + 1) \text{ Arctan } (n + 1)} < \frac{1}{n \text{ Arctan } n}$. Consequently the sequence $\{\frac{1}{n \text{ Arctan } n}\}$ is decreasing, and it is easily seen to converge to zero. The sequence $\{n \frac{1}{n \text{ Arctan } n}\}$ is not a null sequence, however, so $\sum\limits_{n=1}^{\infty} \frac{1}{n \text{ Arctan } n}$ diverges.

305

Exercise 7.1

1. Prove the first corollary to Theorem 7.3.

2. Prove the second corollary to Theorem 7.3.

3. Find the exact sum of $\displaystyle\sum_{n=1}^{\infty} \frac{(-1)^n}{4^{n-1}}$.

4. Prove Theorem 7.4.

5. Use the Cauchy Criterion to prove that $\displaystyle\sum_{n=1}^{\infty} \frac{1}{n(n+1)}$ converges.

6. Prove Theorem 7.8.

7. Find the exact sum of $\displaystyle\sum_{n=1}^{\infty} \frac{1}{n^2 + 4n + 3}$.

8. Prove Theorem 7.11.

9. If $\displaystyle\sum_{n=1}^{\infty} a_n$ has $\left\{ \dfrac{n^2}{n^2 + 1} \right\}$ for its sequence of partial sums, find a formula for a_n.

10. Show that $\displaystyle\sum_{n=1}^{\infty} \frac{n!}{n^n}$ converges, and deduce that $\{\dfrac{n!}{n^n}\}$ is a null sequence.

11. Prove Theorem 7.14.

12. Prove Theorem 7.15.

13. Show that $\dfrac{3}{2} < \displaystyle\sum_{n=1}^{\infty} \frac{1}{n^2} < \dfrac{7}{4}$. Can you improve on this estimate?

14. Prove Theorem 7.16.

15. Prove or disprove: if $\sum_{n=1}^{\infty} a_n$ and $\sum_{n=1}^{\infty} b_n$ are convergent positive term series, then $\sum_{n=1}^{\infty} a_n b_n$ converges.

16. Prove that if $\sum_{n=1}^{\infty} a_n$ is a convergent series with no negative terms, then $\sum_{n=1}^{\infty} \sqrt{a_n a_{n+1}}$ converges.

In Problems 17 - 22 determine convergence or divergence of the given series.

17. $\sum_{n=2}^{\infty} \dfrac{1}{n \ln n}$ 18. $\sum_{n=1}^{\infty} \left(\dfrac{n}{n+1}\right)^n$

19. $\sum_{n=1}^{\infty} \dfrac{\sqrt{n+1} - \sqrt{n}}{\sqrt{n}}$ 20. $\sum_{n=1}^{\infty} \ln \dfrac{n+1}{n}$

21. $\sum_{n=1}^{\infty} \dfrac{1}{n \sqrt[n]{2}}$ 22. $\sum_{n=1}^{\infty} \dfrac{\ln n}{n\sqrt{n}}$

23. Give an example showing that the converse of Theorem 7.17 is false.

24. Prove the <u>Cauchy Condensation Test</u>. If $\{a_n\}$ is decreasing and non-negative for $n \geq 1$, then $\sum_{n=1}^{\infty} a_n$ and $\sum_{n=1}^{\infty} 2^{n-1} a_{2^{n-1}}$ both converge or both diverge.

25. Suppose $\sum_{n=1}^{\infty} a_n$ is a convergent positive term series. Show that if $\{i_n\}$ is any subsequence of $\{n\}$, then $\sum_{n=1}^{\infty} a_{i_n}$ converges.

26. Show that $\sum_{n=1}^{\infty} \frac{1}{(n-1)!} < 3$.

27. Prove or disprove: if $\sum_{n=1}^{\infty} a_n$ is a series with no negative terms such that $\sum_{n=1}^{\infty} \sqrt{a_n a_{n+1}}$ converges, then $\sum_{n=1}^{\infty} a_n$ converges.

28. Suppose $\sum_{n=1}^{\infty} a_n$ is a positive term series and f is a function satisfying the hypothesis of the integral test for $N = 1$. If $s_n = \sum_{i=1}^{n} a_i$ for each positive integer n, prove that $\{s_n - \int_1^n f(x)dx\}$ is a decreasing sequence which converges to a number between 0 and $f(1)$.

29. Use the preceding problem to show that the sequence $\{(1 + \frac{1}{2} + \frac{1}{3} + \ldots + \frac{1}{n}) - \ln n\}$ converges to a number γ, $0 < \gamma < 1$. This number γ is called Euler's Constant.

30. Prove that if $\sum_{n=1}^{\infty} a_n$ is a convergent positive term series and $\{b_n\}$ is positive and bounded, then $\sum_{n=1}^{\infty} a_n b_n$ converges.

308

31. Show that if $\sum\limits_{n=1}^{\infty} a_n$ is a convergent positive term series, then $\sum\limits_{n=1}^{\infty} a_n^2$ converges.

2. General Convergence Tests

Most of our convergence tests so far apply only to positive term series. Before establishing more general results, we need some new terminology which is prompted by the following theorem.

Theorem 7.18: If $\sum\limits_{n=1}^{\infty} a_n$ is a series and the series $\sum\limits_{n=1}^{\infty} |a_n|$ converges, then $\sum\limits_{n=1}^{\infty} a_n$ converges.

Proof: Suppose ε is any positive number. Since $\sum\limits_{n=1}^{\infty} |a_n|$ converges, there exists a positive integer N such that

$$|a_{n+1}| + |a_{n+2}| + \ldots + |a_{n+k}| < \varepsilon$$

for all $n \geq N$ and every positive integer k. Hence

$$|a_{n+1} + a_{n+2} + \ldots + a_{n+k}| \leq |a_{n+1}| + |a_{n+2}|$$

$$+ \ldots + |a_{n+k}| < \varepsilon$$

for all $n \geq N$ and every integer k, so $\sum\limits_{n=1}^{\infty} a_n$ converges by Theorem 7.4. □

Definition 7.19: A series $\sum\limits_{n=1}^{\infty} a_n$ is said to con-verge absolutely if $\sum\limits_{n=1}^{\infty} |a_n|$ converges. If $\sum\limits_{n=1}^{\infty} a_n$ converges and $\sum\limits_{n=1}^{\infty} |a_n|$ diverges, then

$\sum\limits_{n=1}^{\infty} a_n$ is said to <u>converge conditionally</u>.

From Theorem 7.18 we know that $\sum\limits_{n=1}^{\infty} a_n$ must converge if $\sum\limits_{n=1}^{\infty} |a_n|$ converges, that is, absolute convergence implies convergence. The converse is not true--conditionally convergent series exist, and examples will be shortly forthcoming. Loosely speaking, a series having a mixture of positive and negative terms has a greater chance of convergence than one whose terms are all of the same sign.

<u>Theorem 7.20 (Alternating Series Test)</u>*: If $\{a_n\}$ is a decreasing null sequence, then the series

$$\sum_{n=1}^{\infty} (-1)^{n+1} a_n = a_1 - a_2 + a_3 - a_4 + \ldots \text{ converges.}$$

Moreover, if N is a positive integer such that $a_{n+1} \le a_n$ for $n \ge N$, then

$$\left| \sum_{i=1}^{\infty} (-1)^{i+1} a_i - \sum_{i=1}^{n} (-1)^{i+1} a_i \right| \le a_{n+1}$$

for $n \ge N$.

<u>Proof</u>: For each positive integer n let $s_n = \sum\limits_{i=1}^{n} (-1)^{i+1} a_i$. If $2n \ge N$, then

$$s_{2n+1} = s_{2n-1} + (-a_{2n} + a_{2n+1})$$

$$\le s_{2n-1} \text{ since } a_{2n+1} \le a_{2n},$$

*This test was first given by Leibniz in 1705.

proving that $\{s_{2n-1}\}$ is a decreasing sequence.
If $2n + 1 \geq N$, then

$$s_{2n+2} = s_{2n} + (a_{2n+1} - a_{2n+2})$$

$$\geq s_{2n} \text{ since } a_{2n+1} \geq a_{2n+2},$$

proving that $\{s_{2n}\}$ is an increasing sequence.
Since $\{s_{n+1} - s_n\} = \{a_{n+1}\}$ is a null sequence,
the hypothesis of Theorem 2.30 is satisfied.
Therefore $\{s_n\}$ converges and consequently
$\sum\limits_{n=1}^{\infty} (-1)^{n+1} a_n$ converges. (We note in passing
that $\sum\limits_{n=1}^{\infty} (-1)^n a_n = - \sum\limits_{n=1}^{\infty} (-1)^{n+1} a_n$ converges by
Theorem 7.2.) To establish the inequality, let
$s = \sum\limits_{n=1}^{\infty} a_n$. For $2n + 1 \geq N$

$$s_{2n} \leq s_{2n+2} \leq \cdots \leq s \leq \cdots \leq s_{2n+1} \leq s_{2n-1}.$$

Since $s_{2n} \leq s \leq s_{2n-1}$, $s_{2n-1} - a_{2n} \leq s \leq s_{2n-1}$,
so $-a_{2n} \leq s - s_{2n-1} \leq 0$ and $a_{2n} \geq s_{2n-1} - s \geq 0$.
Since $s_{2n} \leq s \leq s_{2n+1}$, $s_{2n} \leq s \leq s_{2n} + a_{2n+1}$,
so $0 \leq s - s_{2n} \leq a_{2n+1}$. In both cases $|s - s_n| \leq$
a_{n+1}. Note that strict inequality holds in case
$\{a_n\}$ is strictly decreasing. $\qquad\qquad\qquad\square$

Example 12: Since $\{\frac{1}{n}\}$ is a decreasing null sequence,
$\sum\limits_{n=1}^{\infty} (-1)^{n+1} \frac{1}{n}$ converges by the alternating series

test. Recalling that $\sum_{n=1}^{\infty} \frac{1}{n}$ diverges, we have our
first example of a conditionally convergent series.

Theorem 7.20 can also be stated as follows:

$\sum_{n=1}^{\infty} a_n$ converges if (1) the terms alternate in
sign (zeros don't matter), (2) $|a_{n+1}| \leq |a_n|$ for
all large enough n, and (3) $\{a_n\}$ converges to
zero. If (3) is false, the series diverges by the
n^{th} term test regardless of (1) and (2). If (2)
fails, the series may or may not converge, but it
cannot be shown to converge by the alternating
series test. Consider the following example.

Example 13: The series $\sum_{n=1}^{\infty} (-1)^{n+1} \frac{|\sin n|}{n^2}$ is
certainly an alternating series. Moreover,
$\{\frac{|\sin n|}{n^2}\}$ is a null sequence. Assume that this
sequence is decreasing. Then there exists a positive integer N such that for all $n \geq N$,

$$\frac{|\sin(n + 1)|}{(n + 1)^2} \leq \frac{|\sin n|}{n^2}.$$

For all $n \geq N$, then,

$$\left|\frac{\sin(n + 1)}{\sin n}\right| \leq \frac{(n + 1)^2}{n^2}$$

and

$$|\cos 1 + \sin 1 \cot n| \leq (1 + \frac{1}{n})^2,$$

313

where we use the fact that $\sin(n + 1) = \sin n \cos 1 + \cos n \sin 1$. This is a contradiction since the left side of the last inequality can be made as large as desired by an appropriately chosen integer $n > N$. Therefore the hypothesis of the alternating series test is not satisfied. Since

$$\frac{|\sin n|}{n^2} \leq \frac{1}{n^2}$$

however, the series converges (absolutely) by the direct comparison test.

Example 14: Consider the alternating series $\sum_{n=1}^{\infty} (-1)^{n+1} \frac{\sqrt{2n - 1}}{n + 1}$. Since $\sum_{n=1}^{\infty} \frac{\sqrt{2n - 1}}{n + 1}$ diverges (using the limit comparison test with $\sum_{n=1}^{\infty} \frac{1}{\sqrt{n}}$, for instance), the original series does not converge absolutely. However, $\left\{ \frac{\sqrt{2n - 1}}{n + 1} \right\}$ is easily seen to be a null sequence, so there is still a chance for conditional convergence. Rather than attempt an induction proof that $\left\{ \frac{\sqrt{2n - 1}}{n + 1} \right\}$ is decreasing, we consider the function $f(x) = \frac{\sqrt{2x - 1}}{x + 1}$. It is not hard to show that $f'(x) = \frac{2 - x}{(x + 1)^2 \sqrt{2x - 1}}$. If $x > 2$, then, $f'(x) < 0$, and f is decreasing. Therefore $\left\{ \frac{\sqrt{2n - 1}}{n + 1} \right\}$ is decreasing, and $\sum_{n=1}^{\infty} (-1)^{n+1} \frac{\sqrt{2n - 1}}{n + 1}$ converges conditionally.

__Theorem 7.21 (Root Test)*__: Suppose $\sum\limits_{n=1}^{\infty} a_n$ is a series.

(1) If there exists a positive integer N and a number $r < 1$ such that $\sqrt[n]{|a_n|} \le r$ for all $n \ge N$, then $\sum\limits_{n=1}^{\infty} a_n$ converges absolutely.

(2) If $\sqrt[n]{|a_n|} \ge 1$ for infinitely many integers n, then $\sum\limits_{n=1}^{\infty} a_n$ diverges.

__Proof__: Suppose there is a positive integer N and a (non-negative) number $r < 1$ such that $\sqrt[n]{|a_n|} \le r$ for all $n \ge N$. Then

$$|a_N| \le r^N$$

$$|a_{N+1}| \le r^{N+1}$$

$$|a_{N+2}| \le r^{N+2}$$

$$.$$
$$.$$
$$.$$

The geometric series $\sum\limits_{n=1}^{\infty} r^n$ converges since $|r| < 1$, so by Theorem 7.10 $\sum\limits_{n=1}^{\infty} a_n$ converges absolutely. If, on the other hand, $\sqrt[n]{|a_n|} \ge 1$ for

*Cauchy published this theorem in 1821.

315

infinitely many n, then $|a_n| \geq 1$ for infinitely many n. Therefore $\{a_n\}$ is not a null sequence, so $\sum_{n=1}^{\infty} a_n$ diverges. □

The following special case of Theorem 7.21 is usually sufficient. For convenience, both the theorem and its corollary will be referred to as the root test.

<u>Corollary</u>: Suppose $\sum_{n=1}^{\infty} a_n$ is a series, and the sequence $\left\{ \sqrt[n]{|a_n|} \right\}$ converges to a number L.

(1) If $L < 1$, $\sum_{n=1}^{\infty} a_n$ converges absolutely.

(2) If $L > 1$, $\sum_{n=1}^{\infty} a_n$ diverges.

<u>Proof</u>: Left as an exercise.

<u>Example 15</u>: Consider the series $\sum_{n=1}^{\infty} (\sqrt[n]{n} - 1)^n$. The sequence $\{ \sqrt[n]{(\sqrt[n]{n} - 1)^n} \} = \{ \sqrt[n]{n} - 1 \}$ converges to 0 by Problem 21 of Exercise 2.3. Hence $\sum_{n=1}^{\infty} (\sqrt[n]{n} - 1)^n$ converges by the root test.

<u>Theorem 7.22 (Ratio Test)*</u>: Suppose $\sum_{n=1}^{\infty} a_n$ is a series, each term of which is non-zero.

*This test was first discovered by the French mathematician Jean d'Alembert.

316

(1) If there exists a positive integer N and a number $r < 1$ such that $\left|\dfrac{a_{n+1}}{a_n}\right| \leq r$ for all $n \geq N$, then $\sum\limits_{n=1}^{\infty} a_n$ converges absolutely.

(2) If there exists a positive integer N such that $\left|\dfrac{a_{n+1}}{a_n}\right| \geq 1$ for all $n \geq N$, then $\sum\limits_{n=1}^{\infty} a_n$ diverges.

Proof: If the hypothesis of (1) is true, then $|a_{n+1}| \leq r|a_n|$ for all $n \geq N$. Therefore

$$|a_{N+1}| \leq r|a_N|$$

$$|a_{N+2}| \leq r|a_{N+1}| \leq r^2|a_N|$$

$$|a_{N+3}| \leq r|a_{N+2}| \leq r^3|a_N|$$

$$\vdots$$

Since $\sum\limits_{n=1}^{\infty} r^n|a_N|$ converges (because $|r| < 1$), $\sum\limits_{n=1}^{\infty} |a_n|$ converges by Theorem 7.10, so $\sum\limits_{n=1}^{\infty} a_n$ converges absolutely. If the hypothesis of (2) is true, then $|a_{n+1}| \geq |a_n|$ for all $n \geq N$. Therefore $|a_{N+1}| \geq |a_N|$, $|a_{N+2}| \geq |a_{N+1}|$, $|a_{N+3}| \geq |a_{N+2}|$, etc. Hence

$$\cdots \geq |a_{N+3}| \geq |a_{N+2}| \geq |a_{N+1}| \geq |a_N| > 0,$$

and consequently $\sum\limits_{n=1}^{\infty} a_n$ diverges since $\{a_n\}$ is not a null sequence. $\qquad\qquad\qquad\qquad\qquad\qquad\quad\square$

The following special case is easier to apply than the theorem itself and is sufficient for most applications. Both results will be referred to as the ratio test.

Corollary: Suppose $\sum\limits_{n=1}^{\infty} a_n$ is a series of non-zero terms, and the sequence $\left\{ \left| \dfrac{a_{n+1}}{a_n} \right| \right\}$ converges to a number L.

(1) If $L < 1$, $\sum\limits_{n=1}^{\infty} a_n$ converges absolutely.

(2) If $L > 1$, $\sum\limits_{n=1}^{\infty} a_n$ diverges.

Proof: Left as an exercise.

Example 16: Consider the series

$$\sum_{n=1}^{\infty} (-1)^{n+1} \frac{1 \cdot 3 \cdot 5 \cdots (2n - 1)}{n!} .$$

If a_n denotes the general term,

$$\left| \frac{a_{n+1}}{a_n} \right| = \frac{1 \cdot 3 \cdot 5 \cdots (2n - 1)(2n + 1)}{(n + 1)!} .$$

$$\frac{n!}{1 \cdot 3 \cdot 5 \cdots (2n - 1)} = \frac{2n + 1}{n + 1} .$$

318

The series diverges since $\{\frac{2n + 1}{n + 1}\}$ converges to 2.

Both the root test and the ratio test are really direct comparison tests, for each compares the given series with an appropriate geometric series. The advantage of these tests over Theorem 7.10 is that no comparison series need be chosen ahead of time, and there is no difficult inequality to establish. With respect to divergence neither test is any more sensitive than the nth term test, for each infers divergence of a series $\sum\limits_{n=1}^{\infty} a_n$ from the fact that $\{a_n\}$ is not a null sequence.

It can be shown that the root test is "stronger" than the ratio test. That is, the root test is conclusive whenever the ratio test is, but there are series for which the root test is conclusive and the ratio test is not. See Problem 5 of Exercise 7.2 for such an example. In practice the ratio test is usually much easier to apply, and it is the most popular of all convergence tests. There are, unfortunately, quite a few series for which the ratio test is inconclusive and no other test seems applicable. Various ingenious tests have been devised to handle such series. The gain in generality is accompanied, however, by a loss in simplicity. A few of these more "delicate" tests are presented here.

Theorem 7.23 (Kummer's Test)*: Suppose $\sum\limits_{n=1}^{\infty} a_n$ is a series each term of which is positive.

    (1) If there exists a sequence $\{b_n\}$ of
           positive numbers, a positive number r,

*Kummer's original version, given in 1835, was slightly different.

and a positive integer N such that

$$b_n \left(\frac{a_n}{a_{n+1}} \right) - b_{n+1} \geq r \text{ for } n \geq N,$$

then $\sum\limits_{n=1}^{\infty} a_n$ converges.

(2) If there exists a sequence $\{b_n\}$ of positive numbers for which $\sum\limits_{n=1}^{\infty} \frac{1}{b_n}$ diverges and a positive integer N such that

$$b_n \left(\frac{a_n}{a_{n+1}} \right) - b_{n+1} \leq 0 \text{ for } n \geq N,$$

then $\sum\limits_{n=1}^{\infty} a_n$ diverges.

Proof: Suppose the hypothesis of (1) is satisfied. Then $a_n b_n - a_{n+1} b_{n+1} \geq r\, a_{n+1}$ for $n \geq N$, so

$$r\, a_{N+1} \leq a_N b_N - a_{N+1} b_{N+1}$$

$$r\, a_{N+2} \leq a_{N+1} b_{N+1} - a_{N+2} b_{N+2}$$

$$r\, a_{N+3} \leq a_{N+2} b_{N+2} - a_{N+3} b_{N+3}$$

$$\cdot$$
$$\cdot$$
$$\cdot$$

$$r\, a_n \leq a_{n-1} b_{n-1} - a_n b_n \; .$$

Adding,

$$r \sum_{i=N+1}^{n} a_i \leq a_N b_N - a_n b_n < a_N b_N \text{ since } a_n b_n > 0.$$

Since r is positive,

$$\sum_{i=N+1}^{n} a_i < \frac{a_N b_N}{r}$$

so

$$\sum_{i=1}^{n} a_i < \sum_{i=1}^{N} a_i + \frac{a_N b_N}{r} \text{ for all } n \geq N.$$

Since the right side of the last inequality is independent of n, the partial sums of $\sum_{i=1}^{\infty} a_i$ are bounded above, and the series converges by Theorem 7.9.

Suppose the hypothesis of (2) is satisfied. Then $a_n b_n \leq a_{n+1} b_{n+1}$ for $n \geq N$, so

$$a_N b_N \leq a_{N+1} b_{N+1} \leq a_{N+2} b_{N+2} \leq \cdot \cdot \cdot \leq a_n b_n$$

and therefore

$$\frac{a_N b_N}{b_n} \leq a_n \text{ for } n \geq N.$$

Since $\sum_{n=1}^{\infty} \frac{1}{b_n}$ diverges, $\sum_{n=1}^{\infty} \frac{a_N b_N}{b_n}$ diverges, and $\sum_{n=1}^{\infty} a_n$ diverges by Theorem 7.11. $\quad\square$

Part (1) of the theorem can be strengthened to include any series $\sum_{n=1}^{\infty} a_n$ whose terms are all non-zero, for the proof above is still valid if absolute values are introduced. Such an improvement cannot be made in (2). Since the sequence $\{b_n\}$ must be carefully chosen, Kummer's Test is not particularly easy to use (the special case below is a little better). Its principal importance is that several more usable tests can be derived from it.

Corollary: Suppose $\sum_{n=1}^{\infty} a_n$ is a series each term of which is positive. Suppose there exists a sequence $\{b_n\}$ of positive numbers such that $\left\{ b_n \left(\dfrac{a_n}{a_{n+1}} \right) - b_{n+1} \right\}$ converges to a number L.

(1) If $L > 0$, $\sum_{n=1}^{\infty} a_n$ converges.

(2) If $L < 0$, $\sum_{n=1}^{\infty} a_n$ diverges.

Proof: Left as an exercise.

Theorem 7.24 (Raabe's Test): Suppose $\sum_{n=1}^{\infty} a_n$ is a series each term of which is positive.

(1) If there exists a number $r > 1$ and a positive integer N such that $n \left(\dfrac{a_n}{a_{n+1}} - 1 \right) \geq r$ for all $n \geq N$, then $\sum_{n=1}^{\infty} a_n$ converges.

322

(2) If there exists a positive integer N
such that $n(\frac{a_n}{a_{n+1}} - 1) \leq 1$ for all $n \geq N$,
then $\sum_{n=1}^{\infty} a_n$ diverges.

Proof: Suppose the hypothesis of (1) is true.
For $n \geq N$

$$n(\frac{a_n}{a_{n+1}} - 1) \geq r$$

$$n \frac{a_n}{a_{n+1}} - n - 1 \geq r - 1$$

$$n \frac{a_n}{a_{n+1}} - (n + 1) \geq t \text{ where } t > 0.$$

Since the hypothesis of (1) in Kummer's Test is
satisfied with $b_n = n$, $\sum_{n=1}^{\infty} a_n$ converges.

Suppose the hypothesis of (2) is true. For
$n \geq N$

$$n(\frac{a_n}{a_{n+1}} - 1) \leq 1$$

$$n \frac{a_n}{a_{n+1}} - n - 1 \leq 0$$

$$n \frac{a_n}{a_{n+1}} - (n + 1) \leq 0.$$

The hypothesis of (2) in Kummer's Test is satis-
fied with $b_n = n$ (note that $\sum_{n=1}^{\infty} \frac{1}{n}$ diverges), so

323

$$\sum_{n=1}^{\infty} a_n \text{ diverges.}$$ □

Corollary: Suppose $\sum_{n=1}^{\infty} a_n$ is a series each term of which is positive, and suppose that $\left\{ n\left(\dfrac{a_n}{a_{n+1}} - 1\right) \right\}$ converges to a number L.

(1) If $L > 1$, $\sum_{n=1}^{\infty} a_n$ converges.

(2) If $L < 1$, $\sum_{n=1}^{\infty} a_n$ diverges.

Proof: Left as an exercise.

Example 17: It can easily be shown that the ratio test is inconclusive when applied to

$$\sum_{n=1}^{\infty} \frac{1 \cdot 3 \cdot 5 \cdots (2n - 1)}{2 \cdot 4 \cdot 6 \cdots (2n)} .$$

If a_n denotes the general term,

$$\frac{a_n}{a_{n+1}} = \frac{1 \cdot 3 \cdot 5 \cdots (2n - 1)}{2 \cdot 4 \cdot 6 \cdots (2n)} \cdot$$

$$\frac{2 \cdot 4 \cdot 6 \cdots (2n)(2n + 2)}{1 \cdot 3 \cdot 5 \cdots (2n - 1)(2n + 1)} = \frac{2n + 2}{2n + 1}$$

and

$$\frac{a_n}{a_{n+1}} - 1 = \frac{1}{2n + 1} \cdot$$

Since $\left\{n\left(\dfrac{1}{2n+1}\right)\right\}$ converges to $\dfrac{1}{2}$, the series diverges by (the corollary to) Raabe's Test.

We saw in Theorems 7.2 and 7.3 how infinite series behave with respect to addition, subtraction, and multiplication by a constant. So far nothing has been said about the multiplication of one series by another. The first problem is finding a suitable definition for such a product. There are several possibilities, but we will consider only one, the Cauchy Product. For convenience in future work the index will begin with zero on all summations involving products.

Definition 7.25: The product of two series $\sum\limits_{n=0}^{\infty} a_n$ and $\sum\limits_{n=0}^{\infty} b_n$ is the series $\sum\limits_{n=0}^{\infty} c_n$, where

$$c_n = \sum_{i=0}^{n} a_i b_{n-i}$$

for each non-negative integer n.

Theorem 7.26: If $\sum\limits_{n=0}^{\infty} a_n$ and $\sum\limits_{n=0}^{\infty} b_n$ are any two series, $\left(\sum\limits_{n=0}^{\infty} a_n\right)\left(\sum\limits_{n=0}^{\infty} b_n\right) = \left(\sum\limits_{n=0}^{\infty} b_n\right)\left(\sum\limits_{n=0}^{\infty} a_n\right)$.

Proof: Let

$$\left(\sum_{n=0}^{\infty} a_n\right)\left(\sum_{n=0}^{\infty} b_n\right) = \sum_{n=0}^{\infty} c_n$$

and

$$\left(\sum_{n=0}^{\infty} b_n\right)\left(\sum_{n=0}^{\infty} a_n\right) = \sum_{n=0}^{\infty} d_n \ .$$

325

By definition, for each non-negative integer n,

$$c_n = \sum_{i=0}^{n} a_i b_{n-i} = a_0 b_n + a_1 b_{n-1}$$

$$+ \ldots + a_{n-1} b_1 + a_n b_0$$

and

$$d_n = \sum_{i=0}^{n} b_i a_{n-i} = b_0 a_n + b_1 a_{n-1}$$

$$+ \ldots + b_{n-1} a_1 + b_n a_0 . \qquad \square$$

Multiplication of polynomials is the motivation for Definition 7.25. When it comes time to consider the product of two power series, it will be evident that this is the only reasonable definition. The following is an example of the multiplication of series, but don't expect the product to be as simple in every case.

<u>Example 18</u>: Suppose we want to multiply $\sum_{n=0}^{\infty} \dfrac{1}{2^n}$

by itself. Then $a_n = \dfrac{1}{2^n} = b_n$, and $c_n = \sum_{i=0}^{n} a_i b_{n-i}$

$= \sum_{i=0}^{n} \dfrac{1}{2^i} \cdot \dfrac{1}{2^{n-i}} = \sum_{i=0}^{n} \dfrac{1}{2^n} = \dfrac{n+1}{2^n}$. Consequently

$$\left(\sum_{n=0}^{\infty} \dfrac{1}{2^n} \right) \left(\sum_{n=0}^{\infty} \dfrac{1}{2^n} \right) = \sum_{n=0}^{\infty} c_n = \sum_{n=0}^{\infty} \dfrac{n+1}{2^n} .$$

It's natural to ask if the product of two convergent series is always convergent. The following example, due to Cauchy, answers this question in the negative.

Example 19: Let $\sum_{n=0}^{\infty} a_n = \sum_{n=0}^{\infty} \frac{(-1)^n}{\sqrt{n+1}} = \sum_{n=0}^{\infty} b_n$.
Convergence of this series is easily established
by the alternating series test. If $\left(\sum_{n=0}^{\infty} a_n\right)\left(\sum_{n=0}^{\infty} b_n\right)$
$= \sum_{n=0}^{\infty} c_n$, then, for each non-negative integer n,

$$c_n = \sum_{i=0}^{n} a_i b_{n-i} = \sum_{i=0}^{n} \frac{(-1)^i}{\sqrt{i+1}} \cdot \frac{(-1)^{n-i}}{\sqrt{n-i+1}}$$

$$= \sum_{i=0}^{n} \frac{(-1)^n}{\sqrt{(i+1)(n-i+1)}}$$

$$= (-1)^n \sum_{i=0}^{n} \frac{1}{\sqrt{(i+1)(n-i+1)}} .$$

In the summation for c_n we have $0 \leq i \leq n$ so that
$1 \leq i+1 \leq n+1$. Since $0 \geq -i \geq -n$, $n+1 \geq$
$n - i + 1 \geq 1$. Therefore

$$|c_n| \geq \sum_{i=0}^{n} \frac{1}{\sqrt{(n+1)(n+1)}} = (n+1)\frac{1}{\sqrt{(n+1)^2}} = 1.$$

It follows that $\sum_{n=0}^{\infty} c_n$ diverges by the nth term
test.

What condition or conditions should be imposed
on two convergent series to insure that their product is convergent? The most useful answer to
this question was given in 1875 by Franz Mertens.

327

Theorem 7.27: If $\sum\limits_{n=0}^{\infty} a_n$ converges absolutely to A and $\sum\limits_{n=0}^{\infty} b_n$ converges to B, their product series $\sum\limits_{n=0}^{\infty} c_n$ converges to AB.

Proof: For each non-negative integer n let

$$A_n = \sum_{i=0}^{n} a_i \qquad B_n = \sum_{i=0}^{n} b_i \qquad C_n = \sum_{i=0}^{n} c_i .$$

Also let $S = \sum\limits_{i=0}^{\infty} |a_i|$. If $S = 0$ the conclusion is obvious, so suppose $S \neq 0$. We will show that the sequence $\{C_n\}$ converges to AB. For each non-negative integer n,

$$C_n = c_0 + c_1 + \ldots + c_n = \sum_{k=0}^{n} c_k$$

$$= \sum_{k=0}^{n} \left(\sum_{i=0}^{k} a_i b_{k-i} \right)$$

$$= (a_0 b_0) + (a_0 b_1 + a_1 b_0) + (a_0 b_2 + a_1 b_1 + a_2 b_0)$$

$$+ \ldots + (a_0 b_n + a_1 b_{n-1} + \ldots + a_n b_0)$$

$$= a_0 (b_0 + b_1 + b_2 + \ldots + b_n)$$

$$+ a_1 (b_0 + b_1 + \ldots + b_{n-1})$$

328

$$+ \ldots + a_{n-1}(b_0 + b_1) + a_n(b_0)$$

$$= a_0 B_n + a_1 B_{n-1} + a_2 B_{n-2} + \ldots + a_{n-1}B_1 + a_n B_0$$

$$= a_0[B + (B_n - B)] + a_1[B + (B_{n-1} - B)]$$

$$+ \ldots + a_{n-1}[B + (B_1 - B)] + a_n[B + (B_0 - B)]$$

$$= B(a_0 + a_1 + \ldots + a_{n-1} + a_n) + a_0(B_n - B)$$

$$+ a_1(B_{n-1} - B) + \ldots + a_n(B_0 - B)$$

$$= BA_n + t_n$$

where $t_n = a_0(B_n - B) + a_1(B_{n-1} - B) + \ldots + a_n(B_0 - B)$. The theorem will be proved if it can be shown that $\{t_n\}$ is a null sequence, since $\{C_n\} = B\{A_n\} + \{t_n\}$ and $\{A_n\}$ converges to A. Examination of the expression for t_n should indicate a way of doing this. See if you can complete the proof before reading on.

Suppose ε is any positive number. The sequence $\{B_n - B\}$ is convergent, therefore bounded, so there is a positive number M such that for every non-negative integer n

$$|B_n - B| \leq M.$$

Since $\{B_n - B\}$ is a null sequence, there is a positive integer N_1 such that

$$|B_n - B| < \frac{\varepsilon}{2S} \text{ for } n \geq N_1.$$

Since $\sum\limits_{n=0}^{\infty} a_n$ converges absolutely, there is by the Cauchy Criterion a positive integer N_2 such that

$$\sum_{i=k}^{j} |a_i| < \frac{\varepsilon}{2M} \text{ for } j > k \geq N_2.$$

Let N be the larger of N_1 and N_2, and consider any integer $n \geq 2N$. Then

$$|t_n| \leq \sum_{i=0}^{n} |a_i||B_{n-i} - B|$$

$$= \sum_{i=0}^{N} |a_i||B_{n-i} - B|$$

$$+ \sum_{i=N+1}^{n} |a_i||B_{n-i} - B|.$$

Note that in the first summation $n - i \geq N$ since $i \leq N$ and $n \geq 2N$. Therefore

$$|t_n| < \frac{\varepsilon}{2S} \sum_{i=0}^{N} |a_i| + M \sum_{i=N+1}^{n} |a_i|$$

$$< \frac{\varepsilon}{2S} (S) + M(\frac{\varepsilon}{2M}) = \varepsilon$$

and the proof is complete. □

Theorem 7.28: If $\sum\limits_{n=0}^{\infty} a_n$ converges absolutely to A and $\sum\limits_{n=0}^{\infty} b_n$ converges absolutely to B, their product series $\sum\limits_{n=0}^{\infty} c_n$ converges absolutely to AB.

Proof: Left as an exercise.

Exercise 7.2

1. Prove the corollary to Theorem 7.21.

2. Prove the corollary to Theorem 7.22.

3. Give an example of a divergent series $\sum\limits_{n=1}^{\infty} a_n$ such that $\left| \dfrac{a_{n+1}}{a_n} \right| < 1$ for every positive integer n.

*4. Show that $\sum\limits_{n=1}^{\infty} \dfrac{c^n}{n!}$ converges for every number c and deduce that $\left\{ \dfrac{c^n}{n!} \right\}$ is a null sequence.

5. Show that the series $\dfrac{1}{2} + \dfrac{1}{3} + \dfrac{1}{2^2} + \dfrac{1}{3^2} + \dfrac{1}{2^3} + \dfrac{1}{3^3} + \ldots$ converges by the root test after showing that the ratio test is inconclusive.

6. (a) Find a convergent series $\sum\limits_{n=1}^{\infty} a_n$ such that $\{ \sqrt[n]{a_n} \}$ converges to 1.

   (b) Find a divergent series $\sum\limits_{n=1}^{\infty} a_n$ such that $\{ \sqrt[n]{a_n} \}$ converges to 1.

7. Prove or disprove: if $\sum\limits_{n=1}^{\infty} a_n$ is a series of positive terms for which $\left\{ \dfrac{a_{n+1}}{a_n} \right\}$ is unbounded, then $\sum\limits_{n=1}^{\infty} a_n$ diverges.

8. Prove that if $\sum\limits_{n=1}^{\infty} a_n$ converges absolutely and $\{b_n\}$ is bounded, then $\sum\limits_{n=1}^{\infty} a_n b_n$ converges absolutely.

9. Give an example of a convergent series $\sum\limits_{n=1}^{\infty} a_n$ such that $\sum\limits_{n=1}^{\infty} a_n^2$ diverges.

10. Show that if $\sum\limits_{n=1}^{\infty} a_n$ converges absolutely, then $\left| \sum\limits_{n=1}^{\infty} a_n \right| \le \sum\limits_{n=1}^{\infty} |a_n|$.

11. Prove the corollary to Theorem 7.23.

12. Prove the corollary to Theorem 7.24.

13. Find the sum of $\sum\limits_{n=1}^{\infty} (-1)^{n+1} \dfrac{1}{(2n-1)!}$ correct to three decimal places.

In Problems 14 through 23 determine convergence or divergence of the given series.

14. $\sum\limits_{n=1}^{\infty} \dfrac{(n!)^2}{(2n)!}$

15. $\sum\limits_{n=1}^{\infty} \dfrac{1}{n \sqrt[n]{n}}$

16. $\sum\limits_{n=1}^{\infty} (-1)^{n+1} \dfrac{(\ln n)^2}{n}$

17. $\sum\limits_{n=1}^{\infty} (-1)^{n+1} \dfrac{n}{2n-1}$

18. $\sum\limits_{n=1}^{\infty} (\dfrac{n}{n+1})^{n^2}$

19. $\sum\limits_{n=1}^{\infty} \sin \dfrac{1}{n}$

20. $\sum\limits_{n=1}^{\infty} (\sqrt[n]{n} - 1)$

21. $\sum\limits_{n=1}^{\infty} (1 - \dfrac{\ln n}{n})^n$

333

22. $\displaystyle\sum_{n=1}^{\infty} \frac{1 \cdot 3 \cdot 5 \cdots (2n - 1)}{2 \cdot 4 \cdot 6 \cdots (2n)} \cdot \frac{1}{2n + 1}$

23. $1 + \dfrac{1}{2} - \dfrac{1}{3} + \dfrac{1}{4} + \dfrac{1}{5} - \dfrac{1}{6} + \dfrac{1}{7} + \dfrac{1}{8} - \dfrac{1}{9} + \cdots$

*24. If r is a number satisfying $|r| < 1$, show that $\{nr^n\}$ is a null sequence.

25. Prove Theorem 7.28.

26. Prove or disprove: if $\displaystyle\sum_{n=1}^{\infty} a_n$ is a convergent series each term of which is non-zero, then $\displaystyle\sum_{n=1}^{\infty} \frac{1}{|a_n|}$ diverges.

27. Suppose the hypothesis of the alternating series test is satisfied. Show that for all $n \geq N$

$$\left| \sum_{i=1}^{\infty} (-1)^{i+1} a_i - \left[\frac{1}{2}(-1)^{n+1} a_{n+1} + \sum_{i=1}^{n} (-1)^{i+1} a_i \right] \right|$$

$$< \frac{1}{2} a_{n+1} ,$$

an improvement on the approximation given in that theorem.

28. Show that both of the series $2 + 2 + 4 + 8 + 16 + 32 + \ldots$ and $-1 + 1 + 1 + 1 + 1 + 1 \ldots$ diverge, but their Cauchy Product converges.

29. Find, in simplest possible form, the Cauchy Product of $\displaystyle\sum_{n=0}^{\infty} \frac{1}{n!}$ with itself.

30. Prove the Cauchy-Schwarz Inequality for Series.

If $\sum\limits_{n=1}^{\infty} a_n^2$ and $\sum\limits_{n=1}^{\infty} b_n^2$ both converge, then

$\sum\limits_{n=1}^{\infty} a_n b_n$ converges absolutely, and

$$\left(\sum_{n=1}^{\infty} a_n b_n\right)^2 \leq \left(\sum_{n=1}^{\infty} a_n^2\right)\left(\sum_{n=1}^{\infty} b_n^2\right).$$

31. Prove the <u>Minkowski Inequality for Series</u>.
If $\sum\limits_{n=1}^{\infty} a_n^2$ and $\sum\limits_{n=1}^{\infty} b_n^2$ both converge, then

$\sum\limits_{n=1}^{\infty} (a_n + b_n)^2$ converges, and

$$\sqrt{\sum_{n=1}^{\infty} (a_b + b_n)^2} \leq \sqrt{\sum_{n=1}^{\infty} a_n^2} + \sqrt{\sum_{n=1}^{\infty} b_n^2}\,.$$

32. Prove that if $\sum\limits_{n=1}^{\infty} a_n^2$ converges, then $\sum\limits_{n=1}^{\infty} \dfrac{a_n}{n}$ converges absolutely.

*33. If $\sum\limits_{n=1}^{\infty} a_n$ is any convergent series, suppose there exists a positive integer N and a positive number r such that $\left|\dfrac{a_{n+1}}{a_n}\right| \leq r < 1$ for all $n \geq N$. Show that the error made in approximating the sum of the series by the nth partial sum ($n \geq N$) is less than $\dfrac{|a_n|r}{1 - r}$.

34. Establish <u>Gauss's Test</u>. Suppose $\sum\limits_{n=1}^{\infty} a_n$ is a series each term of which is positive. Suppose there exists a number r and, for each positive integer n, a number A_n such that

$$\frac{a_n}{a_{n+1}} = 1 + \frac{r}{n} + \frac{A_n}{n^2} .$$

If $\{A_n\}$ is bounded, then $\sum\limits_{n=1}^{\infty} a_n$ converges if $r > 1$ and diverges if $r \leq 1$.

Chapter 8

1. Sequences and Series of Functions; Pointwise and Uniform Convergence

The study of infinite series reaches its full fruition when elements of the series are allowed to be functions, rather than numbers. Most of our attention will be focused on power series, but first we consider some important general results concerning sequences of functions.

Definition 8.1: Suppose S is a set of numbers, and the domain of each of the functions f_1, f_2, . . . , f_n, . . . includes S. If for every x in S the sequence of numbers $\{f_n(x)\}$ converges, then the sequence of functions $\{f_n\}$ is said to converge pointwise on S.

If the above condition holds, then to each number x in S there corresponds a unique number, namely the limit of the sequence $\{f_n(x)\}$. Thus, a function is defined on S, and we introduce the following terminology.

Definition 8.2: If the sequence of functions $\{f_n\}$ converges pointwise on S, the limit function of $\{f_n\}$ is the function f defined by

$$f(x) = \lim_{n \to \infty} f_n(x), \quad x \text{ in } S.$$

Example 1: Consider the sequence $\{f_n\}$ where $f_n(x) = \dfrac{nx}{1 + n^2x^2}$ for each x in $[-2,2]$. Clearly

337

$f_n(0) = 0$ for every positive integer n. For each $x \neq 0$ and for every n

$$f_n(x) = \frac{\dfrac{x}{n}}{\dfrac{1}{n^2} + x^2}$$

so

$$\lim_{n \to \infty} f_n(x) = \frac{0}{x^2} = 0.$$

Therefore $\{f_n\}$ converges pointwise on $[-2,2]$, and the limit function f is given by $f(x) = 0$.

Example 2: Consider the sequence $\{f_n\}$ where $f_n(x) = \dfrac{x^n}{1 + x}$ for each x in $[1,2]$. For every positive integer n, $f_n(1) = \dfrac{1}{1 + 1} = \dfrac{1}{2}$. For x satisfying $1 < x \leq 2$, however, $\dfrac{x^n}{1 + x}$ does not converge. Therefore $\{f_n\}$ does not converge pointwise on $[1,2]$.

Suppose a sequence of functions $\{f_n\}$ converges pointwise on a set S. If all functions of the sequence have a certain property (continuity, integrability, differentiability, say), it's natural to ask if the limit function "inherits" this common property. Consider the following examples.

Example 3: Define a sequence $\{f_n\}$ by $f_n(x) = x^n$ for each x in $[0,1]$. Certainly $f_n(1) = 1$ and $f_n(0) = 0$ for every positive integer n. If x is any number satisfying $0 < x < 1$,

338

$$\lim_{n \to \infty} f_n(x) = 0.$$

Therefore $\{f_n\}$ converges pointwise on $[0,1]$, and the limit function f is given by

$$f(x) = \begin{cases} 0 & \text{if } 0 \le x < 1 \\ 1 & \text{if } x = 1 \end{cases}.$$

Here is a simple example of a pointwise convergent sequence of continuous functions whose limit function is not continuous. The first four functions of the sequence are shown in Figure 8.1.

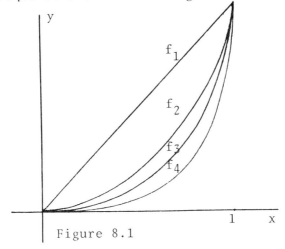

Figure 8.1

Example 4: Define a sequence $\{f_n\}$ by

$$f_n(x) = \begin{cases} nx & \text{if } 0 \le x \le \dfrac{1}{\sqrt{n}} \\ \dfrac{1}{x} & \text{if } \dfrac{1}{\sqrt{n}} < x \le 2 \end{cases}.$$

339

Of course $f_n(0) = 0$ for every positive integer n. For all x satisfying $0 < x \leq 2$, $f_n(x) = \frac{1}{x}$ for all but finitely many integers n. Therefore $\{f_n\}$ converges pointwise on $[0,2]$, and the limit function f is given by

$$f(x) = \begin{cases} \dfrac{1}{x} & \text{if } 0 < x \leq 2 \\[2mm] 0 & \text{if } x = 0 \end{cases}.$$

Although each function in the sequence is integrable, the limit function is unbounded and therefore not integrable. See Figure 8.2.

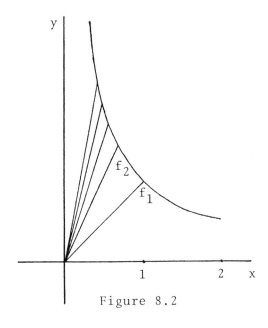

Figure 8.2

As might be expected, the situation with respect to differentiation is just as bad. In Example 3 all the functions are differentiable on [0,1], but the limit function is not differentiable on the entire interval since it is not continuous. Clearly it's necessary to impose additional conditions on a pointwise convergent sequence of functions in order that any common property carry over to the limit function. The crucial condition in this investigation is the one described below.

Definition 8.3: We say that the sequence of functions $\{f_n\}$ converges uniformly on S to a limit function f provided the following is true:

> if ε is any positive number, there exists a positive integer N such that for every integer $n \geq N$ and for every number x in S
>
> $$|f_n(x) - f(x)| < \varepsilon.$$

For brevity the phrase "$\{f_n\}$ converges uniformly on S" will mean that there exists a function f such that $\{f_n\}$ converges uniformly on S to f.

To say that $\{f_n\}$ converges pointwise to f on S means that for each x in S, $\{f_n(x)\}$ converges to $f(x)$. That is, for each $\varepsilon > 0$ a positive integer N exists such that $|f_n(x) - f(x)| < \varepsilon$ for all $n \geq N$ for that particular x. It may very well happen that different x's require different N's for the same ε. In the case of uniform convergence, for each ε there is an N that "works" for every x in S. A geometric interpretation of uniform convergence is given in Figure 8.3 for the case in which S is an interval $[a,b]$.

341

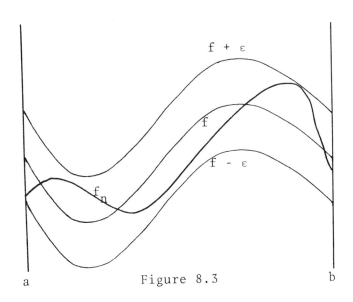

a   Figure 8.3   b

Example 5: Define $\{f_n\}$ on the set S of all non-negative numbers by $f_n(x) = \dfrac{nx}{nx + 1}$. Now $f_n(0) = 0$ for every positive integer n, and for $x > 0$,

$$\lim_{n\to\infty} f_n(x) = \lim_{n\to\infty} \frac{x}{x + \frac{1}{n}} = 1.$$

Hence $\{f_n\}$ converges on S to a function f given by

$$f(x) = \begin{cases} 0 \text{ if } x = 0 \\ 1 \text{ if } x > 0 \end{cases}.$$

We ask now if the convergence is uniform or just pointwise. Suppose ε is a positive number less than 1. If the convergence is uniform, there must exist a positive integer N such that

342

$|f_n(x) - f(x)| < \varepsilon$ for all $n \geq N$ and for all x in S. Since the inequality must hold for $n = N$,

$$\left|\frac{Nx}{Nx + 1} - 1\right| < \varepsilon \quad \text{for all } x > 0.$$

Therefore $\quad \dfrac{1}{Nx + 1} < \varepsilon, \; x > 0$

and consequently

$$\frac{1 - \varepsilon}{x\varepsilon} < N, \; x > 0.$$

The last inequality cannot possibly be true for all x in S since the left side can be made as large as desired by choosing x close enough to zero. Hence the convergence is not uniform.

<u>Theorem 8.4</u>: Suppose $\{f_n\}$ converges uniformly to f on a set S. If a is a point in S at which every f_n is continuous, then f is continuous at a.

<u>Proof</u>: Suppose ε is any positive number. There exists a positive integer N such that $|f_n(x) - f(x)| < \frac{\varepsilon}{3}$ for all $n \geq N$ and every x in S. In particular, $|f_N(x) - f(x)| < \frac{\varepsilon}{3}$ for every x in S. Since f_N is continuous at a, there is a positive number δ such that for every x in S satisfying $|x - a| < \delta$ we have $|f_N(x) - f_N(a)| < \frac{\varepsilon}{3}$. For all x in S satisfying $|x - a| < \delta$, therefore,

$$|f(x) - f(a)| \leq |f(x) - f_N(x)|$$

$$+ |f_N(x) - f_N(a)|$$

$$+ \ |f_N(a) - f(a)|$$

$$< \ \frac{\varepsilon}{3} + \frac{\varepsilon}{3} + \frac{\varepsilon}{3}$$

$$= \ \varepsilon \, ,$$

where the first and third $\frac{\varepsilon}{3}$ come from uniform convergence, while the second is due to the continuity of f_N at a. $\qquad\qquad\qquad\qquad$ □

Corollary: If $\{f_n\}$ converges uniformly to f on S and every f_n is continuous on S, then f is continuous on S.

The contrapositive of Theorem 8.4 is sometimes used to show the lack of uniform convergence.

Corollary: Suppose $\{f_n\}$ converges to f on a set S, and every f_n is continuous on S. If f is not continuous, then the convergence is not uniform.

Example 6: Define $\{f_n\}$ on $[-1,1]$ by $f_n(x) = \dfrac{x^{2n}}{1 + x^{2n}}$.
For each positive integer n, $f_n(1) = \frac{1}{2}$ and $f_n(-1) = \frac{1}{2}$. For x satisfying $-1 < x < 1$, $\lim_{n \to \infty} f_n(x) = 0$. Hence $\{f_n\}$ converges on $[-1,1]$ to a function f given by

$$f(x) = \begin{cases} \frac{1}{2} & \text{if } x = \pm 1 \\ 0 & \text{if } -1 < x < 1 \end{cases} .$$

Each f_n is continuous since it is a rational function whose denominator cannot be zero. Since f
is not continuous, the convergence is not uniform.
(Note that if the domain were $(-1,1)$, the limit
function would be continuous and no conclusion
could be drawn about the type of convergence.)

Theorem 8.5: If $\{f_n\}$ converges uniformly to f on
$[a,b]$ and every f_n is integrable on $[a,b]$, then
f is integrable on $[a,b]$. If c is any number in
$[a,b]$, define a sequence $\{g_n\}$ by

$$g_n(x) = \int_c^x f_n(t)dt, \quad x \text{ in } [a,b]$$

and define a function g on $[a,b]$ by $g(x) = \int_c^x f(t)dt$.
Then $\{g_n\}$ converges uniformly to g on $[a,b]$.
That is,

$$\lim_{n\to\infty} \int_c^x f_n(t)dt = \int_c^x \lim_{n\to\infty} f_n(t)dt.$$

Proof: It follows from Problem 13 of the exercises that f is bounded on $[a,b]$. Suppose ε is
any positive number. Since $\{f_n\}$ converges to f
uniformly, there exists a positive integer N such
that for all $n \geq N$ and for every x in $[a,b]$,
$|f_n(x) - f(x)| < \dfrac{\varepsilon}{3(b-a)}$. In particular,

$$(1) \quad f_N(x) - \frac{\varepsilon}{3(b-a)} < f(x)$$

$$< f_N(x) + \frac{\varepsilon}{3(b-a)}$$

345

for every x in [a,b]. Since f_N is integrable on [a,b], there is a partition $P = \{a = x_0, x_1, x_2, \ldots, x_n = b\}$ such that

$$(2) \quad U(f_N,P) - L(f_N,P) < \frac{\varepsilon}{3} .$$

Denote by M_i and M_i' the least upper bounds of f_N and f, respectively, on $[x_{i-1}, x_i]$. Denote by m_i and m_i' the greatest lower bounds of f_N and f, respectively, on $[x_{i-1}, x_i]$. From (1) we find that

$$U(f,P) = \sum_{i=1}^{n} M_i'(x_i - x_{i-1})$$

$$< \sum_{i=1}^{n} [M_i + \frac{\varepsilon}{3(b-a)}](x_i - x_{i-1})$$

$$= U(f_N,P) + \frac{\varepsilon}{3}$$

and

$$L(f,P) = \sum_{i=1}^{n} m_i'(x_i - x_{i-1})$$

$$> \sum_{i=1}^{n} (m_i - \frac{\varepsilon}{3(b-a)}](x_i - x_{i-1})$$

$$= L(f_N,P) - \frac{\varepsilon}{3} .$$

Hence

$$U(f,P) - L(f,P) < U(f_N,P) + \frac{\varepsilon}{3} - L(f_N,P) + \frac{\varepsilon}{3} < \varepsilon$$

by (2).

Therefore f is integrable on [a,b] by Theorem 6.9.
To prove the rest of the theorem we again suppose
that ε is any positive number. There is a posi-
tive integer N such that $|f_n(x) - f(x)| < \frac{\varepsilon}{b - a}$
for all n > N and for all x in [a,b]. Therefore
for all n ≥ N and for all x in [a,b]

$$|g_n(x) - g(x)| = |\int_c^x f_n(t)\,dt - \int_c^x f(t)\,dt|$$

$$= |\int_c^x [f_n(t) - f(t)]\,dt|$$

$$\leq \int_c^x |f_n(t) - f(t)|\,dt$$

$$< \frac{\varepsilon}{b - a}|x - c|$$

$$\leq \frac{\varepsilon}{b - a}(b - a)$$

$$= \varepsilon$$

so $\{g_n\}$ converges uniformly to g on [a,b].   □

Theorem 8.5 provides a condition under which
the integration and limit operations can be inter-
changed. We next seek conditions which allow
interchange of the differentiation and limit operations. Since differentiation is a "stronger"
condition than integration, more stringent conditions should be expected.

Theorem 8.6: Suppose $\{f_n\}$ is a sequence of functions each of which is differentiable on [a,b],
and each of the functions f_n' is continuous on
[a,b]. Suppose $\{f_n'\}$ converges uniformly on [a,b]

347

to a function g, and suppose also that there exists a number c in [a,b] such that $\{f_n(c)\}$ converges. Then $\{f_n\}$ converges uniformly on [a,b] to a function f, f is differentiable, and for every x in [a,b] $g(x) = f'(x)$, that is,

$$\lim_{n\to\infty} f_n'(x) = (\lim_{n\to\infty} f_n(x))'.$$

Proof*: For every positive integer n, f_n' is continuous and therefore integrable on [a,b]. By Theorem 6.26, for every x in [a,b]

$$(1) \qquad \int_c^x f_n'(t)dt = f_n(x) - f_n(c).$$

Since $\{f_n'\}$ is a uniformly convergent sequence of continuous functions on [a,b], the limit function g is continuous and therefore integrable on [a,b]. By the previous theorem

$$\lim_{n\to\infty} \int_c^x f_n'(t)dt = \int_c^x \lim_{n\to\infty} f_n'(t)dt = \int_c^x g(t)dt$$

for every number x in [a,b]. From (1), then,

$$(2) \qquad \lim_{n\to\infty}[f_n(x) - f_n(c)] = \int_c^x g(t)dt.$$

Since $\{f_n(c)\}$ converges, it follows that $\{f_n(x)\}$ converges for every x in [a,b]. Let f denote the limit function of $\{f_n\}$. Then

$$f(x) = \lim_{n\to\infty} f_n(x), \quad x \text{ in } [a,b]$$

*The same conclusion can be reached without requiring continuity of the derivatives, but the proof is more difficult.

and, by (2), $f(x) - f(c) = \int_c^x g(t)dt$

for every x in [a,b]. Since g is continuous, we know by the corollary to Theorem 6.24 that the indefinite integral $\int_c^x g(t)dt$ is differentiable with derivative g(x). Therefore f(x) - f(c) is differentiable and f'(x) = g(x) for every x in [a,b]. It remains only to show that the convergence of $\{f_n\}$ to f is uniform. Suppose ε is any positive number. Since $\{f_n'\}$ converges uniformly to g on [a,b] and since g = f', there exists a positive integer N_1 such that

$$|f_n'(x) - f'(x)| < \frac{\varepsilon}{2(b - a)}$$

for all $n \geq N_1$ and all x in [a,b]. Since $\{f_n(c)\}$ converges to f(c), there is a positive integer N_2 such that

$$|f_n(c) - f(c)| < \frac{\varepsilon}{2}$$

for all $n \geq N_2$. Let N be the larger of N_1 and N_2. For all $n \geq N$ and for every x in [a,b] we have

$$|f_n(x) - f(x)| = |\int_c^x f_n'(t)dt - \int_c^x f'(t)dt$$

$$+ f_n(c) - f(c)|$$

$$= |\int_c^x [f_n'(t) - f'(t)]dt$$

$$+ [f_n(c) - f(c)]|$$

$$\leq \int_c^x |f_n'(t) - f'(t)|dt$$

349

$$+ \ |f_n(c) - f(c)|$$

$$< \ \frac{\varepsilon}{2(b - a)}|x - c| + \frac{\varepsilon}{2}$$

$$\leq \ \varepsilon \text{ since } |x - c| \leq b - a.$$

Therefore $\{f_n\}$ converges uniformly to f on [a,b]. □

The following theorem is often useful in investigating uniform convergence of a sequence of functions.

Theorem 8.7: Suppose that the sequence of continuous functions $\{f_n\}$ converges pointwise to the continuous function f on a compact set D. If $\{t_n\}$ is defined by

$$t_n = \max \ \{|f_n(x) - f(x)|: \ x \ \varepsilon \ D\},$$

then the convergence is uniform if and only if $\{t_n\}$ is a null sequence.

Proof: Suppose the convergence is uniform. We know that t_n exists for each n since f_n - f is continuous on a compact set. Moreover, there exists a number x_n in D such that $t_n = |f_n(x_n) - f(x_n)|$. If ε is any positive number, there exists a positive integer N such that $|f_n(x) - f(x)| < \varepsilon$ for all $n \geq N$ and every x in D. For $n \geq N$, therefore,

$$|t_n| = t_n = |f_n(x_n) - f(x_n)| < \varepsilon$$

350

and consequently $\{t_n\}$ converges to zero. Suppose, on the other hand, that $\{t_n\}$ is a null sequence. If ε is any positive number, there is a positive integer N such that $t_n < \varepsilon$ for all $n \geq N$. Hence

$$|f_n(x) - f(x)| \leq t_n < \varepsilon$$

for $n \geq N$ and every x in D, and the definition of uniform convergence is satisfied. $\quad\Box$

Example 7: Consider the sequence $\{f_n\}$ where $f_n(x) = \dfrac{nx}{e^{nx}}$ for all x in $[0,2]$. It is not hard to show that $\{f_n\}$ converges pointwise to f on $[0,2]$, where $f(x) = 0$. Differentiating, we find that

$$f_n'(x) = \frac{n - n^2 x}{e^{nx}}$$

for each n and all x in $[0,2]$. If $f_n'(x) = 0$, then $n(1 - nx) = 0$, so $x = \dfrac{1}{n}$. It follows that f_n is increasing on $[0,\dfrac{1}{n}]$ and decreasing on $[\dfrac{1}{n},2]$. Hence f_n has its maximum value at $\dfrac{1}{n}$, and this value is $f_n(\dfrac{1}{n}) = \dfrac{1}{e}$. Moreover, $t_n = \max \{|f_n(x) - f(x)| : x \text{ in } [0,2]\} = \dfrac{1}{e}$. Since $\{t_n\}$ is not a null sequence, the convergence is not uniform.

So far in this chapter we have established several important results concerning sequences of functions. Our ultimate goal, however, is series of functions. From our work in Chapter 7 we know that a series can be studied by means of its sequence of partial sums. After the appropriate terminology has been introduced, we have only to interpret each theorem concerning a sequence of functions as a statement about the sequence of

351

partial sums of a certain series of functions. Most of the work, in other words, has already been done.

Definition 8.8: Suppose S is a set of numbers, and the domain of each of the functions f_1, f_2, . . . , f_n, . . . includes S. The series of functions $\sum_{n=1}^{\infty} f_n$ has as its sequence of partial sums $\{s_n\}$, where s_n is defined for each positive integer n by $s_n = \sum_{i=1}^{n} f_i$. We say that $\sum_{n=1}^{\infty} f_n$ converges pointwise on S provided $\{s_n\}$ converges pointwise on S. We say that $\sum_{n=1}^{\infty} f_n$ converges uniformly on S provided $\{s_n\}$ converges uniformly on S. If $\{s_n\}$ converges (pointwise or uniformly) to a function s, then s is called the sum function of $\sum_{n=1}^{\infty} f_n$, and we write $\sum_{n=1}^{\infty} f_n = s$.

Example 8: Consider the series $\sum_{n=1}^{\infty} f_n$, where $f_n(x) = \dfrac{x}{(x + 1)^n}$ for each x in $[0,2]$. If $s_n = \sum_{i=1}^{n} f_i$ for each positive integer n, we can use the formula for adding terms of a geometric progression to show that

$$s_n(x) = 1 - \frac{1}{(x + 1)^n} \, .$$

For every positive integer n, $s_n(0) = 0$. For all x satisfying $0 < x \le 2$, $\lim_{n \to \infty} s_n(x) = 1$. Hence

352

$$\sum_{n=1}^{\infty} f_n = s, \text{ where}$$

$$s(x) = \begin{cases} 0 \text{ if } x = 0 \\ 1 \text{ if } 0 < x \le 2 \end{cases}.$$

For most series of functions an explicit formula for the sequence of partial sums is impossible. In many cases, however, finding the sum function is not as important as determining the nature of the convergence.

Theorem 8.9: Suppose $\sum_{n=1}^{\infty} f_n$ converges uniformly to s on a set S. If a is a point in S at which every f_n is continuous, then s is continuous at a.

Proof: If for each positive integer n, $s_n = \sum_{i=1}^{n} f_i$, then $\{s_n\}$ converges uniformly to s by hypothesis. By Theorem 4.8 every s_n is continuous at a, and therefore s is continuous at a by Theorem 8.4. $\square$

Corollary: If $\sum_{n=1}^{\infty} f_n$ converges uniformly to s on S, and every f_n is continuous on S, then s is continuous on S.

Corollary: Suppose $\sum_{n=1}^{\infty} f_n$ converges to s on a set S, and every f_n is continuous on S. If s is not continuous, then the convergence is not uniform.

Theorem 8.10: If $\sum_{n=1}^{\infty} f_n$ converges uniformly to s on [a,b] and every f_n is integrable on [a,b], then s is integrable on [a,b]. If c is any number in [a,b], define a sequence $\{g_n\}$ by

$$g_n(x) = \sum_{i=1}^{n} \int_c^x f_i(t)dt, \quad x \text{ in } [a,b]$$

and define a function g on [a,b] by $g(x) = \int_c^x s(t)dt$. Then $\{g_n\}$ converges uniformly to g on [a,b]. That is,

$$\lim_{n \to \infty} \sum_{i=1}^{n} \int_c^x f_i(t)dt = \int_c^x \lim_{n \to \infty} \sum_{i=1}^{n} f_i,$$

which is to say

$$\sum_{n=1}^{\infty} \int_c^x f_n(t)dt = \int_c^x \sum_{n=1}^{\infty} f_n.$$

Proof: Left as an exercise.

This last result is referred to as the theorem on "term-by-term integration." Its proof is immediate from Theorem 8.5. The next result, easily proved by Theorem 8.6, is the companion theorem on "term-by-term differentiation."

Theorem 8.11: Suppose $\sum_{n=1}^{\infty} f_n$ is a series of functions each of which is differentiable on [a,b], and each of the functions f_n' is continuous on [a,b]. Suppose that $\sum_{n=1}^{\infty} f_n'$ converges uniformly on [a,b] to a function t, and suppose also that there exists a number c in [a,b] such that $\sum_{n=1}^{\infty} f_n(c)$ converges. Then $\sum_{n=1}^{\infty} f_n$ converges

354

uniformly on [a,b] to a function s, s is differentiable, and for every x in [a,b] t(x) = s'(x), that is,

$$\lim_{n\to\infty} \sum_{i=1}^{n} f_i'(x) = (\lim_{n\to\infty} \sum_{i=1}^{n} f_i(x))',$$

which is to say

$$\sum_{n=1}^{\infty} f_n'(x) = (\sum_{n=1}^{\infty} f_n(x))'.$$

Proof: Left as an exercise.

The last two theorems are of great importance in treating infinite series of functions. If both term-by-term integration and term-by-term differentiation are permitted, we can say a lot more about the series and its sum function than would otherwise be the case. It becomes desirable to have a simple condition indicating the presence of uniform convergence since this concept plays such a key role in the theory of series of functions. We will consider two theorems dealing with this question. The first is important for theoretical purposes while the second is useful in practice.

Theorem 8.12 (Cauchy Criterion for Series of Functions): The series of functions $\sum_{n=1}^{\infty} f_n$ converges uniformly on S if and only if the following condition is satisfied:

if ε is any positive number, there exists a positive integer N such that $|f_{n+1}(x) + f_{n+2}(x) + \ldots + f_{n+k}(x)| < \varepsilon$ for all $n \geq N$, every positive integer k, and every

355

x in S.

Proof: Left as an exercise.

Theorem 8.13 (Weierstrass M-Test): Suppose $\sum_{n=1}^{\infty} f_n$ is a series of functions each defined on the set S. If there exists a convergent series of non-negative numbers $\sum_{n=1}^{\infty} M_n$ such that for each positive integer n, $|f_n(x)| \leq M_n$ for all x in S, then $\sum_{n=1}^{\infty} f_n$ converges uniformly on S, and $\sum_{n=1}^{\infty} f_n(x)$ converges absolutely for every x in S.

Proof: Suppose x is any element of S. For each positive integer n, $|f_n(x)| \leq M_n$. Since $\sum_{n=1}^{\infty} M_n$ converges, $\sum_{n=1}^{\infty} |f_n(x)|$ converges by Theorem 7.10, so $\sum_{n=1}^{\infty} f_n(x)$ converges absolutely. Suppose now that ε is any positive number. Since $\sum_{n=1}^{\infty} M_n$ converges, there exists by Theorem 7.4 a positive integer N such that for all $n \geq N$ and for every positive integer k,

$$M_{n+1} + M_{n+2} + \ldots + M_{n+k}$$

$$= |M_{n+1} + M_{n+2} + \ldots + M_{n+k}| < \varepsilon.$$

If $n \geq N$, k is any positive integer, and x is any element of S, then

$$|f_{n+1}(x) + f_{n+2}(x) + \ldots + f_{n+k}(x)|$$

$$\leq |f_{n+1}(x)| + |f_{n+2}(x)| + \ldots + |f_{n+k}(x)|$$

$$\leq M_{n+1} + M_{n+2} + \ldots + M_{n+k}$$

$$< \varepsilon,$$

so $\sum\limits_{n=1}^{\infty} f_n$ converges uniformly on S by Theorem 8.12. $\qquad\qquad\qquad\qquad\qquad\qquad\qquad\qquad\quad\Box$

Example 9: Consider the series $\sum\limits_{n=1}^{\infty} f_n$, where $f_n(x) = e^{-nx}$ for $x \geq \frac{1}{2}$. Since each function is strictly decreasing,

$$|e^{-nx}| \leq e^{-\frac{1}{2}n}$$

for every positive integer n and all $x \geq \frac{1}{2}$. Furthermore, the geometric series

$$\sum_{n=1}^{\infty} e^{-\frac{1}{2}n} = \sum_{n=1}^{\infty} \left(\frac{1}{\sqrt{e}} \right)^n$$

converges since $|\frac{1}{\sqrt{e}}| < 1$. Therefore $\sum\limits_{n=1}^{\infty} f_n$ converges uniformly on the given set by Theorem 8.13.

The condition of Theorem 8.13 is quite restrictive and by no means necessary for uniform convergence. Nevertheless, the Weierstrass M-Test is the most popular method of testing for uniform convergence of series of functions. More sophisticated tests are available when this one fails.

In this same connection it should be emphasized that no theorem in this section, with the exception of 8.7 and 8.12, provides a condition which is both necessary and sufficient. It sometimes happens, for example, that the non-uniform limit of a sequence of continuous functions is continuous; or term-by-term integration of a series of functions can be valid in the absence of uniform convergence. Similar comments apply to the other theorems. Examples of this kind are explored in the exercises.

Exercise 8.1

In Problems 1-10 find the pointwise limit f of the given sequence of functions $\{f_n\}$ on the indicated set, and determine whether or not the convergence is uniform.**

1. $\{\dfrac{1}{1 + x^{2n}}\}$, all x
2. $\{\dfrac{x^n}{n!}\}$, $[-8,8]$

3. $\{\sin^n x\}$, $[0,\pi]$
4. $\{(1 + \dfrac{x}{n})^n\}$, $[0,5]$

5. $\{\dfrac{x^n}{n}\}$, $[-1,1]$
6. $\{x(1 - x)^n\}$, $[0,1]$

7. $\{nx(1 - x)^n\}$, $[0,1]$
8. $\{\dfrac{nx}{1 + nx^2}\}$, $x > 0$

9. $\{\dfrac{nx}{e^{nx}}\}$, $[.01,2]$
10. $\{\dfrac{nx^2}{1 + nx}\}$, $[0,2]$

11. Give an example of a sequence of continuous functions converging non-uniformly to a continuous function.

12. Prove that if $\{f_n\}$ converges uniformly to f and $\{g_n\}$ converges uniformly to g on a set S, then $\{f_n + g_n\}$ converges uniformly to f + g on S.

**For simplicity the formula for the general term is shown explicitly in the sequence notation rather than by the circuitous (but more correct) notation used in the examples. A similar comment applies to series of functions.

*13.   Show that if $\{f_n\}$ is a uniformly convergent sequence of bounded functions on a set S, then the limit function f is also bounded.

In Problems 14-17, (a) find the pointwise limit f of the given sequence of functions $\{f_n\}$ on the indicated interval [a,b], (b) determine whether or not $\lim_{n\to\infty} \int_a^b f_n(x)dx = \int_a^b f(x)dx$, and (c) determine whether or not $\lim_{n\to\infty} f_n'(x) = f'(x)$ for all x in [a,b].

14. $\{nx(1 - x)^n\}$, $[0,1]$

15. $\{\dfrac{nx}{1 + n^2x^4}\}$, $[0,4]$

16. $\{\dfrac{x^n}{n}\}$, $[0,1]$

17. $\{\dfrac{nx^2}{1 + nx}\}$, $[1,2]$

*18.   Prove the Cauchy Criterion for Sequences of Functions. Suppose S is a set of numbers, and the domain of each of the functions f_1, f_2, . . . , f_n, . . . includes S. Then $\{f_n\}$ converges uniformly on S if and only if the following condition is satisfied: if ε is any positive number, there exists a positive integer N such that for all integers $n \geq N$ and $m \geq N$ and for every x in S, $|f_n(x) - f_m(x)| < \varepsilon$.

360

19. For each positive integer n define f_n on $[0, \pi]$ by $f_n(x) = \dfrac{\sin nx}{\sqrt{n}}$. Show that $\{f_n\}$ converges uniformly, but $\{f_n'(x)\}$ diverges for every x in $[0, \pi]$.

20. Prove or disprove: if $\{f_n\}$ is a sequence of functions each discontinuous on a set S and $\{f_n\}$ converges uniformly on S to a function f, then f is discontinuous on S.

21. Prove that if $\displaystyle\sum_{n=1}^{\infty} f_n$ converges uniformly on S, then $\{f_n\}$ converges uniformly on S to the function which is identically zero.

22. Give an example of sequences $\{f_n\}$ and $\{g_n\}$ both uniformly convergent on the same set S but such that $\{f_n g_n\}$ is not uniformly convergent on S.

23. If both $\{f_n\}$ and $\{g_n\}$ are uniformly convergent on a set S, find a reasonable condition to impose which will insure that $\{f_n g_n\}$ converges uniformly on S.

24. Prove or disprove: if $\{f_n\}$ is a sequence of uniformly continuous functions converging uniformly to a function f on a set S, then f is uniformly continuous on S.

25. Prove Theorem 8.10.

26. Prove Theorem 8.11.

In Problems 27-31 use the ratio test or any other convenient test to determine all values of x for which the series converges.

361

27. $\displaystyle\sum_{n=1}^{\infty} \frac{x^n}{n}$

28. $\displaystyle\sum_{n=1}^{\infty} \sin^n x$

29. $\displaystyle\sum_{n=1}^{\infty} \frac{1}{5^{nx}}$

30. $\displaystyle\sum_{n=1}^{\infty} \frac{1}{n^x}$

31. $\displaystyle\sum_{n=1}^{\infty} \frac{x^2}{(x^2 + 1)^n}$

32. Suppose $\displaystyle\sum_{n=1}^{\infty} f_n$ and $\displaystyle\sum_{n=1}^{\infty} g_n$ are series, and for each n $|f_n(x)| \leq g_n(x)$ for all x in a set S.

   Show that if $\displaystyle\sum_{n=1}^{\infty} g_n$ converges uniformly on S, then so does $\displaystyle\sum_{n=1}^{\infty} f_n$.

33. Show that if $\displaystyle\sum_{n=1}^{\infty} a_n$ converges absolutely, then $\displaystyle\sum_{n=1}^{\infty} a_n \cos nx$ converges uniformly on any set.

34. Prove Theorem 8.12.

In problems 35-41 determine whether the given series of functions converges uniformly or not on the indicated set.

35. $\displaystyle\sum_{n=1}^{\infty} \frac{x^n}{(n + x)^2}$, $[0,1]$

362

36. $\displaystyle\sum_{n=1}^{\infty} \frac{1}{n^x}$, $x \geq 1.01$

37. $\displaystyle\sum_{n=1}^{\infty} \frac{1}{n} \sqrt{\frac{\cos nx}{n}}$, all x

38. $\displaystyle\sum_{n=1}^{\infty} \frac{1}{1 + n^2 x^2}$, $x \geq \frac{1}{2}$

39. $\displaystyle\sum_{n=1}^{\infty} \frac{x^n}{n!}$, any interval

40. $\displaystyle\sum_{n=1}^{\infty} e^{-nx}$, $[0,1]$

41. $\displaystyle\sum_{n=1}^{\infty} \frac{x^2}{(x^2 + 1)^n}$, all x

42. By Theorem 8.13 the series $\displaystyle\sum_{n=1}^{\infty} \frac{\sin nx}{n^2}$ converges on $[0,\pi]$. If $s(x) = \displaystyle\sum_{n=1}^{\infty} \frac{\sin nx}{n^2}$, show that

$$\int_0^\pi s(x)\,dx = \sum_{n=1}^{\infty} \frac{2}{(2n-1)^3} \quad .$$

43. If $f(x) = \displaystyle\sum_{n=0}^{\infty} \frac{x^n}{n!}$, for what x can you conclude

that $f'(x) = \sum\limits_{n=0}^{\infty} \dfrac{x^n}{n!}$?

2. Power Series

The remainder of this chapter will be devoted to a study of the most important type of series of functions.

<u>Definition 8.14</u>: If x_0 is a number and $\{a_0, a_1, a_2, \ldots, a_n, \ldots\}$ is a sequence of numbers, a series of the form

$$\sum_{n=0}^{\infty} a_n (x - x_0)^n$$

is called a <u>power series</u>.

The series above is also called a "power series in $(x - x_0)$" or a "power series expanded about (centered at) x_0." When $x_0 = 0$ we speak of a "power series in x." To avoid notational problems, it will be understood that $(x - x_0)^0 = 1$, even if $x = x_0$.

If the variable x in a power series is replaced by a particular number, the resulting series of numbers will either converge or diverge. In general, some values of x will produce convergence while others result in divergence. By means of the following theorem we will obtain a simple characterization of the set of numbers for which any power series converges.

<u>Theorem 8.15</u>: If $\sum_{n=0}^{\infty} a_n (x - x_0)^n$ converges for $x = x_1$, then the series converges absolutely for every number x such that $|x - x_0| < |x_1 - x_0|$.

Proof: By the nth term test $\{a_n(x_1 - x_0)^n\}$ is a null sequence and therefore a bounded sequence. Hence there exists a number M such that $|a_n(x_1 - x_0)^n| \leq M$ for every non-negative integer n. Suppose x is any number satisfying $|x - x_0| < |x_1 - x_0|$, and let $r = \left|\dfrac{x - x_0}{x_1 - x_0}\right|$. For all n we have

$$|a_n(x - x_0)^n| = |a_n(x_1 - x_0)^n| \frac{|x - x_0|^n}{|x_1 - x_0|^n}$$

$$= |a_n(x_1 - x_0)^n| \, r^n$$

$$\leq Mr^n.$$

Since $|x - x_0| < |x_1 - x_0|$, $0 \leq r < 1$. Since $\sum\limits_{n=0}^{\infty} Mr^n$ is a convergent geometric series, $\sum\limits_{n=0}^{\infty} |a_n(x - x_0)^n|$ converges by Theorem 7.10. □

Corollary: If $\sum\limits_{n=0}^{\infty} a_n(x - x_0)^n$ diverges for $x = x_1$, then the series diverges for every number x such that $|x - x_0| > |x_1 - x_0|$.

Proof: Suppose x_2 is any number satisfying $|x_2 - x_0| > |x_1 - x_0|$, and assume that the series converges for $x = x_2$. By the theorem $\sum\limits_{n=0}^{\infty} a_n(x - x_0)^n$

366

converges for all x satisfying $|x - x_0| < |x_2 - x_0|$. Since $|x_1 - x_0| < |x_2 - x_0|$, the series converges for $x = x_1$. Contradiction. □

Theorem 8.16: Suppose $\sum\limits_{n=0}^{\infty} a_n(x - x_0)^n$ is any power series. One and only one of the following is true.

   (a) The series converges for $x = x_0$ and for no other number.

   (b) The series converges absolutely for every number x.

   (c) There exists a positive number R such that the series converges absolutely for all x satisfying $|x - x_0| < R$ and diverges for all x satisfying $|x - x_0| > R$.

Proof: Define a set S as follows:

$$S = \{0\} \cup \{t > 0: \sum\limits_{n=0}^{\infty} a_n(x - x_0)^n$$

converges absolutely for all x satisfying

$$|x - x_0| < t\}.$$

Suppose S contains a positive number t. We will show that S contains every number t' such that $0 < t' < t$. Let x' be a number such that $|x' - x_0| = t'$. Then $\sum\limits_{n=0}^{\infty} a_n(x - x_0)^n$ converges absolutely for $x = x'$ by definition of S. By the previous

367

theorem $\sum\limits_{n=0}^{\infty} a_n (x - x_0)^n$ converges absolutely for all x such that $|x - x_0| < |x' - x_0| = t'$. Hence t' is in S. If S is unbounded, then S contains all non-negative numbers, and (b) is true. If S is bounded, then S has a non-negative least upper bound R. If $R = 0$, (a) is true, so consider the case $R > 0$. Suppose x_1 is any number such that $|x_1 - x_0| < R$, and let $|x_1 - x_0| = r_1$. Since R is the least upper bound of S, any number r_1' satisfying $r_1 < r_1' < R$ is in S. Consequently $\sum\limits_{n=0}^{\infty} a_n (x - x_0)^n$ converges absolutely for $x = x_1$ since $|x_1 - x_0| = r_1 < r_1'$. Suppose now that x_2 is any number such that $|x_2 - x_0| > R$, and let $|x_2 - x_0| = r_2$. If $\sum\limits_{n=0}^{\infty} a_n (x - x_0)^n$ converges for $x = x_2$, then the series converges absolutely for all x satisfying $|x - x_0| < r_2$. Hence r_2 is in S. Since $r_2 > R$, this contradicts the fact that R is an upper bound for S. Therefore the series diverges for $x = x_2$. $\square$

If (c) is true in the theorem above, the series converges for all x in the open interval $(x_0 - R, x_0 + R)$. Notice that no statement is made concerning behavior at the end-points $x_0 - R$ and $x_0 + R$. It's customary at this juncture to stretch the definition of interval, referring to the set in (a) as an interval of length zero and to the set in (b) as an interval of infinite length. In each case the relevant interval is called the "interval of convergence," and the following terminology is also used.

Definition 8.17: The radius of convergence of a power series is either 0, ∞, or R, according to whether (a), (b), or (c) is true in Theorem 8.16.*

Example 10: The ratio test will easily establish each of the following statements.

(a) $\sum_{n=0}^{\infty} n^n x^n$ converges only for $x = 0$;

(b) $\sum_{n=0}^{\infty} \frac{(x + 2)^n}{n!}$ converges for every number x;

(c) $\sum_{n=0}^{\infty} \frac{(2x - 5)^n}{\sqrt{n}}$ converges for all x satisfying $2 \leq x < 3$.

In (c) the ratio test gives no conclusion at the end-points, so some other test has to be used for these two series of numbers. Note that the radius of convergence in (c) is $\frac{1}{2}$, not 1.

In a power series $\sum_{n=0}^{\infty} a_n (x - x_0)^n$ the a_n's evidently play a fundamental role in determining the series' properties. It's not unreasonable to seek a formula for the radius of convergence in terms of these coefficients. The simplest result along these lines is the following.

*The symbol $(x_0 - R, x_0 + R)$ will be interpreted as $\{x_0\}$ in case (a) and as the set of all numbers in case (b).

Theorem 8.18: The radius of convergence of $\sum_{n=0}^{\infty} a_n(x - x_0)^n$ is given by

$$\frac{1}{\lim_{n \to \infty} \left| \frac{a_{n+1}}{a_n} \right|}$$

provided $\lim_{n \to \infty} \left| \frac{a_{n+1}}{a_n} \right|$ exists or is ∞ (where we inter-pret $\frac{1}{0} = \infty$ and $\frac{1}{\infty} = 0$).

Proof: Denote the radius of convergence of $\sum_{n=0}^{\infty} a_n(x - x_0)^n$ by R, and let $L = \lim_{n \to \infty} \left| \frac{a_{n+1}}{a_n} \right|$.
In preparation for using the ratio test we calcu-late

$$\lim_{n \to \infty} \left| \frac{a_{n+1}(x - x_0)^{n+1}}{a_n(x - x_0)^n} \right| = \lim_{n \to \infty} \left| \frac{a_{n+1}}{a_n} \right| |x - x_0|$$

$$= |x - x_0| L.$$

If $L = 0$, $|x - x_0|L < 1$ for all x, so $R = \infty = \frac{1}{0}$.
If L is finite and non-zero, $|x - x_0|L < 1$ is true for x satisfying $|x - x_0| < \frac{1}{L}$, so $R = \frac{1}{L}$. If $L = \infty$, $|x - x_0|L$ cannot be less than 1 for any $x \neq x_0$. Hence $R = 0 = \frac{1}{\infty}$. □

Example 11: To find the radius of convergence of

370

$\sum\limits_{n=0}^{\infty} \dfrac{(n!)^2}{(2n)!} (3x + 1)^n$, we first rewrite the series

$\sum\limits_{n=0}^{\infty} \dfrac{(n!)^2 3^n}{(2n)!} (x - [-\frac{1}{3}])^n$, identifying a_n as

$\dfrac{(n!)^2 3^n}{(2n)!}$. It is easily seen that

$$\lim_{n \to \infty} \left| \frac{a_{n+1}}{a_n} \right| = \lim_{n \to \infty} \frac{[(n + 1)!]^2 3^{n+1}}{(2n + 2)!} \cdot \frac{(2n)!}{(n!)^2 3^n}$$

$$= \lim_{n \to \infty} \frac{3n^2 + 6n + 3}{4n^2 + 6n + 2} = \frac{3}{4}.$$

Consequently the radius of convergence is $\frac{4}{3}$. Since $x_0 = -\frac{1}{3}$, it follows that the series converges for x satisfying $|x + \frac{1}{3}| < \frac{4}{3}$ and diverges for x satisfying $|x + \frac{1}{3}| > \frac{4}{3}$. This calculation gives no information about the end-points $-\frac{5}{3}$ and 1.

Theorem 8.19: The radius of convergence of $\sum\limits_{n=0}^{\infty} a_n (x - x_0)^n$ is given by

$$\frac{1}{\lim\limits_{n \to \infty} \sqrt[n]{|a_n|}}$$

provided $\lim\limits_{n \to \infty} \sqrt[n]{|a_n|}$ exists or is ∞ (where we interpret $\frac{1}{0} = \infty$ and $\frac{1}{\infty} = 0$).

Proof: Left as an exericse.

Theorem 8.20: If $\sum\limits_{n=0}^{\infty} a_n(x - x_0)^n$ has radius of convergence R > 0 and D is any compact subset of $(x_0 - R, x_0 + R)$, then $\sum\limits_{n=0}^{\infty} a_n(x - x_0)^n$ converges uniformly on D.

Proof: Since D is a compact and therefore bounded subset of $(x_0 - R, x_0 + R)$, there is a number r < R such that $|x - x_0| \le r$ for every x in D. Hence

$$|a_n(x - x_0)^n| \le |a_n r^n|$$

for every x in D. Since r < R, $\sum\limits_{n=0}^{\infty} |a_n r^n|$ converges by Theorem 8.16. Letting $M_n = |a_n r^n|$ for each non-negative integer n, we conclude uniform convergence of $\sum\limits_{n=0}^{\infty} a_n(x - x_0)^n$ on D by the Weierstrass M-Test. □

Every power series determines a function on its interval of convergence, namely the sum function for that particular series of functions. One of our goals is to investigate the properties of such functions.

Theorem 8.21: Suppose $\sum\limits_{n=0}^{\infty} a_n(x - x_0)^n$ is a power series with radius of convergence R > 0. If f denotes the sum function of the series, f is continuous on $(x_0 - R, x_0 + R)$.

372

Proof: Suppose x_1 is any number in $(x_0 - R, x_0 + R)$. Let $[a,b]$ be a subset of $(x_0 - R, x_0 + R)$ which contains x_1 in its interior. By the previous theorem $\sum_{n=0}^{\infty} a_n (x - x_0)^n$ converges uniformly on $[a,b]$. Every term of the series is a polynomial and is therefore continuous on $[a,b]$, so f is continuous on $[a,b]$ by the first corollary to Theorem 8.9. Hence f is continuous at x_1. $\square$

Suppose a power series falls into category (c) of Theorem 8.16. If the series converges at one of the end-points, then the sum function is automatically defined at that point, but is it continuous there? One would hope so, but Theorem 8.21 gives no assurance. For the time being this remains an open question.

Theorem 8.22: Both of the series $\sum_{n=0}^{\infty} a_n (x - x_0)^n$ and $\sum_{n=0}^{\infty} n a_n (x - x_0)^{n-1}$ have the same radius of convergence.

Proof: Let R denote the radius of convergence of $\sum_{n=0}^{\infty} a_n (x - x_0)^n$ and R' the radius of convergence of $\sum_{n=0}^{\infty} n a_n (x - x_0)^{n-1}$. We will first show that $R \geq R'$. If $R' = 0$, then certainly $R \geq R'$, so consider the case $R' > 0$. Suppose x is any (fixed) number in $(x_0 - R', x_0 + R')$. Let x_1 be a number such that $|x - x_0| < |x_1 - x_0| < R'$. The series $\sum_{n=0}^{\infty} n a_n (x_1 - x_0)^{n-1}$ converges absolutely by Theorem 8.16. Let $r = \left| \dfrac{x - x_0}{x_1 - x_0} \right|$, and note that $r < 1$.

It follows that $\left\{ \dfrac{|x - x_0| r^{n-1}}{n} \right\}$ is a null sequence (remember x is fixed), so there is a positive integer N such that

$$\frac{|x - x_0| r^{n-1}}{n} < 1$$

for all $n \geq N$. For all $n \geq N$, therefore,

$$|a_n (x - x_0)^n| = \left| a_n (x_1 - x_0)^{n-1} \left(\frac{x - x_0}{x_1 - x_0} \right)^{n-1} (x - x_0) \right|$$

$$= \left| n a_n (x_1 - x_0)^{n-1} \right| \frac{|x - x_0| r^{n-1}}{n}$$

$$< \left| n a_n (x_1 - x_0)^{n-1} \right|.$$

Since $\sum\limits_{n=0}^{\infty} |n a_n (x_1 - x_0)^{n-1}|$ converges, $\sum\limits_{n=0}^{\infty} a_n (x - x_0)^n$ converges absolutely by Theorem 7.10. Hence $R \geq R'$. We now show that $R' \geq R$. If $R = 0$ this is obvious, so consider the case $R > 0$. Suppose x is any (fixed) number in $(x_0 - R, x_0 + R)$ different from x_0. Let x_1 be a number such that $|x - x_0| < |x_1 - x_0| < R$. The series $\sum\limits_{n=0}^{\infty} a_n (x_1 - x_0)^n$ converges absolutely by Theorem 8.16. Let $r = \left| \dfrac{x - x_0}{x_1 - x_0} \right|$, and note that $0 < r < 1$. Since $\{n r^n\}$ is a null sequence (Problem 24 of Exercise 7.2), there is a positive integer N such that

$$\frac{n r^n}{|x - x_0|} < 1$$

374

for all $n \geq N$. For all $n \geq N$, therefore,

$$|na_n(x - x_0)^{n-1}| = \left|\frac{na_n(x_1 - x_0)^n}{x - x_0}\left(\frac{x - x_0}{x_1 - x_0}\right)^n\right|$$

$$= |a_n(x_1 - x_0)^n| \frac{nr^n}{|x - x_0|}$$

$$< |a_n(x_1 - x_0)^n|.$$

Since $\sum\limits_{n=0}^{\infty} |a_n(x_1 - x_0)^n|$ converges, $\sum\limits_{n=0}^{\infty} na_n(x - x_0)^{n-1}$ converges absolutely by Theorem 7.10. Hence $R' \geq R$. Therefore $R = R'$, and the proof is complete. □

Corollary: Both of the series $\sum\limits_{n=0}^{\infty} a_n(x - x_0)^n$ and $\sum\limits_{n=0}^{\infty} \frac{a_n}{n + 1}(x - x_0)^{n+1}$ have the same radius of convergence.

Since the relationship between the two series in the corollary is the same as the relationship between the two series in the theorem, this result is immediate. (Remember, the statement that two series have the same radius of convergence is not equivalent to the statement that they converge for precisely the same values of x since behavior at the end-points is unpredictable.) We are now able to prove the following important result.

Theorem 8.23: Suppose $\sum\limits_{n=0}^{\infty} a_n(x - x_0)^n$ is a power

375

series with radius of convergence $R > 0$. If f denotes the sum function of the series, then f is differentiable on $(x_0 - R, x_0 + R)$ and

$$f'(x) = \sum_{n=1}^{\infty} na_n(x - x_0)^{n-1}.*$$

Proof: Suppose x is any (fixed) number in $(x_0 - R, x_0 + R)$. Let $[a,b]$ be any interval which contains x and is a subset of $(x_0 - R, x_0 + R)$. The series $\sum_{n=1}^{\infty} na_n(x - x_0)^{n-1}$ has radius of convergence R by the previous theorem and consequently converges uniformly on $[a,b]$ by Theorem 8.20. It follows from Theorem 8.11 that f is differentiable at x and $f'(x) = \sum_{n=1}^{\infty} na_n(x - x_0)^{n-1}$. ☐

Example 12: The geometric series $\sum_{n=0}^{\infty} x^n$ converges for $|x| < 1$ and

$$\sum_{n=0}^{\infty} x^n = \frac{1}{1 - x}.$$

By Theorem 8.23

$$\sum_{n=1}^{\infty} nx^{n-1} = \frac{1}{(1 - x)^2}.$$

*Since the 0th term is zero, the summation may as well start at 1.

376

Since term-by-term differentiation of a power series produces another power series with the same radius of convergence, Theorem 8.23 can be applied to the new series. In fact, we have the following.

Corollary: Suppose $\sum\limits_{n=0}^{\infty} a_n (x - x_0)^n$ is a power series with radius of convergence $R > 0$. If f denotes the sum function of the series and k is any positive integer, then f is differentiable k times on $(x_0 - R, x_0 + R)$ and

$$f^{(k)}(x) = \sum\limits_{n=0}^{\infty} a_{n+k} \frac{(n + k)!}{n!} (x - x_0)^n.$$

Proof: Left as an exercise.

If we interpret $f^{(0)}$ as f, which is customary, the formula above actually holds for every non-negative integer k. From this formula can be deduced the simple relationship that exists between f and the coefficients of the power series.

Corollary: Suppose $\sum\limits_{n=0}^{\infty} a_n (x - x_0)^n$ is a power series with radius of convergence $R > 0$. If f denotes the sum function of the series, then

$$a_k = \frac{f^{(k)}(x_0)}{k!}$$

for every non-negative integer k.

Proof: Left as an exercise.

377

<u>Corollary</u>: If there exists a positive number δ such that $\sum\limits_{n=0}^{\infty} a_n(x - x_0)^n = \sum\limits_{n=0}^{\infty} b_n(x - x_0)^n$ for all x in $(x_0 - \delta, x_0 + \delta)$, then $a_n = b_n$ for every non-negative integer n.

<u>Proof</u>: Left as an exercise.

According to this last corollary it's impossible for two different power series to have the same sum function on any interval, no matter how small. This result is called the "uniqueness theorem" for power series.

<u>Theorem 8.24</u>: Suppose $\sum\limits_{n=0}^{\infty} a_n(x - x_0)^n$ is a power series with radius of convergence $R > 0$. If f denotes the sum function of the series, then f is integrable on any interval [a,b] which is a subset of $(x_0 - R, x_0 + R)$, and

$$\int_a^b f(x)\,dx = \sum_{n=0}^{\infty} \frac{a_n}{n+1} [(b - x_0)^{n+1} - (a - x_0)^{n+1}].$$

<u>Proof</u>: Each function in the series $\sum\limits_{n=0}^{\infty} a_n(x - x_0)^n$ is continuous and therefore integrable on [a,b]. The series converges uniformly to f on [a,b] by Theorem 8.20. It follows from Theorem 8.10 that f is integrable on [a,b] and

$$\int_a^b f(x)\,dx = \sum_{n=0}^{\infty} [\int_a^b a_n(x - x_0)^n dx].$$

Hence

$$\int_a^b f(x)\,dx = \sum_{n=0}^{\infty} \frac{a_n}{n+1} [(b - x_0)^{n+1} - (a - x_0)^{n+1}] \cdot \square$$

378

One of our main concerns in this section has been the determination of properties of functions defined by power series. We now reverse the point of view and consider the problem of expressing a given function as a power series. If such an expansion is possible, the second corollary to Theorem 8.23 shows exactly what the series must be. Clearly a necessary condition for the existence of the series is that f be "infinitely differentiable."

Definition 8.25: Suppose, for every positive integer n, f is differentiable n times at the point x_0. The power series

$$\sum_{n=0}^{\infty} \frac{f^{(n)}(x_0)}{n!} (x - x_0)^n$$

is called the <u>Taylor Series for f at x_0</u>.*

Despite the new name, we have no knowledge of the series beyond its existence. We do not know if the series converges for any x except x_0. And--most importantly--if the series does converge for some $x \neq x_0$, we do not know if convergence is to the "right" number, namely f(x).

<u>Definition 8.26</u>: The series $\sum_{n=0}^{\infty} \frac{f^{(n)}(x_0)}{n!} (x - x_0)^n$ is said to <u>represent</u> the function f on a set S provided $\sum_{n=0}^{\infty} \frac{f^{(n)}(x_0)}{n!} (x - x_0)^n$ converges to f(x) for every x in S.

*The special case occurring when $x_0 = 0$ is called the <u>Maclaurin Series for f</u>.

379

If f is infinitely differentiable at a point x_0, the Taylor Series for f at x_0 exists. We are faced with the problem of determining whether the series represents f on any set containing x_0. The following theorem is crucial in attacking this problem.

Theorem 8.27 (Taylor's Theorem): Suppose, for some positive integer n, f, f', f", . . . , $f^{(n)}$ are continuous on [a,b], $f^{(n+1)}$ is defined on (a,b), and x_0 is any (fixed) number in [a,b]. If x is any number in [a,b], there exists a number z between x_0 and $x(z = x_0$ if $x = x_0)$ such that

$$f(x) = f(x_0) + \frac{f'(x_0)}{1!} (x - x_0) + \frac{f''(x_0)}{2!} (x - x_0)^2$$
$$+ \ldots + \frac{f^{(n)}(x_0)}{n!} (x - x_0)^n$$
$$+ \frac{f^{(n+1)}(z)}{(n + 1)!} (x - x_0)^{n+1}.$$

Proof: If $x = x_0$ the result is trivial, so suppose $x \neq x_0$. For convenience we rename $x = c$. If $c < x_0$ let $I = [c, x_0]$, and if $x_0 < c$ let $I = [x_0, c]$. Define on I a function F by

$$F(x) = f(c) - f(x) - \frac{f'(x)}{1!} (c - x) - \frac{f''(x)}{2!} (c - x)^2$$
$$- \ldots - \frac{f^{(n)}(x)}{n!} (c - x)^n.$$

(The reason for renaming x now becomes apparent.) Since each of the first n derivatives of f exists on [a,b] and $f^{(n+1)}$ exists on (a,b), F is differ-

380

entiable on (a,b). Hence F is differentiable at every interior point of I. Since all the middle terms conveniently cancel (write it out to make sure),

$$F'(x) = - \frac{f^{(n+1)}(x)}{n!} (c - x)^n.$$

We next define on I a function G by

$$G(x) = \frac{(c - x)^{n+1}}{(n + 1)!}.$$

Certainly G is differentiable on I and

$$G'(x) = - \frac{(c - x)^n}{n!}.$$

At this point we apply the corollary to the Generalized Mean Value Theorem (convince yourself the hypothesis is satisfied). There exists a number z between c and x_0 such that

$$\frac{F'(z)}{G'(z)} = \frac{F(x_0) - F(c)}{G(x_0) - G(c)}.$$

(Note that this equation holds whether I is $[c,x_0]$ or $[x_0,c]$.) Since $F(c) = 0$ and $G(c) = 0$,

$$\frac{F'(z)}{G'(z)} = \frac{F(x_0)}{G(x_0)},$$

so

$$F(x_0) = \frac{F'(z)}{G'(z)} G(x_0).$$

Using the formulas for F', G', and G, we find after simplifying that

$$F(x_0) = \frac{f^{(n+1)}(z)}{(n+1)!} (c - x_0)^{n+1}.$$

Therefore

$$f(c) - f(x_0) - \frac{f'(x_0)}{1!} (c - x_0) - \frac{f''(x_0)}{2!} (c - x_0)^2$$

$$- \cdots - \frac{f^{(n)}(x_0)}{n!} (c - x_0)^n = \frac{f^{(n+1)}(z)}{(n+1)!} (c - x_0)^{n+1},$$

so

$$f(c) = f(x_0) + \frac{f'(x_0)}{1!} (c - x_0) + \frac{f''(x_0)}{2!} (c - x_0)^2$$

$$+ \cdots + \frac{f^{(n)}(x_0)}{n!} (c - x_0)^n + \frac{f^{(n+1)}(z)}{(n+1)!} (c - x_0)^{n+1}.$$

Since $c (= x)$ was any number in $[a,b]$, the proof is complete. □

Definition 8.28: Suppose f is a function which satisfies the hypothesis of Taylor's Theorem. We write

$$P_n(x) = \sum_{k=0}^{n} \frac{f^{(k)}(x_0)}{k!} (x - x_0)^k$$

and call P_n the Taylor Polynomial of degree n for f at x_0. We also write

$$R_{n+1}(x) = \frac{f^{(n+1)}(z)}{(n+1)!} (x - x_0)^{n+1}$$

and call R_{n+1} the <u>remainder after n + 1 terms.</u>*

In using this definition it's assumed that f and x_0 are known since neither is explicitly identified in the notation. If the hypothesis of Taylor's Theorem is satisfied, then $f(x) - P_n(x) = R_{n+1}(x)$ for all x in some interval containing x_0. As n increases without bound, the Taylor Polynomial becomes a Taylor Series. The key to determining whether the series represents the function lies in the nature of the remainder term R_{n+1}. In fact, the following statement should now be evident.

Theorem 8.29: Suppose f is infinitely differentiable on [a,b], and x_0 is a number in [a,b]. The Taylor Series for f at x_0 represents f at the point x in [a,b] if and only if $\lim_{n \to \infty} R_{n+1}(x) = 0$.

Proof: Left as an exercise.

It should be emphasized that a function can have a Taylor Series and yet the series does not represent the function. Two things can go wrong: (1) the series fails to converge for some values of x where f is defined; (2) for some x the series converges, but not to $f(x)$. See Problem 40 of the exercises for a classic example of this pathological behavior.

Example 13: Let $f(x) = e^x$ and $x_0 = 0$. If x is any number, let [a,b] be an interval containing

---

*This is the Lagrange Form of the Remainder. Several other forms are possible.

both x and 0. The hypothesis of Taylor's Theorem is satisfied on [a,b] for any positive integer n, and furthermore, $f^{(k)}(0) = e^0 = 1$ for k = 0, 1, 2, . . . , n. Therefore

$$e^x = \sum_{k=0}^{n} \frac{1}{n!} x^n + R_{n+1}(x)$$

where

$$R_{n+1}(x) = \frac{e^z}{(n+1)!} x^{n+1}$$

with z between 0 and x. We want to show that $\lim_{n \to \infty} R_{n+1}(x) = 0$. Clearly this is true if x = 0, so suppose $x \neq 0$. If x > 0, then 0 < z < x, so $e^z < e^x$ since f is an increasing function. Hence

$$0 < \frac{e^z}{(n+1)!} x^{n+1} < e^x \frac{x^{n+1}}{(n+1)!} .$$

By Problem 4 of Exercise 7.2

$$\lim_{n \to \infty} e^x \frac{x^{n+1}}{(n+1)!} = e^x \lim_{n \to \infty} \frac{x^{n+1}}{(n+1)!} = 0,$$

and Theorem 3.24 tells us that $\lim_{n \to \infty} \frac{e^z}{(n+1)!} x^{n+1} = 0$. If x < 0, then x < z < 0, so $e^x < e^z < e^0$, and consequently $0 < e^z < 1$. Therefore

$$0 < \frac{e^z}{(n+1)!} x^{n+1} < \frac{x^{n+1}}{(n+1)!}$$

or

384

$$0 > \frac{e^z}{(n+1)!} x^{n+1} > \frac{x^{n+1}}{(n+1)!}$$

according to whether x^{n+1} is positive or negative. In either case

$$\lim_{n\to\infty} \frac{e^z}{(n+1)!} x^{n+1} = 0$$

by the same reasoning as before. We conclude by Theorem 8.29 that the Taylor Series for f at 0 represents the function at every number x. In other words, for every x

$$e^x = 1 + \frac{x}{1!} + \frac{x^2}{2!} + \cdots + \frac{x^n}{n!} + \cdots$$

Example 14 (Binomial Series): If c is any number, it will be shown that

$$(1+x)^c = 1 + \sum_{n=1}^{\infty} \frac{c(c-1)(c-2)\cdots(c-n+1)}{n!} x^n$$

for all x satisfying $|x| < 1$. We first determine the radius of convergence. By Theorem 8.18 this number is given by

$$\lim_{n\to\infty} \left| \frac{c(c-1)(c-2)\cdots(c-n+1)}{n!} \cdot \right.$$

$$\left. \frac{(n+1)!}{c(c-1)(c-2)\cdots(c-n+1)(c-n)} \right|$$

$$= \lim_{n\to\infty} \left| \frac{n+1}{c-n} \right|$$

$$= \lim_{n\to\infty} \left| \frac{1 + \frac{1}{n}}{\frac{c}{n} - 1} \right| = 1.$$

We next show that the series represents the func-
tion $(1 + x)^c$ for all x such that $|x| < 1$. Al-
though we could attack the problem directly, using
an explicit formula for the remainder as in the
previous example, this turns out to be quite difficult. The standard procedure is to use an ingenious, roundabout method. Since the series has been
shown to converge for $|x| < 1$, there is a sum func-
tion f for the series, that is,

$$(1) \quad f(x) = 1 + \sum_{n=1}^{\infty} \frac{c(c - 1) \cdots (c - n + 1)}{n!} x^n,$$

$$|x| < 1.$$

Using Theorem 8.23,

$$(2) \quad f'(x) = \sum_{n=1}^{\infty} \frac{c(c - 1) \cdots (c - n + 1)}{(n - 1)!} x^{n-1},$$

$$|x| < 1.$$

Multiplying by x,

$$(3) \quad xf'(x) = \sum_{n=1}^{\infty} \frac{c(c - 1) \cdots (c - n + 1)}{(n - 1)!} x^n$$

$$= \sum_{n=1}^{\infty} n \frac{c(c - 1) \cdots (c - n + 1)}{n!} x^n.$$

From (2),

$$f'(x) = c + \sum_{n=2}^{\infty} \frac{c(c - 1) \cdots (c - n + 1)}{(n - 1)!} x^{n-1}$$

$$= c + \sum_{n=1}^{\infty} \frac{c(c - 1) \cdots (c - n)}{n!} x^n$$

386

by a change in index

(4) $f'(x) =$

$$c + \sum_{n=1}^{\infty} (c - n) \frac{c(c - 1) \cdots (c - n + 1)}{n!} x^n.$$

Adding (3) and (4),

$(1 + x)f'(x) =$

$$c + \sum_{n=1}^{\infty} [n + (c - n)] \frac{c(c - 1) \cdots (c - n + 1)}{n!} x^n$$

$$= c + c \sum_{n=1}^{\infty} \frac{c(c - 1) \cdots (c - n + 1)}{n!} x^n.$$

Therefore, by (1),

$$(1 + x)f'(x) = cf(x),$$

or $\qquad (1 + x)f'(x) - cf(x) = 0.$

Multiplication of this last equation by $(1 + x)^{-c-1}$ produces

$$(1 + x)^{-c}f'(x) - c(1 + x)^{-c-1}f(x) = 0.$$

This can be written $[(1 + x)^{-c}f(x)]' = 0$ where the prime denotes differentiation. A function whose derivative is zero on its entire domain is a constant function by Theorem 5.27. That is,

$$(1 + x)^{-c}f(x) = K$$

for some constant K. By (1), $f(0) = 1$, and it follows that $K = 1$. Hence

$$(1 + x)^{-c} f(x) = 1$$

and therefore

$$f(x) = (1 + x)^c$$

$$= 1 + \sum_{n=1}^{\infty} \frac{c(c - 1) \cdots (c - n + 1)}{n!} x^n$$

for all x satisfying $|x| < 1$. For some additional facts about the binomial series, see Problems 30 and 31 of the exercises.

Many Taylor Series expansions can be obtained without consideration of the remainder term in Taylor's Theorem and without the careful analysis used in the last example. Since the power series for a function at a point is unique (if it exists), it makes no difference how that series is obtained. The simplest device, when it works, is a mere change of variable.

Example 15: Suppose it is desired to find the Taylor Series for $f(x) = \frac{1}{2x + 1}$ at 3. By elementary algebra we write

$$\frac{1}{2x + 1} = \frac{1}{7} \cdot \frac{1}{1 + \frac{2}{7}(x - 3)} .$$

Since
$$\frac{1}{1 - x} = \sum_{n=0}^{\infty} x^n$$

for $|x| < 1$, it follows that

$$\frac{1}{1 + x} = \sum_{n=0}^{\infty} (-x)^n = \sum_{n=0}^{\infty} (-1)^n x^n$$

388

for $|-x| < 1$, that is, $|x| < 1$. Therefore

$$\frac{1}{1 + \frac{2}{7}(x - 3)} = \sum_{n=0}^{\infty} (-1)^n [\frac{2}{7}(x - 3)]^n$$

for $|\frac{2}{7}(x - 3)| < 1$, that is, $|x - 3| < \frac{7}{2}$. Consequently

$$f(x) = \frac{1}{2x + 1} = \frac{1}{7} \sum_{n=0}^{\infty} (-1)^n (\frac{2}{7})^n (x - 3)^n$$

$$= \sum_{n=0}^{\infty} (-1)^n \frac{2^n}{7^{n+1}} (x - 3)^n,$$

and this expansion is valid for $-\frac{1}{2} < x < \frac{13}{2}$.

Theorems 8.23 and 8.24 are indispensable in obtaining new series expansions from old ones. Moreover, the radius of convergence is never a problem when using one of these two theorems, for it is always the same as that of the series from which it was obtained. Finally, power series can be combined algebraically according to the following theorems.

Theorem 8.30: Suppose $f(x) = \sum_{n=0}^{\infty} a_n (x - x_0)^n$ with radius of convergence R_1 and $g(x) = \sum_{n=0}^{\infty} b_n (x - x_0)^n$ with radius of convergence R_2. Then

$$f(x) + g(x) = \sum_{n=0}^{\infty} (a_n + b_n)(x - x_0)^n$$

and

$$f(x) - g(x) = \sum_{n=0}^{\infty} (a_n - b_n)(x - x_0)^n,$$

389

and the radius of convergence of each of these series is at least as large as the smaller of R_1 and R_2.

Proof: Left as an exercise.

Theorem 8.31: Suppose $f(x) = \sum\limits_{n=0}^{\infty} a_n (x - x_0)^n$ with radius of convergence R_1 and $g(x) = \sum\limits_{n=0}^{\infty} b_n (x - x_0)^n$ with radius of convergence R_2. Then

$$f(x)g(x) = \sum_{n=0}^{\infty} \left(\sum_{k=0}^{n} a_k b_{n-k} (x - x_0)^n \right),$$

and the radius of convergence of this series is at least as large as the smaller of R_1 and R_2.

Proof: Left as an exercise.

We complete this section by proving an important theorem which answers the question raised in connection with Theorem 8.21.

Theorem 8.32 (Abel's Theorem): Suppose $\sum\limits_{n=0}^{\infty} a_n (x - x_0)^n$ is a power series with finite radius of convergence $R > 0$. If the series converges for $x = x_0 + R$ and if f denotes the sum function of the series, then f is continuous on $[x_0, x_0 + R]$.

Proof: It will be shown that the series converges uniformly on $[x_0, x_0 + R]$. Suppose ε is any positive number. Uniform convergence will follow from Theorem 8.12 if we can show the existence of a positive integer N such that

$$|a_{n+1}(x - x_0)^{n+1} + a_{n+2}(x - x_0)^{n+2}$$

$$+ \ldots + a_{n+k}(x - x_0)^{n+k}| < \varepsilon$$

for all $n \geq N$, every positive integer k, and every x in $[x_0, x_0 + R]$. Since $\sum\limits_{n=0}^{\infty} a_n R^n$ converges by hypothesis, there is a positive integer N such that

$$|a_{n+1}R^{n+1} + a_{n+2}R^{n+2} + \ldots + a_{n+k}R^{n+k}| < \varepsilon$$

for all $n \geq N$ and every positive integer k. If $x_0 \leq x \leq x_0 + R$, $0 \leq x - x_0 \leq R$, and $0 \leq \dfrac{x - x_0}{R} \leq 1$, so $\left\{\left(\dfrac{x - x_0}{R}\right)^n\right\}$ is a decreasing sequence of non-negative numbers. Suppose now that $n \geq N$, k is any positive integer, and x is any number in $[x_0, x_0 + R]$. Using Abel's Lemma (Problem 36) with the sequences $\{a_{n+1}R^{n+1}, a_{n+2}R^{n+2}, \ldots\}$ and $\left\{\left(\dfrac{x - x_0}{R}\right)^{n+1}, \left(\dfrac{x - x_0}{R}\right)^{n+2}, \ldots\right\}$ (convince yourself the hypothesis is satisfied), we conclude that

$$-\varepsilon\left(\dfrac{x - x_0}{R}\right)^{n+1} < \sum\limits_{i=1}^{k} (a_{n+i}R^{n+i})\left(\dfrac{x - x_0}{R}\right)^{n+i}$$

$$< \varepsilon\left(\dfrac{x - x_0}{R}\right)^{n+1},$$

that is,

$$\left| \sum_{i=1}^{k} a_{n+i} (x - x_0)^{n+i} \right| < \varepsilon \left(\frac{x - x_0}{R} \right)^{n+1} \leq \varepsilon .$$

Therefore $\sum_{n=0}^{\infty} a_n (x - x_0)^n$ converges uniformly on $[x_0, x_0 + R]$. Theorem 8.9 now tells us that f is continuous on $[x_0, x_0 + R]$. □

Corollary: Suppose $\sum_{n=0}^{\infty} a_n (x - x_0)^n$ is a power series with finite radius of convergence $R > 0$. If the series converges for $x = x_0 - R$ and if f denotes the sum function of the series, then f is continuous on $[x_0 - R, x_0]$.

Proof: Left as an exercise.

If $\sum_{n=0}^{\infty} a_n (x - x_0)^n$ has finite radius of con-vergence $R > 0$ and converges at the right end-point $x_0 + R$, then the sum function f is continuous at that point, and by the continuity of f we can conclude that $\lim_{x \to (x_0 + R)-} f(x)$ exists and equals $\sum_{n=0}^{\infty} a_n R^n$. A similar statement can be made about the left end-point.

Example 16: It was shown in the last example that

$$\frac{1}{1 + x} = \sum_{n=0}^{\infty} (-1)^n x^n, \quad |x| < 1.$$

392

By Theorem 8.24 $\int_0^x \frac{dt}{1 + t} = \sum_{n=0}^{\infty} \int_0^x (-1)^n t^n$, $|x| < 1$

so that

$$\ln(1 + x) = \sum_{n=0}^{\infty} (-1)^n \frac{x^{n+1}}{n + 1} = \sum_{n=1}^{\infty} (-1)^{n+1} \frac{x^n}{n},$$

$|x| < 1$. Since the last series converges for $x = 1$, $\lim_{x \to 1^-} \ln(1 + x)$ exists and equals $\sum_{n=1}^{\infty} (-1)^{n+1} \frac{(1)^n}{n}$; that is,

$$\ln 2 = \sum_{n=1}^{\infty} \frac{(-1)^{n+1}}{n} = 1 - \frac{1}{2} + \frac{1}{3} - \frac{1}{4} + \ldots \ldots$$

Exercise 8.2

1. Find the Taylor Series for $f(x) = \dfrac{x}{1 - x^2}$ at -2.

2. Prove Theorem 8.19.

3. Use the identity $\sin^2 x = \frac{1}{2}(1 - \cos 2x)$ to obtain the Maclaurin Series for $\sin^2 x$.

4. Using Taylor's Theorem and Theorem 8.29, show that $\sin x = \sum\limits_{n=0}^{\infty} (-1)^n \dfrac{x^{2n+1}}{(2n + 1)!}$ for every number x.

5. Obtain the Maclaurin Series for $\cos x$ by term-by-term differentiation of the series for $\sin x$.

6. Prove the first corollary to Theorem 8.23.

7. Prove the second corollary to Theorem 8.23.

8. Prove the third corollary to Theorem 8.23.

9. Show that $e = \dfrac{1}{7} \sum\limits_{n=0}^{\infty} \dfrac{(n + 1)(n + 2)}{n!}$.

In Problems 10-14 find the exact sum of the given series.

10. $\sum\limits_{n=1}^{\infty} nx^n$

11. $\sum\limits_{n=1}^{\infty} \dfrac{n}{(n + 1)!}$

12. $\sum\limits_{n=1}^{\infty} x^2 x^n$

13. $\sum\limits_{n=1}^{\infty} \dfrac{(-1)^n}{n(n + 1)}$

14. $\displaystyle\sum_{n=1}^{\infty} \frac{n}{5^n}$

15. Find the Taylor Series for $\sqrt{x}$ at 4.

16. From the geometric series obtain the series for $\dfrac{1}{1 + x^2}$ and then the series for Arctan x.

17. Show that the series in the previous exercise represents Arctan x for all x satisfying $|x| \le 1$, and deduce that $\pi = 4(1 - \frac{1}{3} + \frac{1}{5} - \frac{1}{7} + \ . \ . \ . \ )$.

18. Prove Theorem 8.29.

19. For what values of x does $x - \frac{1}{6} x^3$ approximate sin x correct to three decimal places?

20. Give an example of a power series which converges for x satisfying $5 < x \le 8$ and for no other numbers.

21. Obtain the Maclaurin Series for Arcsin x, and determine all values of x for which the series represents the function.

22. Use Taylor's Theorem to prove that e is irrational.

23. If $f(x) = \tan x$, then $f'(x) = 1 + [f(x)]^2$. Knowing that $f(0) = 0$, use successive differentiation of this equation to obtain the first four non-zero terms in the Maclaurin Series for f.

24. Prove Theorem 8.30.

25. Prove Theorem 8.31.

26. Evaluate $\lim_{x \to 0} \dfrac{e^{x^2} + 2 \cos x - 3}{x^3 \sin x}$ by writing the first few terms of the series for both numerator and denominator and simplifying.

27. Obtain the Maclaurin Series for $\ln\sqrt{\dfrac{1 + x}{1 - x}}$ and determine for which values of x the series represents the function.

28. Use multiplication of series to show that $\sin 2x = 2 \sin x \cos x$.

29. If $\displaystyle\sum_{n=0}^{\infty} a_n (x - x_0)^n$ has radius of convergence R, determine the radius of convergence of $\displaystyle\sum_{n=0}^{\infty} a_n (x - x_0)^{2n}$.

30. In the binomial series for the function $(1 + x)^c$ show the following: (a) if $c > 0$, the series converges absolutely at both end-points; (b) if $c \leq -1$, the series diverges at both end-points.

31. In the binomial series for the function $(1 + x)^c$ show the following: if $-1 < c < 0$, the series converges conditionally at $x = 1$ and diverges at $x = -1$.

32. (a) Prove that $\text{Arctan } \dfrac{1}{2} + \text{Arctan } \dfrac{1}{3} = \dfrac{\pi}{4}$.
    (b) Use the result in (a) together with the series for Arctan x to calculate π correct to four decimal places.

33. Prove or disprove: if $\displaystyle\sum_{n=0}^{\infty} a_n (x - x_0)^n$ has finite radius of convergence $R > 0$, if f

denotes the sum function of the series, and if f is defined at $x = x_0 + R$, then

$$\sum_{n=0}^{\infty} a_n(x - x_0)^n \text{ converges for } x = x_0 + R.$$

34. Evaluate $\int_0^1 e^{-x^2} dx$ correct to three decimal places using term-by-term integration of the series for e^{-x^2}.

35. Give an example of two power series, having radii of convergence R_1 and R_2, such that the radius of convergence of the product series is larger than the smaller of R_1 and R_2.

*36. Prove <u>Abel's Lemma</u>. Suppose $\{a_n\}$ is a sequence and $\{b_n\}$ is a decreasing sequence of non-negative numbers. If $s_n = a_1 + a_2 + \ldots + a_n$ for each positive integer n and if there exist numbers m and M such that $m \leq s_n \leq M$ for each n, then

$$mb_1 \leq \sum_{k=1}^{n} a_k b_k \leq Mb_1$$

for each positive integer n.

37. Verify the identity $\sqrt{2} = \frac{7}{5}(1 - \frac{1}{50})^{-\frac{1}{2}}$ and then calculate $\sqrt{2}$ correct to five decimal places.

38. Calculate the radius of convergence of $\sum_{n=0}^{\infty} \frac{n^n}{n!} x^n$ in two different ways and deduce that $\lim_{n \to \infty} \frac{n}{\sqrt[n]{n!}} = e$.

39. Prove the corollary to Theorem 8.32.

*40. Define a function f by

$$f(x) = \begin{cases} e^{-\frac{1}{x^2}} & \text{if } x \neq 0 \\ 0 & \text{if } x = 0 \end{cases}.$$

Show that the Maclaurin Series for f converges for all numbers but represents the function only at $x = 0$.

Exercise 1.1
Answers and Hints

6. $-\dfrac{3}{4} < x < \dfrac{5}{2}$

9. Use Problem 8.

13. (a) Use mathematical induction. The binomial theorem is not needed.

14. A table of primes is helpful.

15. If k is a positive integer, $\dfrac{1}{(k + 1)^2} < \dfrac{1}{k(k + 1)}$.

17. Work backwards from the desired result to see how to get started.

19. $\left(1 + \dfrac{1}{n^2 - 1}\right)^n \geq 1 + \dfrac{n}{n^2 - 1} > 1 + \dfrac{1}{n}$

21. Show that if the theorem is not true, the set $A = \{a:\ a < s$ for every $s \in S\}$ contains every positive integer, a contradiction.

24. Apply the Well-Ordering Principle to the set S of all positive integers for which $P(n)$ is false.

25. Use the Second Principle of Mathematical Induction.

31. Show that the least upper bound of A (or the greatest lower bound of B) is the desired number.

34. Define $s_0 = 0$. Then $\displaystyle\sum_{k=1}^{n} a_k b_k = \sum_{k=1}^{n} (s_k - s_{k-1})b_k$

$= \displaystyle\sum_{k=1}^{n} s_k b_k - \sum_{k=1}^{n-1} s_k b_{k+1}.$

35. $[f(g)](x) \neq x$

37. Consider the standard functions of calculus.

40. Write the positive rational numbers in an infinite matrix array so that $\frac{m}{n}$ is in the nth row and mth column. Then "count" the numbers by traversing the various diagonals, deleting any that have already been encountered.

42. If the set is countable, then all numbers in $[0,1]$ can be written in decimal form in a table:

$$0. \quad a_{11} \ a_{12} \ a_{13} \ \cdot \ \cdot \ \cdot$$

$$0. \quad a_{21} \ a_{22} \ a_{23} \ \cdot \ \cdot \ \cdot$$

$$0. \quad a_{31} \ a_{32} \ a_{33} \ \cdot \ \cdot \ \cdot$$

$$\cdot$$
$$\cdot$$
$$\cdot$$

Show that a number in $[0,1]$ can be "constructed" in such a way that its nth decimal place differs from the nth decimal place of the nth number in the table. Remember that some numbers have two different infinite decimal expansions.

43. Use Problem 39.

2. Strictly speaking, problems of this kind have infinitely many correct answers. Usually, however, one answer seems more "natural" than any other. In part (c) consider a quadratic function of n.

3. (a) 10

7. This is easier than it looks.

8. The algebra can be simplified by considering two cases. You can show the following:

   if $\varepsilon < 1$, choose $N > 2/\varepsilon$

   if $\varepsilon > 1$, choose $N > 2\varepsilon$.

9. $|1 - 2n| = 2n - 1$ since $n \geq 1$. Also

$$\frac{1}{|n + (-1)^{n+1}|} \leq \frac{1}{|n - 1|} = \frac{1}{n - 1} \text{ for } n \geq 2.$$

16. Use Problem 13 and Example 3.

17. Assume that $\{a_n\}$ is bounded and get a contradiction.

3. $\{\frac{\cos n}{n}\} = \{\cos n\} \cdot \{\frac{1}{n}\}$

6. Use Theorem 2.18.

8. 0

9. Use Theorem 2.15.

11. Assume $A > B$ and get a contradiction.

14. $\sqrt{a_n} - \sqrt{A} = \dfrac{a_n - A}{\sqrt{a_n} + \sqrt{A}}$ provided the denominator

   is not zero.

16. The statement is false.

17. Use Example 6.

18. Don't make this one too hard.

22. $\left| \dfrac{a_1 + a_2 + \ldots + a_n}{n} - A \right|$

   $= \left| \dfrac{(a_1 - A) + (a_2 - A) + \ldots + (a_n - A)}{n} \right|$

   $\leq \left| \dfrac{(a_1 - A) + (a_2 - A) + \ldots + (a_N - A)}{n} \right|$

   $+ \left| \dfrac{(a_{N+1} - A) + \ldots + (a_n - A)}{n} \right|$

   for $n > N$.

   Show that if N is properly chosen, each of the two terms on the right is small.

Exercise 2.3
Answers and Hints

2. If $\{a_n\}$ is decreasing and bounded below, then $\{-a_n\}$ is increasing and bounded above.

5. If D is a neighborhood of x, D contains an element y of S' different from x. Consider a neighborhood of y which is a subset of D.

8. (a) Let $k = n + 1$. Then $(1 + \frac{1}{n + 1})^n =$
   $(1 + \frac{1}{k})^k \cdot (1 + \frac{1}{k})^{-1}$ for $k \geq 2$. Of course
   $\{(1 + \frac{1}{k})^k\}$ converges to e.
   (c) $1 + \frac{2}{n} = (1 + \frac{1}{n})(1 + \frac{1}{n + 1})$
   (d) Use Problem 14 of Exercise 2.2.

10. The limit is $\frac{1}{2}$.

11. Use Theorem 2.18.

14. If $\{a_n\}$ converges, what is the limit?

16. (b), (c), (d) need not be increasing

19. $a_5 = \frac{665857}{470832}$

21. For each positive integer n, if $y_n = n^{\frac{1}{n}}$, there exists a positive number x_n such that $y_n = 1 + x_n$. It suffices to show that $\{x_n\}$ is a null sequence. But
   $$y_n^n = n = (1 + x)^n > \frac{1}{2} n(n - 1)x_n^2$$
   by Example 8 of Chapter 1.

403

5. $\dfrac{2}{3}$

6. (a)   only 0

8. Consider two cases: (1) the range of $\{a_n\}$ is finite; (2) the range of $\{a_n\}$ is infinite.

11. $|a_{n+k} - a_n| = \dfrac{1}{(n+1)^2} + \dfrac{1}{(n+2)^2} + \ldots + \dfrac{1}{(n+k)^2}$

$< \dfrac{1}{n(n+1)} + \dfrac{1}{(n+1)(n+2)}$

$+ \ldots + \dfrac{1}{(n+k-1)(n+k)}$

$= (\dfrac{1}{n} - \dfrac{1}{n+1}) + (\dfrac{1}{n+1} - \dfrac{1}{n+2})$

$+ \ldots + (\dfrac{1}{n+k-1} - \dfrac{1}{n+k})$

12. The converse is false.

14. This is very much like Example 20.

15. After writing out a few terms, you should be able to guess an explicit formula for a_n and prove it by induction.

19. The set of limiting points is the entire interval [0,1] no matter how the rationals are arranged in a sequence.

22. $\sqrt[3]{4}$

1. (b) $\delta = \dfrac{1}{400}$

4. If $|x - 5| < 1$, how small can $|2x - 3|$ be?

6. The functions are identical where they are both defined. However 2 is in the domain of g, and 2 is not in the domain of f.

8. See the note following Definition 3.9.

10. $\dfrac{x + 1}{x^3 + 1} = \dfrac{1}{x^2 - x + 1}$ for all $x \neq -1$.

14. Get an idea from the function in Example 11.

15. (1) Consider two sequences converging to a, one from the left and one from the right.

16. $\left| |a| - |b| \right| \leq |a - b|$ for all numbers a and b.

18. (c) Opinion is divided as to whether 0 should be considered in the domain of the function. Whether it is or not, 0 is certainly not a limit point of the domain.

4. See Problem 10 of Exercise 2.2.

8. Use the preceding lemma, Theorem 3.14, and the corollary to Theorem 3.16.

9. Use Theorems 2.15, 3.5, and 3.6.

10. (a) If $\lim\limits_{x \to \infty} f(x) = L$, for any positive number ε there exists a positive number N such that $|f(x) - L| < \varepsilon$ for all x in D satisfying $x > N$. This is equivalent to saying that there exists a positive number δ such that $|f(x) - L| < \varepsilon$ for all x in D satisfying $0 < \frac{1}{x} < \delta \ (= \frac{1}{N})$.

11. Verify that $(x^{\frac{2}{3}} + a^{\frac{1}{3}} x^{\frac{1}{3}} + a^{\frac{2}{3}})(x^{\frac{1}{3}} - a^{\frac{1}{3}}) = x - a$ so that

$$|\sqrt[3]{x} - \sqrt[3]{a}| = \frac{|x - a|}{\left| x^{\frac{2}{3}} + a^{\frac{1}{3}} x^{\frac{1}{3}} + a^{\frac{2}{3}} \right|} \quad .$$

15. Use Problem 10 and Theorem 3.23.

16. (a) does not exist

17. $\sqrt{x^2 + 1} = \begin{cases} x\sqrt{1 + \dfrac{1}{x^2}} & \text{if } x > 0 \\[4mm] -x\sqrt{1 + \dfrac{1}{x^2}} & \text{if } x < 0 \end{cases}$

19. $-\dfrac{1}{2}$

25. Show that if $P(a) \neq 0$, the limit does not exist, and if $P(a) = 0$, the limit may exist.

5. You might require that δ be less than $\frac{1}{2}$ (so that $|x + 3| > \frac{1}{2}$) and impose other conditions on δ as needed.

7. (a) no discontinuities; (b) if $f(2) = \frac{1}{3}$, then f is continuous at 2.

9. (b) The only numbers not in the domain of f are $1 + \sqrt{2}$, $1 - \sqrt{2}$, $-1 + \sqrt{2}$, and $-1 - \sqrt{2}$.

11. (b) f can be made continuous at -1 with the proper definition.

13. Use Problem 19 of Exercise 3.1 and Theorem 4.4.

14. Let $g(x) = -f(x)$ and use Theorem 4.12 (as well as the corollary to Theorem 4.10).

17. Modify Example 2.

18. Use Theorem 3.21.

22. Either give a proof modeled on that of Theorem 4.17 or express cos x in terms of sin x and use the result of Theorem 4.17.

26. Use Theorem 3.22.

3. Define a function g by $g(x) = f(x) - c$, and show that Bolzano's Theorem is applicable.

8. All that is necessary is to collect the pertinent facts already proved in theorems throughout the section.

9. Use mathematical induction.

10. Assume that f is not strictly monotonic, and deduce a contradiction. You may want to consider different cases and use the Intermediate Value Theorem.

12. Explain why this function has no inverse.

14. $f^{-1}(x) = 1 + \sqrt[3]{x}$

15. A graph is helpful.

17. By Theorem 4.28 there is at least one such number b.

20. Let $r = \dfrac{m}{n}$, where m and n are integers, $n > 0$. Then use Example 10.

23. Consider the basic functions of calculus.

25. The line $y = x$ plays an important role in this discussion.

26. "Guess" the numbers $f(a)$ and $f(b)$, and prove your conjecture.

27. Show that, for each x in D,
$$M(x) = \frac{f(x) + g(x)}{2} + \frac{|f(x) - g(x)|}{2}$$
and find a similar expression for $m(x)$.

Exercise 4.3
Answers and Hints

7. To show that every infinite subset of elements of S has a limit point in S, you might want to use the Bolzano-Weierstrass Theorem. For the converse, try using Theorem 4.38.

8. Consider the proof of Theorem 4.33.

12. Show that the set $\{x:\ f(x) \le c\}$ is closed.

13. Use an indirect proof and the fact that a convergent sequence is a Cauchy Sequence.

18. The domain of f can consist of two separated sets.

19. To say that g is bounded away from zero on D means the following: there exists a positive number ε such that $|g(x)| \ge \varepsilon$ for all x in D.

21. Uniformly continuous.

22. Not uniformly continuous.

25. Let [a,b] be a closed interval containing S_1 (and therefore every S_n). For each positive integer n let $T_n = C(S_n) \cap [a,b]$. If the theorem is not true, then $\{T_1,\ T_2,\ T_3,\ \cdots\}$ is an open cover of [a,b].

27. Use Theorem 4.43.

Exercise 5.1
Answers and Hints

4. The domain of f does not contain 0.

7. You have to be concerned about zeros in the denominators.

9. First prove the theorem for $r = \frac{1}{n}$, n a positive integer.

11. The answer is not 1.

17. 1

22. $\dfrac{2x(x^2 - 3)}{|x^2 - 3|}$

23. Use the definition to check differentiability at 0.

25. A rational function is differentiable at every point in its domain.

27. Recall that $|a| = \sqrt{a^2}$ for every number a.

32. Existence of the given limit does not guarantee differentiability.

4. Assume the theorem is not true, and use the Mean Value Theorem.

6. Use Theorem 5.27.

7. Use the Mean Value Theorem.

10. Get an idea from the function in Example 9.

12. All you need to do is show that $g(b) - g(a)$ cannot be zero.

14. Does it matter that the interval is open instead of closed?

18. With $f(x) = x^2 - x \cos x + \sin x - 2$, use Bolzano's Theorem to find two intervals each of which contains at least one root. Then use Problem 16 to show that two roots is the maximum number possible.

20. Apply Theorems 5.20 and 5.21 to the function f'. Other results are also needed.

23. (a) $\dfrac{1}{|x|\sqrt{x^2 - 1}}$ (b) The answer is not the same as in (a).

26. The inequality holds for $0 < x < 1$ as well as all $x > 1$.

28. 0

31. (a) Use Problem 10 of Exercise 3.2, Example 12, and Theorem 3.24.

Exercise 6.1
Answers and Hints

4. If [c,d] is any subinterval of [a,b], apply
Theorem 6.10 to [a,b] and then to either [a,d]
or [c,b].

6. Consider several cases.

7. Note that the function is increasing on part
of the interval and decreasing on part of the
interval.

8. If P is any partition of [a,b], show that
$U(f + g,P) \leq U(f,P) + U(g,P)$ and $L(f + g,P) \geq L(f,P) + L(g,P)$. Then show that

$$\overline{I}\ _a^b(f + g) \leq \int_a^b f(x)dx + \int_a^b g(x)dx \text{ and}$$

$$\underline{I}\ _a^b(f + g) \geq \int_a^b f(x)dx + \int_a^b g(x)dx.$$

Take care with the details.

9. Divide [0,1] into n equal parts, and use the
fact that f is increasing.

13. If a < c < b, show that there exists an interval [c - δ, c + δ] and a partition P of
that interval such that $U(g,P) - L(g,P)$ is as
small as desired.

17. Use the corollary to Theorem 6.16.

19. First prove that $\frac{1}{g}$ is integrable. Then use
Theorem 6.19.

25. Since $\int_a^b [z\ f(x) + g(x)]^2 dx \geq 0$ for every number z, the quadratic equation in z

$$z^2 \int_a^b f^2(x)dx + 2z \int_a^b f(x)g(x)dx + \int_a^b g^2(x)dx = 0$$

cannot have two distinct real roots.

412

4. 0

5. You have already seen an example of such a
    function.

8. $\frac{1}{2}$ e(e - 2)

9. Define on D a function F by $F(x) = \int_a^x f(t)dt$.
    Then $G(x) = F(v(x)) - F(u(x))$.

13. $f'(x) = 2x \cos x^4 - \cos x^2$

15. The answer is not xe^{x^2}.

17. Use Theorem 4.12.

19. Use Theorem 6.29 twice, with a different f
    and g each time.

21. $\int_{\frac{\pi}{6}}^{\frac{\pi}{2}} \frac{\sin x}{x} \, dx \leq \ln 3$.

24. Use the Cauchy-Schwarz Inequality.

26. Define on [a,b] a function h by $h(x) =$
    $f(a)\int_a^x g(t)dt + f(b)\int_x^b g(t)dt$ and use Theorem
    6.29.

Exercise 7.1
Answers and Hints

4. The series $\sum\limits_{n=1}^{\infty} a_n$ converges if and only if its sequence of partial sums is a Cauchy Sequence.

5. $\dfrac{1}{n(n+1)} = \dfrac{1}{n} - \dfrac{1}{n+1}$

9. $s_n - s_{n-1} = a_n$ for $n \geq 2$

10. $\dfrac{n!}{n^n} = \dfrac{1 \cdot 2 \cdot 3 \cdots n}{n \cdot n \cdot n \cdots n} \leq \dfrac{1 \cdot 2}{n \cdot n} \left(\dfrac{n \cdot n \cdots n}{n \cdot n \cdots n}\right)$ for $n \geq 2$

13. $\left(\dfrac{1}{n} - \dfrac{1}{n+1}\right) < \dfrac{1}{n^2} < \dfrac{1}{2}\left(\dfrac{1}{n-1} - \dfrac{1}{n+1}\right)$ for $n \geq 2$

14. Use the limit comparison test.

16. $\sqrt{ab} \leq \dfrac{a+b}{2}$ by Theorem 1.1 (g)

18. Use the nth term test.

20. Find an explicit formula for s_n.

22. converges

24. If n and k are positive integers, let $s_n = a_1 + a_2 + \ldots a_n$ and $t_k = a_1 + 2a_2 + 4a_4 + \ldots 2^k a_{2^k}$. If $n < 2^k$, then $s_n \leq a_1 + (a_2 + a_3) + (a_4 + a_5 + a_6 + a_7) + \ldots + (a_{2^k} + a_{2^k+1} + \ldots + a_{2^{k+1}-1}) \leq t_k$.

8. Show that the sequence of partial sums of
$\sum\limits_{n=1}^{\infty} |a_n b_n|$ is bounded above.

9. Recall Problem 31 of Exercise 7.1.

15. Use Theorem 7.17.

16. Use the method of Example 14.

21. diverges

22. Use Raabe's Test.

25. The product of $\sum\limits_{n=1}^{\infty} |a_n|$ and $\sum\limits_{n=1}^{\infty} |b_n|$ converges by Theorem 7.27.

29. Use Problem 26 of Exercise 1.1.

30. Use Theorem 1.4.

32. Use Problem 30.

33. The absolute value of the error is

$$\left| a_{n+1} + a_{n+2} + a_{n+3} + \cdots \right|$$

$$= \left| a_n \left(\frac{a_{n+1}}{a_n} + \frac{a_{n+2}}{a_n} + \frac{a_{n+3}}{a_n} + \cdots \right) \right|$$

$$= |a_n| \left| \frac{a_{n+1}}{a_n} + \frac{a_{n+2}}{a_{n+1}} \cdot \frac{a_{n+1}}{a_n} \right.$$

$$\left. + \frac{a_{n+3}}{a_{n+2}} \cdot \frac{a_{n+2}}{a_{n+1}} \cdot \frac{a_{n+1}}{a_n} + \cdots \right|$$

34. For $r = 1$ let $b_n = n \ln n$ in Kummer's Test.

Exercise 8.1
Answers and Hints

1. not uniform

5. Since max $|f_n(x) - f(x)| = \frac{1}{n}$, the convergence is uniform by Theorem 8.7.

6. uniform

7. Show that the maximum value of f_n is $(\frac{n}{n+1})^{n+1}$.

9. uniform

13. There exists a positive integer N such that $|f_n(x) - f(x)| < 1$ for every $n \geq N$ and all x in S.

14. (b) yes, (c) $\lim_{n \to \infty} f_n'(0)$ does not exist

15. (c) yes

17. (b) yes

21. Use Theorem 8.12.

27. $-1 \leq x < 1$

29. $x > 0$

32. Use Theorem 8.12.

34. Use Problem 18.

37. Use Theorem 8.13 with $\sum_{n=1}^{\infty} \frac{1}{n^{3/2}}$.

39. Recall Problem 4 of Exercise 7.2.

41. Work with the sequence of partial sums.

Exercise 8.2
Answers and Hints

1. $\dfrac{1}{1 - x} = \dfrac{\frac{1}{3}}{1 - \frac{x + 2}{3}}$ and $\dfrac{1}{1 + x} = \dfrac{-1}{1 - (x + 2)}$

6. Use mathematical induction.

9. Start with $e^x = \sum\limits_{n=0}^{\infty} \dfrac{x^n}{n!}$, multiply by x^2, differentiate twice, and set $x = 1$.

11. 1

14. $\dfrac{5}{16}$

16. $\sum\limits_{n=0}^{\infty} \dfrac{(-1)^n x^{2n+1}}{2n + 1}$

19. Note that $x - \dfrac{1}{6} x^3$ is really the Taylor Polynomial of degree 4 for $\sin x$ at 0.

21. $x + \sum\limits_{n=1}^{\infty} \dfrac{1 \cdot 3 \cdot 5 \cdots (2n - 1)}{2 \cdot 4 \cdot 6 \cdots (2n)} \cdot \dfrac{x^{2n+1}}{2n + 1}$,
    $|x| \leq 1$

22. Assume $e = \dfrac{p}{q}$, where p and q are positive integers. Choose $n > q$. Then

    $$e - (1 + \dfrac{1}{1!} + \dfrac{1}{2!} + \cdots + \dfrac{1}{n!}) = \dfrac{e^z}{(n + 1)!}$$

    where $0 < z < 1$. If both sides are multiplied by $n!$, the left side is an integer and the right side is not (if $n \geq 2$).

417

25. Use Theorem 7.28.

29. $\sqrt{R}$

30. (a) Use Raabe's Test after noting that $\dfrac{a_n}{a_{n+1}} = \dfrac{n+1}{n-c}$ for $n > c$.

    (b) $\dfrac{a_{n+1}}{a_n} \geq 1$ for all n

31. Raabe's Test is needed for both end-points.

34. 0.747

35. One of the "series" can be a polynomial.

36. Use Abel's Summation by Parts Formula.

37. You can use the error estimate of Problem 33, Exercise 7.2.

40. See Problem 31 of Exercise 5.2.

INDEX

ABOUT THE AUTHOR

After receiving his B.A. from Rice University and M.A. from The University of Texas at Austin, Vance Underhill spent two years on active duty in the U.S. Army. He then began working for TRACOR, Inc. and resumed his graduate studies, earning his Ph.D. in Mathematics at The University of Texas at Austin in 1972. He is now Professor of Mathematics at East Texas State University in Commerce. Dr. Underhill is deeply committed to mathematics education and has been active in the Mathematical Association of America and the American Mathematical Society for several years. He and his wife Charlotte have one child, a daughter, Erin.